The Art of
Slow Writing

The Art of Slow Writing

Reflections on Time, Craft, and Creativity

LOUISE DeSALVO

ST. MARTIN'S GRIFFIN ⚏ NEW YORK

www.stmartins.com

Designed by Steven Seighman

Library of Congress Cataloging-in-Publication Data

DeSalvo, Louise A., 1942–
    The art of slow writing : reflections on time, craft, and creativity / Louise DeSalvo.
        p.   cm.
    Includes bibliographical references.
    ISBN 978-1-250-05103-5 (trade paperback)
    ISBN 978-1-4668-5198-6 (e-book)
    1. Authorship—Psychological aspects.   2. Creative writing.
3. Creation (Literary, artistic, etc.)—Psychological aspects.   I. Title.
    PN171.P83D46 2014
    808.02019—dc23

                                                    2014028473

St. Martin's Griffin books may be purchased for educational, business, or promotional use. For information on bulk purchases, please contact Macmillan Corporate and Premium Sales Department at 1-800-221-7945, extension 5442, or write specialmarkets@macmillan.com.

First Edition: October 2014

10 9 8 7 6 5 4 3 2 1

For
Ernie DeSalvo, Edvige Giunta, and Amy Jo Burns
with thanks

Contents

Part Three: Challenges and Successes

Part Four: Writers at Rest

Part Five: Building a Book, Finishing a Book

Epilogue: Beginning Again

Preface

It's late April and I'm sitting in my office at Hunter College in New York City, talking to a student writer about her work in progress. I've witnessed this writer's struggle to get to the heart of her story—a memoir about how her family was affected by her father's experience as a first responder to the Twin Towers tragedy. She tells me she'd like to finish her book by the end of the summer. She has a fine first draft in hand. But this is a big subject; its significance can't be plumbed quickly. My job, now, is to help her realize it'll take time to achieve the complexity she desires. On the bulletin board behind my desk, I've posted lines from the poem, "A Lazy Thought," by Eve Merriam: "It takes a lot / Of slow / To grow." And by the end of our meeting, she understands that, yes, her work is too significant to rush.

Beginning—and even accomplished—writers often expect to complete an essay in a few weeks, a book in a year. As Roxane Gay has written in *Salon*, we have a "cultural obsession with genius." Yet the best writing grows by accretion, over time. As John Updike said, "I try to be a regular sort of fellow—much like a dentist drilling his teeth every morning—except Sunday. . . ." Taking time prevents us from writing knee-jerk responses to challenging material.

It encourages us to reflect upon, and express, the complexity of our subjects. It allows us to understand that creating fine work can only be achieved by a slow, consistent dedication to our craft.

The Art of Slow Writing: Reflections on Time, Craft, and Creativity is based not upon how I believe writers *should* work, and not upon how *I* work, but upon decades of research into the writing process and the work habits of real writers. If we understand the writing process, learn how real writers work, and use that information to develop our unique identity as writers, we'll transform our writing lives. In reading the letters, journals, and interviews of well-known writers, I learned that virtually all described the process I refer to here as "slow writing," one that paradoxically allows us to take risks and make intuitive leaps in our work.

In *The Art of Slow Writing*, you'll find slow writing anecdotes from writers of classic works like D. H. Lawrence, Virginia Woolf, Henry Miller, and John Steinbeck. But I also include reflections from contemporary writers—Jo Ann Beard, Michael Chabon, Junot Díaz, Jeffrey Eugenides, Mary Karr, Maxine Hong Kingston, Ian McEwan, and Salman Rushdie, among others.

The Art of Slow Writing begins with an introduction articulating how I developed the slow writing concept. Part One, "Getting Ready to Write," explores the beginning stages of the writing process, how we find our authentic subjects, how we discover our way of working. Part Two, "A Writer's Apprenticeship," examines how long it takes us to learn our craft or develop a new project. Part Three, "Challenges and Successes," addresses learning patience, overcoming a fear of failure, and cultivating determination. Part Four, "Writers at Rest," rethinks writing blocks as moments when we step back and regroup before resuming our work; it discusses, too, writing when we're ill. Part Five, "Building a Book, Finishing a Book," illuminates the hurdles we encounter and surmount to successfully complete our work. An epilogue suggests how we can begin the process of writing our next work.

The reflections in *The Art of Slow Writing* are an invitation for us to think about specific techniques we can use to enter the slow writing life; find ways to deal with the emotional pitfalls—fear, anxiety, judgment, self-doubt—that inevitably accompany our work; delve into what it means to live a healthy and productive creative life; and celebrate our tenacity and our accomplishments. In our rush-rush world, if we allow ourselves to slow down our lives and our writing process, we'll discover that we'll connect—or reconnect—with the wellspring of our most profound work.

Introduction
The Art of Slow Writing

I love visiting writers' houses. I imagine a writer sitting at a desk; taking time to craft each sentence of a work in progress; living the unhurried, unharried writer's life I desire, the one I try (sometimes successfully, sometimes not) to enact myself.

When my husband and I planned a trip to Verona, Italy, we decided to also journey to Gargnano on Lake Garda to visit the house where D. H. Lawrence lived while he revised *Sons and Lovers* (1913). I was researching an essay about the impact of the places Lawrence lived upon his work. In exile from England, writing at a desk positioned so he could view the changing light on Monte Baldo across the lake, Lawrence re-created his childhood in Eastwood, Nottinghamshire. He described his collier father and his grueling work, his proper mother who wanted a better life for her children, the violent arguments between his parents. He wrote about his early, unsuccessful efforts at love, his struggle to free himself from his mother's dominion, his response to her death, and how he became a writer.

On Lake Garda, Lawrence went back and transformed his manuscript *Paul Morel* into *Sons and Lovers*. He'd begun the work in the autumn of 1910; the draft he produced on Lake Garda was his fourth—the novel took two years and four drafts to complete. In this revision, Lawrence transformed the work from a rather straightforward autobiographical novel into a study of a young man's growing understanding of his own troubled sexuality. Lawrence wrote his friend Edward Garnett that in Gargnano he "made [*Sons and Lovers*] patiently, out of sweat as well as blood."

As I planned our trip, I was beginning to think about the process of slow writing. Visiting Lawrence's house would be a pilgrimage, a reminder of my own desire to work as patiently as Lawrence had. I was in the midst of writing a chapter for a book in progress about my parents' lives during World War II, describing how they found and decorated an apartment near the docks in Hoboken, New Jersey. The United States hadn't yet entered the war. Still, my parents knew war was imminent and that my father would be called back into service because he'd been in the navy before and was an expert airplane machinist.

I knew how much that apartment meant to them, and how hard they worked to make it beautiful. But I suspected there was far more to the story. Writing about my father's wartime absence, the terrible carnage of that war, and how the war changed him was difficult. I knew there was no way to rush this. Each time I worked, I'd have high expectations—I'd want to write four, five, maybe six pages. After all the time I'd spent researching and writing preliminary drafts, I expected myself to complete the chapter quickly and well.

I'd noticed how my students at Hunter College often told me they wanted to finish their memoirs in a year or two, a condition I jokingly referred to as "terminal hurriedness." "What's the rush?" I'd ask, even as I was pushing myself, too.

After I'd published *Writing as a Way of Healing* (1999), I'd communicated with scores of writers who'd begun important projects. They also complained about how long their works were taking. To help them—and myself—understand how long it took to complete a work, I'd begun collecting anecdotes about how slowly many famous writers and artists worked. Salman Rushdie, in his memoir, *Joseph Anton*, described that it took him thirteen years to understand that his identity as a writer was that of a migrant "who ended up in a place that was not the place where he began." After finding the right voice, Rushdie worked for three more years to complete his first novel, the Booker Prize–winning *Midnight's Children* (1981). Vincent van Gogh also took long to perfect his talent; "'he had no talent for drawing'"—his early work was horrible; but he persisted: "'If he couldn't do it, he tried it 50 more times.'"

We live in a world that values speed. Messages that used to take days or weeks to reach their recipients arrive in our e-mail in-boxes instantly. By comparison, James Clavell's *Shōgun* (1975) describes how, in the sixteenth century, a person would receive a reply to a letter sent to Europe four years later—if none of the ships carrying either missive sank. The people we communicate with expect our responses immediately. And all this back and forth e-mailing or texting, innocuous as it seems, shifts our attitude to time so we might begin to value only that which happens quickly. It can also rob us of our precious writing time—a writer friend having difficulty completing a book discovered she'd written more than three thousand words in e-mails in one day.

An article in *The New York Times*—"Writer's Cramp: In the E-Reader Era, a Book a Year Is Slacking"—described the pressure publishers put on bestselling writers. The Edgar Award–winning author Lisa Scottoline is now publishing two books a year. Her writing schedule is brutal: "2,000 words a day, seven days a week, usually 'starting at 9 a.m. and going until Colbert.'" Publishers now act as if writing is the same as typing.

"'It seems like we're all running faster to stay in the same place,'" the British thriller writer Lee Child, also urged by his publisher to write more quickly, declared. That's one downside of the fast-paced world we live in. We've internalized the idea that the only actions worth undertaking are those that can be accomplished quickly. (New presidents are expected to solve every major crisis immediately—think of those "First Hundred Days" articles.) And we get frustrated when, say, writing a chapter takes a long time. We blame ourselves for ineptitude or conclude that lengthy projects aren't worthwhile. We push aside work that takes long—novels, poetry collections, biographies, articles, memoirs—to write e-mail messages that take little time while complaining we have no time to write.

We expect ourselves to work quickly. We tell ourselves that if our writing takes so long, we might not be cut out for the writing life. We might equate our worth as writers with the number of pages we write rather than with the excellence of our work.

In the journal John Steinbeck kept while writing *East of Eden* (1952), he described how, in the eighth month of his novel's composition, his editor, Pascal Covici, urged him to work faster than Steinbeck's self-assigned two handwritten pages of manuscript a day. "I [now] find I am hurrying to get through my day's work. . . . It is a destructive suggestion. . . . A book, as you know, is a very delicate thing. If it is pressured, it will show that pressure. So—no more increases." Steinbeck refused to yield; he knew how he needed to work and he stuck to the plan he'd steadfastly adhered to since beginning the novel in late January 1951.

I'm a teacher and writer. But I'm also a passionate foodie. So as I planned our trip to Lake Garda, I looked for a special restaurant, preferably a Slow Food establishment, overlooking the lake, where we could eat local freshwater fish. Slow Food, which began as a movement to resist the opening of a McDonald's near the Spanish Steps in Rome, at its most basic means slowing down enough to understand our relationship to what we eat—where it comes from, how it's grown or raised, how we prepare it, and our rituals in consuming it. Many of the fundamental ideas of the Slow Food movement can be adapted to describe the slow writing process.

As Adam Gopnik has written of the Slow Food movement in *The Table Comes First*, in a world that values speed, if we make a commitment to take time, we commit to an important set of values. Slow writing, I thought, could be one way to slow down time, to "articulate time." A way, too, to "slow down life." Like Slow Food, "slow writing" doesn't "just take time, but *makes* time." Slow writing is a meditative act: *slowing down* to understand our relationship to our writing, *slowing down* to determine our authentic subjects, *slowing down* to write complex works, *slowing down* to study our literary antecedents.

I was looking forward to visiting D. H. Lawrence's house, looking forward to gazing at the window through which Lawrence viewed Monte Baldo when he paused in his difficult work on *Sons and Lovers*. But I had an accident.

A few days before our scheduled departure, I was racing around New York City wearing ill-fitting, floppy shoes, and developed a stress fracture of my left foot, and we had to postpone our trip. That accident and its aftermath forced me to undergo what Virginia Woolf in *On Being Ill* describes as a spiritual change that can accompany a life-altering event. Needing to slow down—I couldn't walk at first, and when I could again, only slowly—I started to understand my relationship to my writing differently. I read about the lives of writers who composed important works while they or their partners were ill—Marcel Proust, Mark Doty, and Elizabeth Bishop, among them.

When I was beginning to walk again, our back fence neighbors had their annual Memorial Day party to which my husband and I were invited. We drove, though their house is just around the corner. When it was time to leave I decided to walk home. It would be my first solo walk since my injury.

I began with trepidation. At first I was disgruntled with my slow pace, eager to get home. But soon I started noticing my surroundings.

A neighborhood teenager was throwing a party. I heard her classmates' jokes, their comments on the music playing, their boy/girl antics. I smiled, remembering the gathering where I met my husband. I observed how a breeze made the leaves reveal their silvery undersides. Needing to rest, I paused before flowers in a neighbor's yard. Late spring had never smelled sweeter. And I wondered why hurriedness had taken over my life. This newfound sense of peace from taking time to linger and enjoy the world was a benefit from my injury I hadn't anticipated.

And because I needed to walk slowly, I needed to do many things slowly. The first day I resumed cooking, I made focaccia. It took long, but the experience was blissful. When I was out in my garden, having remembered my book but forgotten my reading glasses, I was forced to sit and "be" until I could summon the energy to retrieve them. I saw birds washing themselves in the pool above our little waterfall, a chipmunk dashing into its nest, a dragonfly hovering over water. I'd sat in this garden for years, writing or reading, but I hadn't ever spent this much "slow time" there.

When I returned to my study, I took down the published edition of Virginia Woolf's handwritten draft of *To the Lighthouse* (1927). I was curious about how many words Woolf had written in one day. I knew I was living too fast, trying to work too quickly, and my injury was teaching me the necessity and the benefits of slowing down. Maybe I could learn something more about the creative act from the way Woolf worked.

I'd studied the earlier versions of Woolf's published novels—what she deleted or added to a page, whether key scenes or images existed in the earliest version. I believe we can deepen our understanding of the writing process by examining writers' early drafts, reading their journals or transcriptions of interviews with them. Whenever I get stuck, it's time for me to turn to the experts for help.

My students are often stunned to learn that famous writers revise more and take longer to complete their works than my students think necessary. Ernest Hemingway penned about forty-seven alternate endings of *A Farewell to Arms* (1929) before deciding on the one he used. The Pulitzer Prize winner Michael Chabon took almost five years to complete his novel *Telegraph Avenue* (2012). "If you want to write like the pros," I thought, "you have to work like the pros."

Woolf usually wrote fiction for two and a half to three uninterrupted hours, from about ten in the morning to twelve thirty or one in the afternoon. Did she write a thousand words, two thousand?

I opened the early draft of *To the Lighthouse* to May 9, 1926, and learned that Woolf penned roughly 535 words and crossed out 73 of them, netting her 462 words for her day's work. Let's say she worked for three hours. That's about 178 words an hour including the words she deleted—and Woolf was writing at the height of her creative powers.

Once I'd learned how many words Woolf wrote, I thought about how many words I expected myself to write. If I sat down to write for two and a half to three uninterrupted hours, did I expect to draft a scene, a short essay, revise an entire piece of writing? How many words did I hope to write? Far more than Woolf, I had to admit.

While Woolf was carefully composing those 535 words of *To the Lighthouse*, she was also experiencing a life-altering event. England was in the midst of its most disabling strike. There were no trains, no subways, no taxis. A few busses driven by special constables plied London's streets but riding in them was dangerous— strike sympathizers attacked the vehicles. Everyone worried about having enough food as supplies dwindled. The country seemed on the brink of civil war.

Living a life so adversely affected by the strike, Woolf was forced to contemplate the contribution of working-class people to her country's stability. And so she introduced Mrs. McNab, the charwoman who restores the chaos of the Ramsay summer home to order by her hard labor, into her narrative. Woolf became newly aware that workers keep civilization afloat, and that her privileged life depended upon someone else's efforts.

Woolf used her writing as a way to think about and report on what she observed. Though she'd planned this book carefully, because Woolf worked slowly, she could also ponder the changing condition of her world, the effect of the general strike, and allow a new character to emerge from this act of attention, a stunning breakthrough made possible only because of her slow writing.

During the months of my recovery, I worked to slow down my writing process. Not at first, but over time, I learned that my unease about the chapter I was writing was based upon my not having taken the time to learn enough about what was happening in the world as my parents spent their evenings creating their first home, papering walls, painting trim, laying a carpet, positioning furniture they'd bought with savings.

I did more research, wrote in my process journal, and realized something I'd overlooked. As my parents worked through the summer of 1941, they listened to the radio broadcasting news of bombing raids over London, the German invasion of the Soviet Union, the uncovering of a Nazi spy network in the United States that planned to bomb docks like the ones at the end of my parents' street. Nor had I taken time to think about what my parents must have felt like creating a home at this time.

Because I'd wanted to finish this chapter quickly, I'd missed its fundamental significance. My parents were creating their first home when homes created with as much care as theirs were being obliterated. They were beginning their life together knowing it would soon be wrenched apart. No home, no matter how lovingly created, could insulate them from the tragedy of war.

Although I've been writing since 1975, I'm still a beginner. I'm still learning my craft; I'm still learning what it means to be a writer; I'm learning what it means to be a slow writer.

Most of the writers I work with have a hard time getting themselves to the desk, thinking about their works in progress, thinking about the act of writing, finding a space for their writing within the context of their busy lives, dealing with the emotional roller coaster attending their work, expecting themselves to produce more than they can, continuing to write through all the vicissitudes of the writing process, and finishing the works they've started. Most writers I know expect more from themselves than is humanly possible and this often derails their work.

I like to think of *The Art of Slow Writing* as a report of the on-going conversations I've had with writers about the act of writing since the publication of *Writing as a Way of Healing*. There I wrote about how writing could help us overcome trauma and how many published writers (Isabel Allende, Henry Miller, and Alice Walker, among others) described how they were inspired to begin a major work because of a deep wound they'd received. In *Writing as a Way of Healing*, I articulated the process whereby writing can serve as a healing art.

In *The Art of Slow Writing*, I write about that major challenge affecting *all* writers: our need to slow down to understand the writing process so we can do our best work. I'm inviting you on a journey to think about how to work at writing day by day. I'm providing a path—a slow writing path—to think about preparing to write, beginning to write, writing an extended work, and completing a work. This book isn't prescriptive. It isn't about how to write. It's about how to think about working at writing and slowing down our process so we can become self-reflective writers so we can find our own way.

Finding our way as writers is a daily, ever-changing process. As soon as we've figured out how to work, something happens and everything falls apart and we need to learn how to work all over again. This happened to many novelists after the 9/11 tragedies. Ian McEwan took a long while trying to absorb its meaning. It took him until 2005 to publish *Saturday*, his fictional response to "a general darkening and gathering pessimism since the . . . attacks." When our lives change, when the world changes, we must reinvent ourselves as writers.

Through the years, I've learned that the most successful writers I've worked with are those who've learned to think about their process and who've learned to reflect upon their work. Writers who, as

Zadie Smith, author of *NW* (2013), says, are "always hard at work; refining, improving, engaged by and interested in every step in the process." Writers who are slow writers.

This book will work best if you start or continue a writing practice. You can read straight through the book. Or you can read a section that strikes your fancy. But let's imagine what we might gain from becoming slow writers, from allowing ourselves to really be in our work and with our work. What we might gain from thinking about the process of our work and not the product. From learning how real writers work. From not judging our work (which doesn't mean not evaluating our work) but just doing our work. From congratulating ourselves on work well done. Let's imagine how we might grow as writers if we work in a slow writing way rather than rushing through our work trying to accumulate a pile of pages. Just imagine what we might gain from being writers who move slowly through our work and slowly through our lives.

Slow writing is a meditative act. It acknowledges that we are all beginners and insists we cultivate empathy for ourselves because being a writer isn't easy. Slow writing is a way to resist the dehumanization inherent in a world that values speed. It's one way to find—or return to—our authentic selves.

Part One

GETTING READY TO WRITE

Introduction

It's essential for me to understand where I am in the writing process with a particular work. Am I getting ready to write—doing research, scribbling notes, assembling the bits and pieces I've written? Am I writing a first draft—trying to get my work into a provisional order? Revising or deepening a draft? Ordering a work? Completing it? Polishing a piece, readying it for an audience?

Unless I know where I am in the process, I expect too much too soon. I criticize myself for not accomplishing the impossible. When I'm preparing a new work, if I expect myself to know precisely how to work or what to say, I might forestall my process. If, instead of playing with the project for a time, I expect to write beautiful, lucid sentences, I'll become frustrated.

Random, hazy, unclear attempts at meaning often characterize the earliest stages of the creative process. We work in the dark, not yet knowing the direction our work will take, trusting this early work will be rewarded. When Margaret Atwood, author of the Booker Prize–winning *The Blind Assassin* (2000), starts a novel, she doesn't yet know where it will lead—it "seems a process of working [the problems] out." She begins with something small, "an image, scene, or voice," and discovers the "structure or design" as she writes. When she was writing *Surfacing* (1972), Atwood wrote two parts of her novel five years before writing the remainder. To know too much at first, Atwood maintains, would be "too much like paint-by-numbers." Often, beginning writers skip this stage and try to write a first draft too soon. But many successful writers linger here for years. Trying to work too quickly, trying to work in too polished a way too quickly, expecting clarity too soon, can set us up for failure.

Margaret Drabble took time to learn about jigsaw puzzles before composing *The Pattern in the Carpet* (2009). Originally intended as a history of puzzle making, the memoir interleaves Drabble's life story, her passion for games, and a history of puzzles. The choreographer Twyla Tharp collects objects, images, and ideas for future work in a special container long before she understands how to use them: "There are separate boxes for everything I've ever done."

When we begin a new project, as embryonic or unsatisfactory as our early work may seem, we're readying ourselves for the deeper work that comes later. We learn about ourselves as writers. We establish our work's foundation. We permit ourselves to play and explore. We commit—or recommit—to working steadily and purposefully.

Michael Chabon stumbled in the dark for four years before beginning *The Mysteries of Pittsburgh* (1988). He honed his craft by writing imitative novels, "quasi-Calvino, and neo-Borges." He studied the structure of F. Scott Fitzgerald's *The Great Gatsby* (1925) and Philip Roth's *Goodbye, Columbus* (1959); each work, he learned, took place in a single summer, a scheme he borrowed, setting his novel in Pittsburgh, a place he understood. As Orhan Pamuk, author of *My Name Is Red* (2001), has said, "most of art . . . is really craft." Learning technique requires a patient apprenticeship—Pamuk worked for seven years before publishing his first novel, *Cevdet Bey ve Oğulları* (*Cevdet Bey and His Sons*) (Istanbul: Karacan Yayınian, 1982) . Like these authors, in the beginning stage, we can learn how to work at our craft and learn what this particular work requires of us.

Though this may be unsettling, we continue to work even if we don't yet understand what we're doing or where the work is heading. Nicole Krauss, describing how she wrote *The History of Love* (2005), said, "I never know where the story is going until it gets there." For Krauss, "Getting completely lost, coming unstrung and unbound, arriving at unknown and unexpected places, is, for me, a critical part of writing." She worked herself out of many corners, having "no idea how the book would end." Dealing with the anxiety of not knowing where our work is headed or whether it'll be successful is essential. Krauss worked steadily though she thought *The History of Love* might fail. She took risks because she focused on the *process* of doing her work, rather than on the end product. As we begin a work, remembering we needn't know how it'll turn out or whether it'll be successful might be comforting. And we can cultivate our ability to work despite confusion as Krauss does.

Our early attempts will most likely be muddled, like Virginia Woolf's first draft of *Between the Acts* (1941), at first called *Pointz Hall*. The beginning of this draft—"Oh beautiful and bounteous light on the table; oil lamp; ancient and out-of-date oil lamp; upholding as on a tawny tent the falling grey draperies of dusk"—was nothing like the final draft—"It was a summer's night and they were talking, in the big room with the windows open to the garden, about the cesspool." The early version was muddled and flowery, like a prolonged play period with the language, subject matter, images, and characters Woolf developed and changed over time. The final version gets right down to business: cultured people are gathered around a lamp talking about how to dispose of human waste, retaining only the first version's oil lamp.

We can take as much time as we need in our projects' initial stages, allowing ourselves to be unsure of what we're doing or whether we'll succeed. We can commit to the process of learning and honing our craft even as we acknowledge the anxiety and frustration that often occur early on. We can commit to working slowly, taking time to figure out our work, one slow step at a time.

There will, of course, be occasions in our writer's lives when we might find ourselves working quickly. Times when we're in the flow of the work and we give ourselves over to it as it seems to come to us, unbidden. Times when we are trying to meet a self-imposed deadline. Times when we have a contractual deadline to meet. But working quickly does not mean rushing the process to get to the end no matter what. And even if we work quickly now and then, for the greater part of the writing process, by working slowly and steadily, we will produce our finest work.

1

Learning How to
Work at Writing

I remember a meltdown I had in college when I was writing an essay. You were given an assignment. You had to hand in a perfect paper on a due date. There were no opportunities for revision, no comments on a draft to help you improve.

So there I was, sitting at my desk. I'd reel a sheet of erasable paper into my typewriter and begin. And I'd expect myself to do everything at once—present a coherent argument; write an organized essay in syntactically correct, perfectly punctuated prose.

I was writing about Dostoyevsky, my favorite author. I knew what I wanted to say. But I had no notes, no draft. I had an outline, but it felt like a straitjacket. I kept having new insights as I wrote, but instead of tossing my outline, I tossed away my pages. When I wrote an incoherent sentence, I'd tear the paper out of the typewriter and begin anew.

Halfway through the night, I was so muddled, so incapable of working, that I began crying and couldn't stop. A friend calmed me down and sat beside me while I did the best I could. But the paper was a disaster. "You write primer English," the professor commented. Afraid of making a mistake, short on time, I'd simplified my writing and my argument.

I wanted to be a writer. But if this was what writing was like, I couldn't do it—I didn't have the necessary skills. I didn't know it was all right to start anywhere. That most writers compose more than one draft. That it was impossible to do everything at once. But that's how I thought writers wrote, and no one—not my professors, not the books I read about literature (we were steered away from biography)—told us anything different about how writers worked. The closest I came to seeing a writer's process was when I typed a few drafts of a collection by a poet who taught at my college.

Now, when I teach the craft of memoir, I invite Kathryn Harrison to my class to describe how she wrote *The Mother Knot* (2004), her memoir describing her tangled relationship with her mother. My students are eager to pen their first full-length work; still, many want to rush the process and don't yet know how to work at writing. Hearing Harrison discuss the many stages of her work provides them with important information about how to write their own memoirs.

Harrison arrived in class with a stack of manuscripts—ten drafts of *The Mother Knot* that she composed from autumn 2002 through summer 2003. She began the work as a long essay; she realized she was writing a book in the seventh draft. Seeing that pile of drafts was an important learning experience for my students. As one said, "I realized that if it took Harrison that many drafts, it'd take me that long, too."

Because Harrison knows she'll work through many drafts, she gives herself permission to write badly at first. Although the book's skeleton—having her mother's body exhumed and cremated—existed in the first draft, Harrison deleted or shortened self-indulgent material that wasn't germane to the book. Other subjects—her anorexia, for example—that she raced through, she had to later develop. In time, Harrison deepened the meaning of what breast-feeding and her mother's sadism meant to her. And what she'd reported—her mother's behavior, conversations with her own therapist—she later revised into scenelets and full-fledged scenes.

Harrison took time between drafts—a few days, a month—and that helped her understand how to fix problems. She often dealt with challenges one draft at a time—how she presented character A, how she presented character B. In another draft, she focused on how she treated images of water that had been present early, refining and expanding them. In later drafts, she worked by association to fill in the blanks of her narrative.

The structure of Harrison's work had been established from the beginning: a linear narrative combined with flashbacks in scenelets, scenes, or exposition. But until almost the last draft, Harrison didn't know how the memoir would end. From the first draft, it began with a scene of her finding frozen breast milk. She thought she'd end with casting her mother's ashes into the water. But she intuitively wrote a scene describing her Quaker wedding, which, she realized, was a more apt resolution to the theme of how she came to terms with her mother's adverse effect upon her.

Witnessing how Harrison wrote and revised *The Mother Knot* helped my students understand that it takes many drafts to create a work of art, that we can't tackle all our challenges at once, and that composing and revision proceed in stages. After Harrison's visit, we discussed the stages of the writing process.

First, you imagine the work, think about it, and take notes about it, perhaps long before you actually begin writing. (Harrison, though, began the work immediately after a telephone conversation with the undertaker who would exhume her mother's body.)

Second, once you start, you work provisionally, knowing you'll have many opportunities to get it right.

Third, you work in stages, writing, revising, letting yourself learn what your subject is really about as you work.

Fourth, you figure out order, structure, and image patterns late in the process, though you may have some ideas from the start. You revise accordingly.

Fifth, you fine-tune the work, tightening where necessary, adding information your reader needs when necessary. You go through the work word by word, sentence by sentence, and paragraph by paragraph.

Sixth, you don't show your work until late in the process. And then you revise again, based upon feedback. (After Harrison showed a draft to her editor, she deleted a hospital scene, material about her son, and revised again.)

Whether we're beginning writers or beginning a new project, understanding that working *with* the stages of the writing process, rather than *against* it, can help our work immeasurably, as my students learned from Harrison's visit and her generosity in describing her composition of *The Mother Knot*.

2

Finding Our Own Rhythm

Interviewers always ask writers "When do you write? *What's your writing schedule?*" I love learning how writers organize their lives because I hope I can apply something I've learned to my own writer's life.

J. D. Salinger, author of *The Catcher in the Rye* (1951), started work each morning at 6 a.m., but not later than 7 a.m., and he wrote, without interruption, throughout the day, and sometimes well into the night. Margaret Atwood, author of *The Handmaid's Tale* (1986), writes from ten in the morning until four in the afternoon. Peter Carey, author of *Oscar and Lucinda* (1988), writes "[m]ostly in the mornings"; "making stuff up for three hours, that's enough," although he sometimes returns to the work late in the day to revise it. Jonathan Franzen, author of *The Corrections* (2001), has said that he can write eight to ten hours a day.

Often, I compare my own writing regimen with that of other writers—I write for about two hours a day, fewer when I'm teaching—and sometimes chastise myself for not writing longer. I imagine setting my alarm so I can be at my desk early like Salinger, and working throughout the day and into the night. But I soon realize Salinger's rhythms aren't mine; his life wasn't like mine.

One of my jobs as a writer is to learn what my rhythms are. That's not easy because when it's best for me to write changes throughout the year, when I'm teaching, from one year to the next, from one project to the next, sometimes even from one day to the next. For years, I worked mornings. Then when I wrote my memoir *Vertigo* (1996), I discovered I worked best on this particular book during the afternoons. (I later read memory functions best then, so that might be why.)

Edward M. Hallowell's *CrazyBusy: Overstretched, Overbooked, and About to Snap!* (2006) suggests strategies we can employ so we can understand our work rhythms, reclaim the time we need to write, and discover when we work best.

- Limit your commitments so you have time to do what you want to do.
- Reserve time to do what matters rather than frittering time away on what isn't important.
- Use the time of day when you're most alert on what matters most to you.
- Train yourself to stay on task—write down what you're working on and post it close to you.
- Sculpt your day to do what matters most to you.
- Keep adjusting the way you spend your time until you find what works for you.
- Find your own rhythm. Don't assume someone else's will work for you.
- And understand that sculpting your day will be an ongoing task.

Early in my writing life I read Virginia Valian's essay "Learning to Work," which taught me how to work at writing. Set a timer,

Valian said, and work however long you decide to write. Begin with only five minutes and move on from there. Learning how to sit at our desks without interruption is a necessary skill we can learn. It's the first—and one of the most difficult—assignments I give my writing students. I like to use a meditation timer; it keeps me focused and helps me regard my writing time as a meditative task.

These days, when I'm not teaching, I'm at my desk, and writing, by 10 a.m. I can't settle down to write unless I meditate, exercise, write in my journal, shower, and dress in something I wouldn't mind being seen in. I sometimes chide myself for not getting to the desk earlier. But I know that's when I work best now. As Hallowell suggests, I must sculpt my day to do what matters most to me right now—write that book about my parents' lives during World War II—during the morning, my most productive time, when I've found I work best on this book. And each day, I'll assess what worked and what didn't, and make changes when necessary. I also ask my students to discover, and continually reassess, what time of day works best for them.

All of us can write. Few of us know how to work at writing. And even fewer of us know how to sculpt our lives so we can write. These are learned skills, acquired through time and practice. And, Hallowell says, it seems more difficult to practice these skills now, because learning how to think deeply about our writing lives is different from just being busy. Reflection takes time, quiet, and patience.

Michael Chabon, author of *Wonder Boys* (1995), has described how he and his wife, the novelist Ayelet Waldman (who was a lawyer before she became a novelist), plan their writing around the demands of raising four children. When an interviewer asked, "How do you make space to craft your work?" Chabon responded that, during the school year, when their children are at school, Waldman works "almost entirely during that period," getting "her word count in every day," a routine that "works well for her."

Chabon's "natural rhythm," though, "is to work at night, stay up late and to sleep late." But "that schedule does not work at all well in a family with small children" because Chabon likes to be with them early in the morning. He envies Waldman because she works so well during the day. He's been struggling with his schedule of "staying up late, and getting up early" for years. To work with, rather than against, his natural writing rhythm, he has to "go away [to write]," to a writing colony, a friend's cabin, or a hotel. Then he can write late into the night, sleep late, get sufficient rest, and "get a lot done." In a few days, he can compose what would ordinarily take him a month to write at home.

Chabon and Waldman have accepted the reality of their lives with children, and sculpt their days so they can parent their children but also write. Waldman's solution is different from Chabon's because their writing rhythms are different.

Colum McCann, author of *TransAtlantic* (2013), has said that although he would work every waking hour if he could, he's chosen to limit his writing time: "there is also a life to lead—travel, family, the odd jaunt down to the pub." Writing is an essential part of McCann's life. Still, "I don't live my life as a writer," he says. "It's what I do, but not necessarily what I am." McCann has reflected upon what matters most to him, and he organizes his life so that writing, though it is an important part of his life, doesn't dominate it.

3.

Where to Begin

When my students begin their first major projects, they often say, "I don't know where to begin," and they sometimes ask me where I think they should begin. I'm inclined to say "Just begin, and see what happens" because there's no right answer to this question. Successful writers have different ways of launching their works, and it takes a period of experimentation to learn what works best for each of us. And I know, too, that many writers shift the way they enter their projects from one time in their writing lives to another.

What worked best for me when I began writing was to begin a book by writing an essay for someone else. I wrote for a magazine and for other people's essay collections as often as I could. Beginning a book without having something in hand was too scary for me. But if I wrote for someone else's magazine or book, I felt far less pressure and far more freedom than if I were beginning to write the same material for a book of my own. This wasn't *my* book; it was someone else's, I'd tell myself. And although I was responsible to make my work as good as I could make it, I'd have an editor's help in refining the work for publication. This freed me to figure out the voice of the book beforehand so that when I turned from writing the essay to writing the book, I had a sense of what the work would sound like, what its subject matter would be, and how it would be structured.

I began my biography of Virginia Woolf by writing an essay about when she was fifteen for a friend's collection. I began my novel, *Casting Off* (1987), by writing a story, "Gluttony and Fornication," for *Chicago* magazine. I began my memoir *Crazy in the Kitchen* (2014) by writing an essay called "Cutting the Bread" for *The Milk of Almonds: Italian American Women Writers on Food and Culture* (2002) that I was editing with Edvige Giunta.

Getting a book off the ground is sitting down, starting to work, witnessing what happens, and moving on from there. As Anne Tyler, author of *The Beginner's Goodbye* (2012), a novel about a man dealing with his wife's death, has said, "It doesn't take very long for most writers to realize that if you wait until the day you are inspired and feel like writing you'll never do it at all." She's learned "just to go to my room and plug away." She keeps a quotation by Richard Wilbur from the poem "Walking to Sleep" in her study about plunging directly into the work—to reassure her that once she begins, she'll figure out what to do.

Tyler has described the challenges she's faced as a writer in "Still Just Writing"—her kids' vacations, a sick dog, visits from repairmen, a sick child, long visitations from foreign relatives, grocery shopping, bathroom scrubbing. She feels she's always "hewing . . . creative time in small, hard chips from . . . living time." She's learned the necessity of boundaries: how to write when she can but to be fully engaged with the rest of her life when she's not writing.

Tyler doesn't begin from scratch. She keeps "an index box in which she has written ideas . . . and left them to ripen for years . . . until she feels she can make something of it." After she settles on something that captures her fancy, she plans for "exactly a month" before she begins working. Her plan enables her to feel "very sure how a novel is going to end." She writes "detailed background notes on each of her characters," much of which goes unused because the work often takes a different, unexpected turn. Tyler's way into her work has remained consistent for the nineteen novels she's written.

Zadie Smith began writing her novel *On Beauty* (2005), about the lives of two families, by reworking the "first twenty pages for almost two years." She'd shift from "first-person present tense, to third-person past tense, to third-person present tense, to first-person past tense, and so on." As she worked, she paid close attention to voice; she learned that the nature of the work would shift dramatically "by the choice of a few words."

The time Smith spent on these first pages was necessary: she unconsciously worked out many of the project's challenges during this time. Staying with those pages was one "way of working on the whole novel, a way of finding its structure, its plot, its characters." Smith felt like she'd wound "the key of a toy car tighter and tighter. . . . When you finally let it go, it travels at a crazy speed." Once Smith felt satisfied with those pages, she finished *On Beauty* in five months. Smith's method of beginning the novel worked well for her, although it was difficult.

When Smith started work on her most recent novel, *NW* (2012), she began very differently, improvising "'like a jazz musician'" with "'some scales, some tone, a colour'" about her subject, "the intricate class system that operates in London, with poverty and wealth existing cheek by jowl."

Smith's life differed dramatically from when she wrote *On Beauty*. She was married; she'd given birth to her first child; her father had died. Her writing rhythms were different; she'd been through a period of mourning. Because of these changes, she wrote about "the 'genuine relativity' of time speeding up as one gets older." Unlike the speed with which she completed *On Beauty*, *NW* proceeded far more slowly and took her eight years. A process that had worked for her when she was a young writer had to be adjusted. As a writer with a young child, she's "on a different schedule."

Before Virginia Woolf began composing *Mrs. Dalloway* (1925), she wrote a short story "Mrs. Dalloway in Bond Street." She'd also written another story in which a shell-shocked veteran of the Great War "plots to assassinate the prime minister." She then realized she could use both stories in her novel. In time, Woolf intertwined the story of Mrs. Dalloway, the wife of a member of Parliament, with that of the veteran Septimus Smith.

When Woolf began *To the Lighthouse*, the novel she wrote after *Mrs. Dalloway*, the idea for it came to her "in a great involuntary rush" while she was taking a walk. She then sketched a plan for the novel in her notebook. She decided that she would leave many of the characters of the Ramsay children undifferentiated; that time would become a character in the work; that she would describe her father, mother, St. Ives (her family's summer home), and her childhood, "& all the usual things I try to put in—life, death &c."

Woolf worked out some of the issues she faced in the novel in stories she was writing at the same time. One, "Ancestors," describes her parents and her childhood. It's a preliminary sketch for material she was describing in her evolving novel. The composition of *To the Lighthouse* was successful, in part, because she honored a moment of inspiration and then spent time planning and thinking about what she wanted to achieve. But Woolf also felt free to improvise on the page, even as she stuck to the original structure of the work.

4

Routine

Establishing a consistent writing practice is essential if we are to realize our dream of writing a full-length work. Most aspiring writers have other compelling needs—day jobs, child care, relationships, household tasks—that take time and are essential. Still, what we want—or need—to do most days is write.

Beginning writers often ask "How do you do it?" which means "How can I do it?" I suggest they learn about the early writing life of a writer like Carol Shields, author of the Pulitzer Prize–winning *The Stone Diaries* (1993), who published two poetry collections before she wrote fiction.

When Shields started writing fiction, she enacted a simple routine: "I used to try and catch that hour just before [the children] came home for lunch, between 11:00 and 12:00." She wrote an hour a day, aiming for two pages. Later, if she had time, she'd read her work and plan what came next. "If you write two pages a day," Shields said, "you have ten pages at the end of the week. At the end of a year, you have a novel, and I did have a novel." Shields was surprised that "these writings, these little segments, added up to something larger."

Before Shields wrote her first novel, *Small Ceremonies* (1976), she decided to first determine its structure—nine chapters corresponding to an academic year, beginning with September. She didn't fully understand her main character. But she wanted to write about a biographer, who goes on sabbatical with her husband, finds the notes of a failed novelist, decides to steal them, and writes a novel using them. She attends a writing workshop and has her stolen work appropriated by her professor. "Develop a certain faith in your process," Shields advises. Keep working through difficult times and trust that "somehow you're going to work it out as you go."

When I started to write, I was raising two toddlers, teaching full-time, dealing with health issues, caring for aging parents, running a household. My husband shopped, cleaned, took care of household maintenance, and coparented. I tried to write two hours a day when I could, less when I couldn't, but I tried to write every day, no matter what. I wrote when my children were napping, or, later, when they attended school. Many parents squander that precious time on household tasks. Instead, I did laundry, shopped, and cooked when my children were around.

I recently spoke with a writer trying to finish a book who was miserable because she said she couldn't write. "I yell at my kids all the time," she said. "I need to write; I want to write, but I can't find time to write."

"You don't find time to write," I said. "You make time to write." She could write when her children were at school, organize caregivers to trade kids off a few hours each day, write when her kids were home by giving them some quiet time in their rooms instead of trying to keep them amused.

Early in my writing life, a mentor advised me that if you want to write, you have to give something up. Often, you have to give up a great deal. He said that everything we do, we've chosen to do. And everything we choose to do means there's something we've chosen not to do. All too often, aspiring writers choose to give up writing. My mentor said it's important to say "I'm choosing to do the laundry instead of writing," instead of saying "I don't have time to write." Jeffrey Eugenides has said that, in order to write, he's had to "sacrifice things I can get along without: a frisky social life," for example.

I protect my writing time. I don't engage in long telephone conversations, lunches with people I don't love, most meetings, Facebook, net surfing, e-mailing more than once a day, shopping for the sake of shopping, boozy nights out, television (except for movies), most parties, readings. When my kids were small, I didn't bake for sales, attend every game they played, drive them places—they rode their bikes or used skateboards.

I spend some time in a cost-benefit analysis of the opportunities that come my way. Do I really want to do it? What will it cost? What will I gain? If the cost outweighs the gain, I don't do it. I know writers who act as if they have an infinite amount of time and energy, and who say yes to more than they should. When they get serious about their work, they learn they need to scale back their activities.

Eviatar Zerubavel's *The Clockwork Muse* (1999) suggests that, before we figure out when we *can* write, we mark all the times we *can't* write on a calendar—preparing for work, work, self-care, household tasks, child care, etc. This gives us a realistic sense of the time we have available. It helps us understand if we need to make changes in our lives to write each day.

David Allen's *Getting Things Done* (2001) suggests making a giant list of every project we're engaged in. This reveals how busy we are and how many commitments we have. When a writer friend of mind did this, she was horrified at the number of projects she'd taken on. She learned why she didn't have time to write; she realized she had to drastically scale back her commitments.

Most beginning writers I work with are far busier than they realize. They're shocked when they learn how little time they have to write. They learn they must not waste the time they *do* have. If we want to write, we must actively choose how we spend our time rather than assume that writing time will magically come our way. Still, if we wait for the perfect time to write, we'll never write.

I have some guiding principles I've evolved over the years.

Establish a simple routine. (Shields's hour before lunch; two pages a day.)

Be realistic. (It's better to commit to one hour we can manage than to three we can't.)

Touch the work every day. (I write five days a week; weekends, I scribble thoughts into a process journal.)

Give yourself the gift of uninterrupted time. (It takes about twenty minutes to get back into flow after each interruption.)

Without a simple routine, each new writing day can become an existential dilemma that takes an enormous amount of energy away from our writing. The time we take deciding when to write, whether to write, whether we're up to writing, or whether we should do something else is time wasted. If we develop a routine that permits slow, steady accomplishment, we won't waste time and energy rethinking our routine each day.

5

Tools of the Trade

I'm always asked—and other writers are, too—how I write. By hand? On a computer? A combination of both? I've learned it takes time for beginning writers to discover what process works best. But hearing how other writers compose can help us understand our options. And what works for one writer might not work for another.

So much about the writing process is uncontrollable that we writers sometimes staunchly adhere to our idiosyncratic, proven ways of working. Some even become fetishistic about the process. For if the way we wrote one book worked, we trust that if we work the same way again, we'll successfully complete the next.

Many of Paul Auster's novels, including *Mr. Vertigo* (1994), describe the mechanics of the writing process. His *City of Glass* (1985), *The Book of Illusions* (2002), and *Oracle Night* (2003) describe characters that compose, as Auster does, in notebooks, which he calls "a house for words." Auster isn't only interested in the product his efforts will produce, "but in the process, the act of putting words on a page."

When Auster begins, like many of his characters, he writes "by hand," with "a fountain pen, but sometimes with a pencil—especially for corrections" because he confesses that keyboards intimidate him: "I've never been able to think clearly with my fingers in that position." When Auster writes by hand, he has an intimate, visceral connection to his work: "You feel that the words are coming out of your body and then you dig the words into the page." He has "a particular fetish for notebooks with quadrille lines—the little squares."

Auster has described his longstanding relationship with his Olympia typewriter in *The Story of My Typewriter* (2002). He's owned it "since 1974" after buying it "second-hand from a college friend" and "[i]t's never broken down." Auster fears when "there won't be any ribbons left to buy"—he's stored about seventy of them—and he'll have to work on a computer.

Although Auster admits his process is "cumbersome and inconvenient," beginning his books by hand and then typing a draft on his Olympia forces him "to start all over again. . . ." The process is tedious because, once you've completed a handwritten draft, "you have to spend several weeks engaged in the purely mechanical job of transcribing what you've already written." Because of this process, Auster experiences "the book in a new way," and understands "how it functions as a whole." Inevitably, Auster discovers necessary changes that would have eluded him.

Norman Rush, author of *Mortals* (2003), writes in "his one-room attic," cluttered with the accumulation of treasures he collected in the years he served in the Peace Corps in Botswana and junk he can't part with. He works at a "large U-shaped assemblage of tables and doors on sawhorses that incorporates, also, a desk." On the agglomeration are "three manual typewriters, each a gorgeous antique," together with all the tools of a writer's craft: "Wite-Out, pencils, scissors, and glue." Like Auster, Rush fears running out of typewriter ribbons.

As he works, Rush "rolls his writing chair from one station to another many times." He composes "the main narrative" of his novels on one of two vintage Royal typewriters; he reworks "earlier sections" on a second Royal; he writes freely, "generating fresh associations" on an Underwood typewriter. This "ludicrous" process ensures that Rush inhabits "the novel in different stages. . . ." On "an ideal day," Rush works in the morning on new material that is "raw, highly associative, difficult-for-anybody-else-to-interpret"; he then spends the afternoon revising it and trying to make it readable. When he's completed twenty-five pages, he retypes a draft on yellow sheets on one of the Royals. His wife, Elsa, reads it; they review her comments; he revises. Then the "draft goes to a typist." They edit the final copy together.

Anne Tyler, author of *Dinner at the Homesick Restaurant* (1982), works section by section on her novels, employing a "'very mechanical process.'" She composes by hand, on white, unlined paper using "'the miraculous Pilot P500 gel pen,'" then revises "tiny sections in 'quite small and distinct handwriting.'" Her process "'is almost like knitting a novel.'"

When Tyler is satisfied, "she types it up, then writes the whole manuscript out in longhand again." She then "reads it into a tape-recorder to listen for false notes or clumsiness." Instead of retyping, she "plays it back . . . on a stenographer's machine with a pedal to pause" so she can insert material. She works in this carefully calculated way, accumulating the building blocks of her novel, because she's learned that, for her, "'[s]pontaneity is not always a good thing.'"

Margaret Atwood, author of *Bodily Harm* (1981), works by hand, too. But, unlike Tyler, she doesn't necessarily work scene by scene. "Scenes present themselves," she says. "Sometimes it proceeds in a linear fashion, but sometimes it's all over the place."

Atwood writes "in longhand and preferably on paper with margins and thick lines with wide spaces between the lines." She prefers "pens that glide very easily over the paper" because she writes quickly. Even so, she doesn't "churn out finished copy quickly." She returns to her handwritten sheets to revise and rewrite: "I have to scribble over it and scratch things out." After she's revisited her handwritten draft, she "transcribe[s] the manuscript, which is almost illegible. . . ."

Ian McEwan, author of *Atonement* (2001), used to work by hand and with a typewriter early in his writing life. He wrote "longhand with a fountain pen." Then he'd "type out a draft, mark up the manuscript, type it out again." When computers arrived in the mideighties, McEwan was "a grateful convert." For McEwan, using a computer "is more intimate, more like thinking itself."

McEwan likes "the provisional nature of unprinted material held in the computer's memory"—it's like "unspoken thought." The computer allows "sentences or passages [to] be endlessly reworked" and "this faithful machine remembers all your little jottings and messages to yourself.

"Until, of course, it sulks and crashes."

I began my writing life composing by hand—computers weren't yet available. Writing, for me, then, was a slow, deliberate, methodical act. I wrote on lined yellow sheets of paper with a fountain pen, composing one chapter at a time. I revised on the page. Like Atwood's, my pages became virtually indecipherable, with insertions above the line, in the margins, on the back of the sheet. When I finished a draft, I'd recopy the chapter by hand and revise, again by hand. When I was satisfied, I'd type out a penultimate version, edit that by hand, and retype. Typing was slow and tedious until I bought an IBM Selectric typewriter.

Before computers, once a page was typed, if you made changes, you had to retype the entire page. And if you made a change on the typescript of a previous chapter—adding new material, say—you'd have to retype everything that came after that insertion and so I worked differently and revised differently than I do now that I use a computer. Once you committed to a final version, you were committed. There was no going back to noodle with language at the beginning of a book. Retyping was too hard and took too long.

The three books I wrote by hand and with a typewriter took less time than the ones I've written using a computer. Composing on a computer lets me be tentative for some time, encourages me to play with language, lets me work piecemeal. Because it's a freer process, I often postpone decisions I had to make early when I worked by hand. To complete a book, now, means I have to decide what material to use of the vast quantity I've generated. And this sometimes causes anxiety—which version of a scene I've rewritten a dozen times should I use?

I won't go back to composing by hand. But I do understand how different a process writing has become for me using a computer. My books have become less formal, less constrained, more experimental. But the writing process, paradoxically, has become far more difficult for me and has taken longer.

6

A Writer's *Mise en Place*

Several times a year my husband and I visit the New York apartment of Michele and Charles Scicolone. Michele is a cookbook author specializing in Italian cuisine; Charles is an expert in Italian wines. An invitation to their home, with its view of the Empire State Building, is always delightful because Michele cooks for us, often trying a dish she's discovered on a recent trip to Italy, while Charles finds the perfect regional wine to accompany the meal.

A few weeks ago, Michele cooked pasta amatriciana for a first course. The main course was a cottechino—a sausagelike delicacy—that Michele served with lentils. For dessert, Michele made a simple tart with a combination of fruit jams. And, of course, the food was magnificent in the way that simply prepared Italian food can be—clean, clear, rich flavors; every mouthful a treasure.

I was struck by how calm Michele is in the kitchen. She moves slowly and deliberately, attending to the meal in progress with total focus. And like all good cooks, she prepares a *mise en place* with her ingredients prepped, measured, and organized. When she's ready to cook, her ingredients are at hand, ready for when she needs them.

I love to cook. But as my memoir *Crazy in the Kitchen* describes, my kitchen is often a place where tempers (often mine) flare. That's because I usually adhere to the rule of "Fire, ready, aim." I'll start a soup without checking whether I have onions. Or the pasta will be ready to drain, but the colander will still be wedged in the back of a cabinet. But today I decided to work as Michele does to make an Umbrian lentil soup, with my ingredients prepped, measured, and ready by the stove. Cooking that soup was a pleasure, and it's sitting on my stove, ready for my lunch.

I'm now writing a chapter of my book about my father's life in World War II, dealing with Japan's surrender, mop-up operations on the island in the Pacific where he was stationed during the war, and my father's journey back home several months later. It's a fascinating and, I think, important story—this glimpse of what bases in the Pacific were like after the war was over, how the men and women stationed there felt and how they behaved, what shutting down a forward base in the Pacific entailed, how personnel disposed of wartime matériel, and how they awaited their turn to go home. I have many juicy tidbits to recount that I've never read in other WWII accounts, so I'm psyched.

I've been at this chunk for a few days, and although my writing seems to be fluid enough, still, I've been doing the equivalent of searching in the back of the cabinet for a colander while I'm holding the steaming pasta pot over the sink with one hand. I'm writing about the day news about the Japanese surrender came to the base, how the radio announcers there reported that news, and how soldiers and sailors reacted.

I'd write a few sentences, run to the closet where I store my materials, unearth the right notes, find a first-person account I needed, find my notes from my interviews with my father, run back to my desk, leaf through the accounts and the notes, write a few

lines, until I'd learn that I needed further documentation. So back
to the closet for yet another search.

Not a good way of working when you're using documentary
material or when you have earlier drafts to consult or when you
have notes from interviews with people you're writing about. As
Twyla Tharp writes in *The Creative Habit* (2003), "A writer with a
good storage and retrieval system can write faster."

While thinking back on our wonderful day with Michele and
Charles, I realized that if I *always* approached my cooking as Michele does, I'd be better off. Then I started thinking that if I approached my *writing* like Michele approaches her cooking, I'd be
better off. If I think about the writing I'll be doing on a given day,
search out the ingredients for that day's work, and put together a
writer's *mise en place* before I begin, then maybe I'll be able to maintain my focus without those interruptions that take me away from
the work.

Any way of working, no matter what it is, has costs and benefits. One challenge of having a *mise en place* for a chapter might be
that my work might become overly source driven and that the voice
I'm using will stop being authentic and start sounding derivative,
and that's not a good thing. Haven't you read biographies or historical novels where you feel as if the writer has put her or his notes
down next to the computer and written without synthesizing the
information that was there, without giving the material any flair,
or providing a narrative drive?

The benefit, though, is that with notes assembled, sources
checked, earlier drafts reviewed, we might write more freely and
spontaneously. What truly kills the flow of my writing, I've learned,
is having to stop in the middle of a sequence I'm building to find,
say, how bomber pilots behaved when they learned the war was
over and they wouldn't be flying any more missions. (Samuel Hynes

tells the story of how, after hostilities ceased, two pilots, still hungry for action while awaiting discharge, took two fighter planes into the air and pretended to engage in a dogfight. They swooped and climbed, and dove and leveled off, and crashed into each other and died.)

I want details that only a first-person account can provide in my book. But for my work to proceed as well as it can, it's best for me to think ahead, figure out what I need, find it, and set up my writer's *mise en place*. Then I can work without those constant interruptions that interfere with the process of writing in my own voice.

Many of Peter Carey's novels—*True History of the Kelly Gang* (2000), about the outlaw Ned Kelly; *My Life as a Fake* (2003), "inspired by a notorious Australian poetry hoax"; and *Parrot and Olivier in America* (2009), a reimagining of Alexis de Tocqueville's journey to America—required a substantial amount of research, although Carey does not strictly adhere to the historical record in his work. In order to write *Parrot and Olivier in America*, for example, Carey read and studied more than forty works, among them, Hugh Brogan's *Alexis de Tocqueville*, Max Doerner's *The Materials of the Artist and Their Use in Painting*, and Doris S. Goldstein's *Trial of Faith: Religion and Politics in Tocqueville's Thought*.

Carey prepares for his novels by using index cards and divides them into chapters. He thinks of each chapter as a room, and he asks himself "what happens within each room."

Carey has drafts of his novels "bound into what he calls 'working notebooks,'" his personal version of a writer's *mise en place*. He highlights the places in the work "where further research is necessary." In the margins, Carey affixes "chapter plans and plot points, calendars and timelines, and occasionally pasted-in postcards—anything relevant to the story in progress." The notebooks permit Carey to interweave his research with "his own richly invented worlds." Because everything he needs to rewrite and revise his draft is at his fingertips, Carey doesn't need to spend time looking for necessary materials. Even so, Carey uses his sources judiciously: "For a writer, . . . the greatest thing is to be able to pare away."

7

Deliberate Practice

When I meet writers who are beginning to work seriously, I recommend Geoff Colvin's *Talent Is Overrated* (2008) and Daniel Coyle's *The Talent Code* (2009), describing the habits of high performance. Working hard is not enough: we all know writers who've labored for years on unsuccessful manuscripts that don't improve with time. Coyle and Colvin outline the specific practice—Coyle calls it "deep practice"; Colvin, "deliberate practice"—that differs from simply writing. In deliberate practice, we engage in structured activities designed to improve our craft and overcome our weaknesses.

Colvin outlines five key elements of deliberate practice.

First, deliberate practice is "designed specifically to improve performance" and move us beyond our current abilities. We identify elements of our work that need development. We isolate one, structure activities designed to help us improve, then move on to the next.

Second, deliberate practice must be repeated.

Third, deliberate practice requires feedback about our progress from a mentor or writing partner.

Fourth, deliberate practice demands focus and concentration; it must be undertaken slowly for short sessions.

Fifth, deliberate practice isn't fun. If the activities necessary for achieving greatness were "easy and fun," Colvin says, "then everyone would do them."

Coyle outlines three rules of deep practice.

"Rule one: Chunk it up." First, engage in "fruitful imitation" to learn technique. For a writer, this might mean reading to understand a novel's construction. Second, break it into chunks. For a writer, this means learning, say, how to write dialogue, describe place and time, develop character, structure a novel. Third, slow it down. Taking our time allows us to carefully attend to errors and learn how to correct them.

"Rule two: Repeat it." The simplest way to degrade skills is to stop practicing. To improve or maintain skills, we must continually practice. According to K. Anders Ericsson, a leading researcher in the acquisition of expertise, most "world-class experts" practice "between three and five hours a day."

"Rule three: Learn to feel it." Deep practice teaches us to sense errors in our performance. The most productive sessions elicit sensations of "straining toward a target and falling just short." We pick a goal; we try to reach it; we evaluate the distance between our performance and our goal; we work to improve; we pick another goal and repeat the process. "[T]o get good, it's helpful to be willing, or even enthusiastic, about being bad."

Lucy Corin, author of the novel *Everyday Psychokillers: A History for Girls* (2004), describes how she taught herself about the structure of fiction by the practice described below that helped her organize her novel. (She also deliberately studied image patterns and character descriptions.)

In one exercise, Corin compared her diagram of a page from

Samuel Beckett's *Molloy* (1951) with one from Ernest Hemingway's "A Clean Well-Lighted Place" (1933). Beckett's page consisted of a single paragraph: it appeared dense and rich. Hemingway's consisted of short lines interspersed with white space: it appeared airy. The pages depict "different sorts of worlds." In studying J. M. Coetzee's *Waiting for the Barbarians* (1980), Corin learned that Coetzee's short scenes, separated by asterisks, made reading this book feel like "falling in and out of a dream." Form, Corin learned, "is indistinguishable from content." Corin then studied her work the same way and made deliberate changes to achieve her desired effects.

Corin suggests we engage in the deliberate practice of analyzing the physical layout of our pages. We can contemplate the effect we desire (density, thoughtfulness, complexity; simplicity, directness, straightforwardness) and then retool our work's appearance to alter its meaning. As we revise, Corin suggests reading our drafts in a "dynamic and playfully analytic way," just as we might read "a great piece of writing you are trying to learn from."

If we want to improve our writing, we, too, must engage in deliberate practice. We must assess our performance, work to improve what we do well, and learn how to remediate our shortcomings. As one athletic coach told me, "If we work within the middle range of our talent, we'll never excel." Many writers stay within their comfort zones.

We assess our work, determining its strong points and weaknesses, and we set up structured activities to improve both. Let's say that in assessing a memoir in progress, we discover we don't describe place—we write as if the events could have taken place anywhere. So we devise structured activities to improve. We choose a novel or memoir that treats place brilliantly, and we study twenty pages, underlining instances where the writer describes place and its impact on character. We copy key passages—copying is an excellent device to improve our work. Then we analyze when that writer used setting and how it affects the work's meaning.

We can study a passage describing place from Mark Doty's coming-of-age memoir, *Firebird* (1999), where we find the following description: "We live on East Twenty-second Street, a busy thoroughfare, on a strip of low-slung cinder-block ranch houses where there aren't many trees to absorb the heat. Some of our neighbors have given up on lawns like the ones they had back East and gone to tinted gravel instead." We can then turn to our work and underline every instance where we describe place and note every instance where such a description is missing.

In studying how specifically Doty describes the location of his childhood home, we can learn how to incorporate a similarly precise description where it's missing in our work. We can take time to deliberately write about place in our pages. Or we can write descriptions to use later. (My writing partner, Edvige Giunta, generated pages about Gela, Sicily, her hometown, before working to incorporate them into her memoir.)

In a memoir class I taught, my students' works were consistently unclear about when events in their narratives occurred. To begin our deliberate practice of delineating time in our work, we studied Kathryn Harrison's *The Mother Knot* and highlighted every instance where Harrison tells the reader when the event happened. On a single page, describing when Harrison weaned her youngest child, we found the following references to time: "By May 2002," "twenty-six months old," "only at bedtime," "At the end of that month," "All day and all night for a week," "For a few days," "a sudden June heat wave."

As we studied *The Mother Knot*, we learned that although the memoir moves forward in time—it begins in May 2002 and finishes in March 2003—the narrative is consistently interrupted by memory, backstory, and reminiscence. These are clearly marked— "I was thirteen," "My earliest memory of my mother"—so the reader knows when the events took place.

Students then studied several pages of their work and marked every reference to time. Several immediately understood they'd never told their readers when the events transpired. I next asked them to write a chronology of the events in their narrative and to decide how to indicate when these events occurred.

It takes daily, deliberate practice to become a proficient writer. We might not at first understand how focused our practice must be and how long it will take to develop our craft. As Colvin and Coyle state, we're not born with talent; we find it through the deliberate practice of cultivating the qualities necessary for us to become writers.

8

Writing and Real Life

When I was in my thirties and decided to start writing, the only model that I had for a writer's life was Virginia Woolf's. Although I learned much from her example, unlike me, Woolf was a member of a privileged class. She had a cook and people who took care of her home. Her example of working during uninterrupted writing time between ten and one couldn't help me with my fundamental challenge—how to interweave taking care of children, running a household, and teaching with a writing life— that many of my students face. For a time, I didn't believe an ordinary person like me could find time to write; I thought I might have to wait until my children were grown, even as I knew I couldn't—the need to write was so great.

And then I read Anne Tyler's essay "Still Just Writing," and a writing life became possible for me. Here was a person who'd figured out a way to write in the midst of life's chaos.

Tyler describes how, while she was "painting the downstairs hall," she imagined a character "wearing a beard and a broad-brimmed leather hat"—he became the central character in *Morgan's Passing* (1980). She wanted to sit down and figure out "this character on paper"—she trusted "a novel would grow up around him." But her children's spring vacation intervened, and she had to wait.

When her children returned to school, Tyler's dog "got worms," and she "lost a day." Then she lost Friday—she shopped for groceries and supplies for the gerbils' cage, and cleaned bathrooms. Still, she figured she had "four good weeks in April to block out the novel."

Tyler was ready to begin by May. But she had to write "in patches." There was the dog to deal with, the washing machine repairman, the tree man, the meter reader, a baby born to her husband's cousin, the death of a relative, shopping for a black coat for a relative in mourning. After these interruptions, Tyler "wrote chapters one and two." Although she wanted to write until three thirty in the afternoon, that rarely happened: there were dental appointments, a cat's shots, gymnastic meets, where Tyler tried to convince herself she could use this material in a novel some day. By the time she finished chapter three, "it was Memorial Day and the children were home again."

In June, Tyler put her novel aside to take care of her children. By then she'd forgotten "what I'd planned to do next." She had "high hopes for July," but one of her daughters became seriously ill.

Tyler says it isn't only women who must determine how to find time to write. Her husband, a child psychiatrist and a writer, faced the same challenge. Tyler says she's learned how to write when she can, but also how to be fully engaged with the rest of her life when she's not writing. She believes that putting work away and connecting with whatever else is happening may slow writing down. "[B]ut when I did write," Tyler remarks, "I had more of a self to speak from."

It helps for a writer to develop a "sense of limitless time" so that whatever happens in life can be attended to. Tyler sees herself slipping "gracefully through a choppy life of writing novels, plastering the dining room ceiling, and presiding at slumber parties." If we imagine living "unusually long" lives, Tyler says we can write while still being fully engaged with the rest of our lives.

I seek out writers like Anne Tyler to tell my students about, who write in the midst of the clamor and business of life. A writer like Mary Karr, who was a single parent and teaching full-time while writing *The Liars' Club* (1995); the memoir took her two and a half years to write; she wrote "every other weekend" while her son's father cared for him, and during "every school holiday, including the whole summer vacation."

Or, a writer like the Nobel laureate Alice Munro, who married at twenty, had her first child at twenty-one, published her first book at thirty-six, and who said she wrote "desperately all the time I was pregnant because I thought I would never be able to write afterwards." But she continued to write while raising children, dealing with pets, running a bookstore with her first husband, and caring for a household.

When Munro's children were small, she wrote while they napped—from "one to three in the afternoon." When she wrote her second book, *Lives of Girls and Women* (1971), she was raising four children (her three and a daughter's friend), working in the bookstore, and writing until "one o'clock in the morning." That year, she was working so hard, she was afraid she'd have "a heart attack." At times when her daughter approached her at the typewriter, Munro "would bat her away with one hand and type with the other," about which she feels terrible. Still, it was an enormously productive time and she was proud of the work she accomplished in the midst of such a hectic life.

When Munro's children were older, she started writing "as soon as they left for school." She'd write until noon, when she was "supposed to be doing housework," then she'd work at the book-store. When she wasn't working at the bookstore every day, she'd "write until everybody came home for lunch and then after they went back, probably till about two thirty." Then she'd stop for a cup of coffee and frantically try to get all her housework done "be-fore late afternoon" when her children came back from school.

Like Munro, I've learned there's no correlation between the amount of time I have to write and the amount of writing I've ac-complished. With me, there's an almost inverse correlation—the more writing time I have, the more likely I am to worry every word onto the page, to have difficulty making decisions, to lose focus, to waste time. I wrote more, and published more books, when my kids were small and when I was teaching more classes than I do now. And the hardest writing times for me are always summers and sabbaticals. As Zadie Smith has said, writers with a lot of time "'don't always use it well.'" After the birth of her child, Smith's writing time became limited to "four or five hours a day," and she learned to begin work immediately. It also changed her aesthetic: "'I wasn't interested in 80-page chapters any more—I couldn't stay in that mind-set for that period of time.'"

I prefer writing in real time—a day when I prepare a class, read student work, do laundry, straighten up, run an errand, organize a closet, see my family, make meals, watch a movie. Knowing there are other tasks I must accomplish helps my work. Knowing that I must write during my allotted time or I won't get to write at all urges me to get right to work, draft a few pages. If all I have to do is write, writing becomes too fraught for me.

I can't imagine being that writer who goes up to the desk after breakfast and emerges at the end of day, while someone else takes care of the cooking, cleaning, child rearing, and the business of life. I like to think of writing as "my work," not as "MY WORK." And

I believe that this image of the ideal writing life—writing all day long in a room with a closed door while someone else tends to all life's necessities, Virginia Woolf's proverbial "a room of one's own"—is one reason many people don't begin writing because that so-called idyllic writing life is impossible for most of us who have to earn livings.

Munro has remarked she never understood "that you could have conditions for writing that would be any better than any other conditions." The only time she stopped writing was when she was given a private place to work, an experience she drew upon for her short story "The Office" (1968).

"I did get an office," Munro remarked, "and I wasn't able to write anything there at all—except that story. . . . So I had all this time, and I was in this office, and I would just sit there thinking. I couldn't reach anything; I meant to, but it was paralyzing."

9

Raw Material

Writers have their own ways of beginning projects. Some may favor planning beforehand and making detailed outlines; others prefer plunging into the work without knowing very much, trusting that, in the process of writing, a subject will reveal itself. Still, virtually every writer I know doesn't start from scratch. Many collect material before they know what to do with it; others go in search of material once they've begun to work.

Elizabeth Jolley, who wrote about life in Western Australia in novels like *Foxybaby* (1985), never began by writing "a synopsis or an outline," fearing she might have forced her work into too rigid a scheme before she even began. She needed, instead, to discover "the energy and rhythm" of the particular language she required for a particular story through trial and error.

The beginning of Jolley's process was "a ragged and restless activity" during which she accumulated the raw material for her work—"scattered fragments" of writing. Moving from that initial stage into the process of making a book involved Jolley taking those bits and pieces and piecing them together "rather like a patchwork quilt." After, there was a lot of rewriting. And she often wrote "the first pages last and often put off writing the end for a long time."

Jolley's way of producing the raw material that became her novels involved risk taking—keeping herself free enough to witness the work that was emerging, keeping herself open to decide upon the design of the work after she accumulated much writing, keeping herself from even considering the beginning and concluding pages of her books until the end of the process.

Norman Rush, author of *Mortals*, refused to serve in the military during the Korean War when he was a young man, and he spent two years in a minimum security prison. There, any writing would be confiscated, so he wrote a novel in secret "on onionskin, jamming tiny letters onto both sides of each page." He built a chessboard with a hidden compartment in the prison's wood shop in which he stashed half of his novel. He secreted the other half in the "cardboard tube of a roll of toilet paper" for a friend to smuggle out of prison. When he was released, he assembled the novel.

Rush called it an absurd first effort, "set in a mythical South American dictatorship, involving a peaceful uprising organized by three smart people" against a fictional dictator named Larco Tur. Rush never published that work; he didn't publish his first book until he was fifty-three years old after a Peace Corps stint in Botswana with his wife, Elsa. Still, the subject of insurrection continued to fascinate him, and he drew upon the subject matter of that first novel in *Mortals*.

When Rush was in Botswana, he "carried a spiral notebook everywhere," capturing everything he witnessed; he collected "school journals and periodicals, newspapers and bureaucratic papers"— the raw material for *Mortals* about an insurrection in Botswana involving a local leader, a contract CIA agent, and an idealistic physician. When Rush returned to the United States, he had "cartons of material" that he would draw upon for *Whites* (1986), a story collection filled with "expatriate intrigues—sexual, political, and folk-medicinal"; for the National Book Award–winning *Mating* (1991), about a woman graduate student "who crosses the Kalahari alone to find a secretive utopian village"; and for *Mortals*. While Rush collected that raw material, he trusted he would one day put it all to good use. And he did.

Rush's example illustrates the virtue for writers of carrying notebooks everywhere and recording whatever seems important at the time, even without knowing its potential use. Isabel Allende keeps a notepad by her bedside to collect material that comes to her in dreams. Margaret Atwood thinks writers "should carry notebooks with them at all times just for those moments because there's nothing worse than having that moment and finding that you're unable to set it down except with a knife on your leg or something." Atwood also loves "sticky notes," and she, too, keeps a "bedside notebook" for gathering material that she might use in her work.

Many writers describe how some of their best ideas for a project, or the inspiration for a project, occurs when they're away from the desk. We get a gift from our subconscious writer's mind, and our obligation is to record it. This is raw material we might not yet know how to use in our work but that we might, one day.

I once went into New York City to see a rerun of the film *Breathless*. I was preparing to write *Breathless*, a book about my life as a person with asthma. As is my habit, I arrived at the theater early—I like to have quiet time in public places before a meeting or a movie or a meal.

The theater was dim. The seats were cushy. I was relaxed. I sat there, happily occupied with the pleasure of doing nothing, when, out of nowhere, I "saw" the entire book I was writing. It came to me as a diagram, and I fished out my pen and my notebook and drew a diagram of the book that I would subsequently write. I included that diagram in the book. It was one of those moments of insight I couldn't have anticipated. That moment provided me with all the raw material I would need for my book. But if I didn't have pen and paper, I suspect I would have lost much of that immensely detailed flash of insight, because I never could have remembered it in its entirety. So I consider it to be part of my job as a writer to be ready to collect the raw material for my work wherever I am and whenever an idea comes to me.

Alice Munro has described how, after writing about her childhood for years, she decided to move on to writing "stories that are more observation." To write about lives other than her own and her family's, Munro says she waits for material to turn up, and it always does. When she settles on a story, she often has to search for raw material to transform in her work. Once, when writing a story about a Victorian woman writer, she searched through newspaper clippings, getting "very strong images of the town" where the writer lived, which she called Walley. When she needs specific material to draw from—finding "out things about old cars or something like that, or the Presbyterian church in the 1850s"—she engages the help of a librarian to gather material she can transform in her stories.

When Margaux Fragoso was writing her memoir *Tiger, Tiger* (2011) about her sexual relationship with Peter, a man far older than herself, she realized that the work was too unclear and that it didn't represent her life as she was living it as a child and adolescent, moment by moment. Because her memories were unclear, and because she wanted "to have a lot of real detail," she decided to draw upon the material she'd collected for years: her old journals and the man's letters to her that she'd saved. She went back to the place where the events occurred with a notebook in hand and wrote down "everything to capture the feel" of the place.

Fragoso then went back to her draft and she began to re-create what had transpired from the point of view of the young child who had experienced them, basing the voice upon the material she discovered in her journals. In one sense, having all this information complicated the process because, as Fragoso says, "it takes a lot of work to decide how you're going to shape the material." Without her journals and Peter's letters, though, it would have been impossible for Fragoso to recapture the voice of the child who had experienced sexual abuse for so many years, who nonetheless loved her abuser. The material Fragoso saved helped her decide to reveal she "loved and had affection for Peter," an admission that radically complicates the portrait of her as a young girl.

10

Walking and Inspiration

Many writers I've met, or whose lives I've studied, remark on how they take long walks each day, and that these walks are an integral part of their creative process.

Ian McEwan often hikes with his friend Ray Dolan. They sometimes joke that, if one of them gets Alzheimer's, the other will "take him off to Amsterdam and have him legally put down."

On one of his hikes with Dolan in the Lake District, McEwan imagined "two characters who might make such an agreement, then fall out and lure each other to Amsterdam simultaneously for mutual murder." McEwan was writing another novel, so he "sketched the idea out that night" and put it away. When he turned to writing *Amsterdam* (1998), which he'd conceptualized on that walk, the work took on "a life of its own." He included his and Dolan's walk in the novel—the "route that the character Clive Linley takes."

Alice Munro walked three miles a day. Her walk, like her writing, was a daily practice. (Now in her eighties and frail, Munro no longer writes.)

Munro walked because she felt it was necessary for her to continue to be alert, to train her "capacity for responding to things," rather than "being shut off in some way." This allowed her to be "totally alive" to whatever she was writing.

Munro's daily walk was essential to the vitality that she believes every writer must cultivate lest this capacity to witness the world "shut [itself] off in some way." This required Munro's vigilance in maintaining her daily walking and writing practices. She linked her capacity to generate new work with her compulsivity to stay active. "Yes," she said, "I don't stop [writing] for a day. It's like my walk every day. . . . The vigilance has to be there all the time."

In March 1927, before Virginia Woolf began writing *Orlando* (1928), her love letter to Vita Sackville-West, she promised herself to be alert to the "symptoms of this extremely mysterious process" of when and how she conceptualized a new book. She had become interested in her own creative process, not to try to control it but to try to understand it so she could work with its mystery rather than subvert it. Woolf was finishing correcting the proofs of *To the Lighthouse* at the time, and she believed she was "passive, blank of ideas."

A few weeks before, Woolf had pledged herself to a series of "long romantic London walks" to relieve the intensity of the work she was doing. She understood how these walks refreshed her but also how necessary they were to her creative process. During the night of March 14, 1927, Woolf suddenly conceptualized a new book, a "fantasy to be called 'The Jessamy Brides.'" She began to see characters—"[t]wo women, poor, solitary at the top of a house. . . . [T]he Tower Bridge, clouds, aeroplanes. . . . Sapphism is to be suggested. . . . The Ladies are to have Constantinople in view. . . . Everything mocked. And it is to end with three dots . . . so."

Woolf would have to wait before beginning the book that

became *Orlando*—she had other projects to complete—but she wanted to record and remember "the odd hurried unexpected way in which these things suddenly create themselves—one thing on top of another in about an hour."

Woolf remembered how she'd "made up The Lighthouse one afternoon in the square here" (Tavistock Square in London). In her memoir "A Sketch of the Past" (1939), Woolf recalled how "one day walking round Tavistock Square I made up, as I sometimes make up my books, *To the Lighthouse*; in a great, apparently involuntary, rush. One thing burst into another. Blowing bubbles out of a pipe gives the feeling of the rapid crowd of ideas and scenes which blew out of my mind."

While Woolf walked, and relaxed, and turned her mind to the sights she was seeing—"The greed of my eye is insatiable," she said—she entered that receptive, passive, meditative, yet alert state that created the optimum condition for the inspiration for a new work to surface in enormous detail. And Woolf trained herself to be alert to when that process was occurring, so that she could capture it, remember it, and record it.

Robert Stone, author of *Outerbridge Reach* (1992), about an ordinary man testing his endurance in an around-the-world boat race, finds that movement helps him when he's writing: "I pace a lot," he says. Part of Stone's process involves working freely, which is risky—"You have to be able to surprise yourself." Stone makes a short list of subjects indicating a very loose sequence: he says "I know the beginning and usually the end. My problem is the middle."

To work in such an open-ended way, Stone believes that it's essential for a writer to work to "eliminate self-consciousness"—this doesn't come naturally and must be cultivated. The more consciously a writer works, Stone believes, "the more difficult it is" to create. Stone's solution is to "do a lot of walking. I really like walking and I do a lot of thinking when I walk."

But as he thinks, Stone doesn't ruminate about his work; instead, he tries to let "the story take over," surrendering and becoming involved in the process. Stone believes that a writer can't be outside the work, "constructing it consciously, self-consciously, moment by moment." Instead, "You've got to let your imagination go. And begin to hear voices, figuratively speaking. . . . Beguile yourself. Entertain yourself. And keep yourself inside it." Or, as Stone says, it's important to "[R]elax into the story."

Which is what Stone did as a young child. He was, by his own description, a solitary child, who often listened to the radio, which, he said, "fashioned my imagination." Narrative in radio fascinated him; it embodied both "action and scene." When he was "seven or eight," Stone would "walk through Central Park like Sam Spade, describing aloud what I was doing, becoming both the actor and the writer setting him into the scene." That early habit of simultaneously walking and creating, and acting and writing, Stone says, was how he "developed an inner ear."

I once met a full-time writer who told me he walked to work but that he wrote at home.

"You walk to work?" I asked, perplexed. "But you write at home?"

Each day, after breakfast, this writer walks his kids to school, returns home, takes a shower, dresses in nicer clothes than the sweats he wears when he drops his kids off, goes back outside, and walks back to his house to work. He walks the same route each day, around the block, past a newsstand where he buys a paper, past a deli where he buys himself a cup of coffee, and past a vegetable stand where he picks something up for supper. His walk takes fifteen, maybe twenty minutes. On his walk, he sees people on *their* way to work; he's walking to work, just like them, and it makes him feel professional. By the time he reaches his desk, he told me, he always knows what he needs to do next. On his walk, he's unlocked a puzzle in a chapter, or imagined a scene—sometimes, even, a whole book.

Part Two

A WRITER'S
APPRENTICESHIP

Introduction

One false assumption many of us have about published writers is that they were gifted from childhood and in maturity used their innate ability to write their works. But not every famous writer showed early signs of talent. And literary history is filled with stories of writers investing years of apprenticeship before completing a successful work. The more we learn about how long it takes published writers to achieve their first success, the better we'll understand the slow process of a writer's apprenticeship and the more patient we'll be as we begin learning and perfecting our craft. As Margaret Atwood remarked, writing is "acquired through the apprentice system, but you choose your own teachers. Sometimes they're alive, sometimes dead."

The Brontës' childhood work was poorly written, filled with misspellings and syntactical errors. But the brilliance of their published works came only after many years of constant writing practice. As children, they created Glass Town and wrote, in tiny handwriting in handmade books, about it in tales of magic, mystery, and political intrigue, often modeled upon their reading. Near adolescence, the Brontës wrote melodramas about romantic love. As they aged, their work became more sophisticated. Yet, until each found an authentic voice, their work remained imitative—in 1831, Charlotte's characters were "dark-eyed beauties" and "amoral male characters" borrowed from Sir Walter Scott and Lord Byron.

W. Somerset Maugham in his preface to *The Painted Veil* (1925) describes the "laborious days" he spent in Florence in a room on the via Laura overlooking the Duomo preparing himself to be a writer. He began each day by translating a few pages of Ibsen "so that I might acquire mastery of technique and ease in writing dialogue." He stated few people understand how long it takes to become a writer.

When Henry Miller moved to Paris in 1930, he took carbons of two novels he'd written in New York to revise his manuscripts *Moloch* (about his first marriage to Beatrice Sylvas Wickens) and *Crazy Cock* (about his second marriage to June Miller). He'd been writing seriously for six years, had published a few small pieces, and yet hadn't fulfilled his dream of becoming a "working-class Proust." He also had an outline of a magnum opus recounting his tortured life with June; he'd drafted it when he was thirty-six and working in the parks department in Queens. Miller always wanted to be a writer, but he thought he lacked talent: "Who was I to say *I am a writer?*"

While he was living a poverty-stricken life in Paris, cadging lodgings and meals when he could, living rough when he couldn't, Miller began writing *Tropic of Cancer* (1934), the first novel in his own voice, using "the first person spectacular." It took him two years to complete and he published it privately because he feared it would be declared obscene. The novel had a small but steady readership during and after the war. But it wasn't published in America until 1961, twenty-seven years after it was published in France. Another writer would have become discouraged, but not Miller. He continued writing nonstop despite the attacks on his work.

Nor does our apprenticeship end after we've penned our first full-length work. When we embark upon a new project, or try a new structure or style, we once again become students as we learn what we must for the next phase of our work.

Although Mary Karr was a published poet, when she decided to write her memoir, *The Liars' Club*, she had to begin afresh and learn the memoir form. As she prepared to write, she engaged in a self-designed tutorial. Reading Maya Angelou's *I Know Why the Caged Bird Sings* (1969) was a revelation because Karr learned that writing about ordinary folk was important. She read Harry Crews's *A Childhood* (1978), which became a useful model for describing a rough place and a difficult childhood.

Karr knew it would take time to master the memoir form and find an appropriate voice to describe her girlhood in an East Texas oil-refining town, "our little armpit of the universe." During the two and a half years it took to write her memoir, which won the PEN/Martha Albrand Award for First Nonfiction in 1996, Karr developed a voice combining poetic diction, a tough-minded Texas vernacular, and a brutally sardonic sense of humor. She found the work so "physically enervating" she had to nap each day.

Jennifer Egan, author of the Pulitzer Prize–winning *A Visit from the Goon Squad* (2010), has reinvented herself with each book. To develop a new design, Egan must distance herself from her previous work between books, "a severing of contact with the approach and voice and mood and tone of the previous project." During this interim, Egan reenters a period of apprenticeship and becomes a novice again, rethinking her craft and learning what she needs to know for her next novel. It's as much a process of forgetting what she's learned as it is a process of learning what she needs to craft the next work.

While reading Marcel Proust, Egan was also watching *The*

Sopranos. She asked herself "how to technically accomplish what Proust accomplishes but in a different and, most importantly, compressed way." For *A Visit from the Goon Squad* she also decided to use "some of the techniques of a series like *The Sopranos*," in which a minor character becomes a major character, disappears for a time, then reappears in another guise.

The crime novelist Sue Grafton has stated that far more writers would achieve success if they developed their capacity to endure. "[S]o many people have the ability but they can't withstand the long apprenticeship that every artist must go through," she remarked. Too often beginning writers "get discouraged and disheartened and give up way too prematurely." But "if they . . . can hang in there long enough to learn their craft, they might be fine writers." Grafton's advice is worth remembering as we engage in our apprenticeships.

11.

Apprenticeship

Many beginning writers expect miracles; they plunge headlong into composing a long work before learning the rudiments of their craft, expecting themselves to complete a work in a year or two.

Beginning writers with unrealistic expectations might profit from reading Howard Gardner's *Creating Minds* (1993) that states a decade of concentrated study and practice "heightens the likelihood of a major breakthrough" in our work. It takes time to learn the language of our art, perfect our craft, harness our skills, and develop our own particular form of expression. Because we've used language since childhood, it might seem no apprenticeship is necessary for writers before we begin our first full-length work. But that's not the case: it takes time to learn our craft, and it's time well spent. Studying the early lives of famous writers and patterning an apprenticeship upon theirs can help us achieve success.

Before I started writing, I studied Virginia Woolf's apprenticeship and fashioned one for myself by imitating hers. I learned she kept a journal in which she summarized the day's events, her reflections upon her reading, descriptions of people she knew. When she traveled, she practiced writing by composing sketches of people, places, and conversations. As a mature writer, she used her journals as a source for her work—she used notes from a trip to Greece for her third novel, *Jacob's Room* (1922). So I, too, began keeping a journal. My first entries were nothing more than lists. But in time they became full reports of the events in my life. Like Woolf, I used them as an invaluable resource for, say, describing my sister's suicide and my mother's death in my memoir *Vertigo*.

Woolf improved her prose by setting herself reading programs. She didn't just read; she read with pen in hand to improve her work. She read to learn how to write scenes, describe landscape, construct image patterns, depict the passage of time. She kept notebooks in which she evaluated what she read and copied passages that helped her learn her craft. In one, Woolf describes what she learned about form from reading the novels of Ivan Turgenev. So I, too, set myself reading programs.

My first reading program was studying all Woolf's works. (My most recent, and most enjoyable, was studying novels of the 1940s while I was writing about World War II.) I learned how to write prose by hand-copying more than a thousand pages of Woolf's drafts of *The Voyage Out* (1915), her first novel. This taught me to slow down to see how a writer at work constructs sentences, paragraphs, and scenes. I learned how to revise by studying what Woolf deleted, added, or changed. I never before understood how much published writers revised. The earliest draft of that novel, originally titled *Melymbrosia*, is vastly different from the final version, and so I learned how we can think about the effect we want to achieve—Woolf describes this in her diary—and drastically change our work over time. But perhaps the most important thing I learned was that Woolf's first novel took seven years to complete.

By studying Woolf's apprenticeship, I learned about her work habits and daily routine. I learned to treat a writing apprenticeship

like any other job by going to the desk regularly. To make learning
to write an essential part of our lives. To enlist the support of loved
ones. To join a community of artists. To exercise daily before or
after the day's work.

Zadie Smith has written that it's necessary for writers to have a
model throughout the apprenticeship period to keep them focused
on their work. Smith thinks of John Keats "slogging away, de-
vouring books, plagiarizing, impersonating, adapting, struggling,
growing, writing many poems that made him blush and then a few
that made him proud, learning everything he could from whom-
ever he could find, dead or alive, who might have something useful
to teach him."

Henry Miller's apprenticeship before he wrote *Tropic of Cancer*
lasted for years. Still, he knew he had to learn about Paris, which
would figure importantly in that novel. He set himself the task of
learning all he could about the city by walking its streets. He took a
notebook with him, and later wrote sketches of what he saw and experienced (including his sexual escapades). When he began writing,
he was prepared and he had a wealth of material to draw upon. Like
Woolf, he read to improve his art; the books that most influenced
him—among them, Victor Hugo's *Les Misérables* (1862) and Thomas
Mann's *The Magic Mountain* (1924)—are discussed in *The Books in
My Life* (1969). He studied vocabulary and made lists of words to use
in his work. Before he began the novel, he made outlines, charts, and
graphs of characters and events. *Tropic of Cancer*, which seems to be a
quickly penned free-for-all, was meticulously planned and carefully
prepared for by Miller's long apprenticeship. His spontaneity was
born from years of apprenticeship and preparation.

But some promising writers might keep themselves from engaging in this preparatory work because they don't think of themselves as gifted enough to warrant the time it takes to learn to craft

a book. The Pulitzer Prize winner Carol Shields, author of *The Stone Diaries*, stated she thought it was "a very presumptuous thing" to think about becoming a writer. "Why would anyone care about anything I had to put on the page?"

Although Shields was encouraged to write, she had "very little mentorship." Like Woolf and Miller, Shields's reading was "very tightly bound up" with her writing; the authors of the books she read—particularly Jane Austen—acted as mentors as she studied their works, to learn her craft. Once, when she was writing a series of poems and wanted to perfect her work to enter a competition, she asked herself, "Is this what I really mean?" This single question—one that she continually asked herself throughout her career—was the method Shields devised to develop her singular voice.

I like to remember that someone as supremely gifted as Luciano Pavarotti knew he had to engage in a long apprenticeship because he wanted to build his career upon the firmest possible foundation. He eschewed early success by postponing performance, but he gained something far more important: a stellar, long-lasting career.

Writing for publication is a kind of performance. And expecting to perform too soon might be as risky for writers as Pavarotti believed it was for singers. Like Virginia Woolf and Henry Miller, too, we writers can construct our own apprenticeships; a period of apprenticeship is as necessary for us to learn our craft as it was for Pavarotti to perfect his talent. And like Shields, we can work to perfect our art even if we worry that doing so might be presumptuous.

12.

Writing Outside and Elsewhere

Years ago I had a student in a beginning memoir class whose work took place on Fire Island. The memoir she'd begun described her complex relationship to her mother, and was potentially fine apprenticeship work, but it could have taken place anywhere. The impact of living on Fire Island on her, her mother, and their relationship—a fascinating subject—was missing. A mother and daughter had to relate to one another differently there, I told her, than in Manhattan.

This student also had great difficulty writing in her apartment. She'd do laundry, mop floors, talk on the telephone and her precious writing time—she worked part-time while attending classes—ebbed away.

"What can I do?" she asked during a conference.

"Get out of the house," I answered. "Write in a café. And take your notebook, go to Fire Island, and write there. See if it helps you remember what happened."

I told her to try writing elsewhere because I remembered what a boon leaving the house was when I was a beginning writer. Like her, I'd find any household task I ordinarily despised—cleaning the bathroom, scraping sludge off the inside of the oven—became more compelling than the chapter I was writing.

I never would have finished that first book had I stayed home. I wrote most of the first draft sitting at a table at the Ramapo College library, overlooking a stand of evergreens during fall, winter, and spring. During summer, I wrote sitting on a lounge chair at our local pool as my kids swam, on a park bench near my house, at a bistro table under a huge shade tree. When I wrote outside, I focused only on my work. After a year, I wound up with a very rough first draft that I later refined. I never would have gotten that far had I stayed home.

When I began teaching, if I found that students were having difficulty working, I suggested they work outside their homes. I'd describe how Ernest Hemingway wrote *The Sun Also Rises* (1926) sitting at a table at the Closerie des Lilas in Paris, the "nearest good café" to where he lived on the rue Notre-Dame-des-Champs, with the "afternoon light coming in" over his shoulder.

When I left the house to work, writing didn't seem as scary as it did at home. I was often surrounded by people, which somehow made my project seem less daunting. The work seemed improvisational rather than something very serious and important. I didn't yet know that improvising is a far better way to begin a work than aiming for perfection from the start.

I continue to write outdoors. If I only write at my desk, my work becomes too reflective and introspective. Writing away from my desk feels different from composing inside, either on a computer or by hand. Time slows down. I pause, stop, gaze at my surroundings, and consider what I want to say next. I don't feel as if I'm rushing pell-mell through my work. I find myself inspired by my surroundings rather than oppressed by the solitude of my study. And often, when I'm away from home, my writing feels like sheer pleasure.

On a holiday to Mexico, I took my notebook to the veranda of a hotel overlooking the Pacific. I could see whales breaching, fishing boats, speckles of light shining on the surface of the sea, waves pounding a rocky escarpment. As I tried describing what I saw, I realized that when I write indoors, I rarely pause and look up from my work to see what's around me—my study is too familiar for me to take notice of it. But when I write elsewhere, I notice where I am, and that act of witnessing my surroundings slows me down and enriches the act of writing without taking me away from my work. Sometimes I pen short descriptions of what I see for a few minutes. But sometimes what I see inspires me to think about something in my work in progress I would have otherwise ignored.

As I wrote about the way the ocean looked, I began thinking about the chapter I was writing about my father's stay on a Pacific island during World War II. I realized I needed to learn more about that island—how hot it was, what the Pacific looked like, what the sand on the beaches was like, what the vegetation was like, whether there was potable water available, and so much more. I realized I needed to try to *reimagine* my father's experience on that island—not only to retell what happened to him there but to try to re-create what it must have felt like for him to *be* there. I doubt I would have understood that locked away in my study.

D. H. Lawrence often wrote by hand outside. When he and his wife, Frieda, lived in a humble cottage in Higher Tregerthen in Cornwall, England, Lawrence wrote outside when the weather was fine. He'd brace himself against a pale gray outcropping of rocks facing the sea and write with his notebook on his knees. Writing outside, he said, made him feel "safe and remote." He wrote, too, under a tree looking at the distant mountains in New Mexico, under a tree to escape the scorching sun in Mexico, sitting in the shade in the countryside in the English Midlands, even sitting outside in the snow in Germany. Writing outside soothed Lawrence's restless spirit.

Each novel he wrote incorporated the landscapes he'd lived in, wrote in, and studied. The Abruzzi in Italy of *The Lost Girl* (1920), the Australia of *Kangaroo* (1923), the New Mexico of *The Woman Who Rode Away* (1928), the Mexico of *The Plumed Serpent* (1926). Had Lawrence written indoors exclusively, could he have penned those exquisite descriptions of place in his novels? Could he have represented so tellingly the relationship between his characters and their environments?

My student did go to Fire Island. She learned that the island had gotten its name because fires were set on its sands to warn ships away—the barrier island was a great hazard. And she wrote there and recalled the look of the island on the day of a great fire that became the climax of her memoir, a fire that claimed the life of her mother. That visit prompted an extraordinary breakthrough in her work and enabled her to write a sophisticated first effort.

13.

Process Journal

From 1915 to 1965, the novelist Dawn Powell, author of *A Time to Be Born* (1942), kept forty-three volumes of diaries, an essential part of her process. Some entries describe the "what ifs" of her writing—what if I do this, what if I do that. Others record life events and accounts of her friendships.

Powell's journals provide a detailed account of her writing life. They record her process. Plans for future projects (in May 1965, a possible essay rebutting Ernest Hemingway's detractors). Drafts of potential scenes. Discussions about structure. Triumphs, disappointments, and accomplishments (in January 1942, pride in composing thirty-three hundred words of "The Auditions" in about four hours).

Powell took her journal when she ventured into New York society, the setting for her work. She recorded conversations wherever she went, descriptions of whatever she witnessed, sketches of people's behavior, notes toward scenes she'd later elaborate.

One of the most important items in my writer's toolbox is my process journal. I first learned about keeping one when I heard the novelist Sue Grafton, author of the Kinsey Milhone mysteries, speak at the University of South Carolina in 2001. Grafton keeps a separate journal for each novel; they're about four times longer than the novel itself. She writes an entry each day before she begins work. She records her feelings—especially if she's anxious—so they won't interfere with her day's work, a brief account of daily events, helpful dreams, ideas about the direction her work might take.

The journal stands as a record of the conversation she has with herself about the work in progress. She describes what's troublesome in a scene, a puzzle she can't resolve, lines she's imagined but doesn't know how to use, snippets of dialogue. Grafton maintains that every solution to her work's challenges occurs, not when she's composing, but in her writer's journal. There, she steps back and reflects upon her work; there, she articulates problems and solves them.

Grafton keeps her process journal on her computer so she can transfer material into the draft of her manuscript when appropriate. She can also quickly search the journal to find all the entries about a given topic. (Searching for notes about a subject in a handwritten process journal is difficult.)

Periodically, Grafton prints her journal's pages. She reviews them, looking for solutions to challenges and highlighting anything that's useful. She finds she's often "already solved the problem and it's sitting right there."

When she begins a new book Grafton uses her old journals to face her fear. She rereads them to remind herself she *always* feels inadequate at the start.

After I heard Grafton speak, I began keeping my process journal on my computer. This practice has helped my work immeasurably. I used it to plan the various voices in my memoir *Crazy in the Kitchen* about my family's history in southern Italy. My greatest challenge was determining how to relate what I'd learned about the brutal living conditions in Puglia, the region in which my paternal grandparents lived. Some information came from family stories, much more from research. In the journal, after many false starts, I stumbled upon writing about what I *didn't know* about my family's history. This technique permitted me to write about what I'd learned; it underscored that my grandparents had hidden the abysmal facts about their lives.

I use my process journal to plan a project, list books I want to read, list subjects I want to write about, capture insights about my work in progress, discuss my relationship to my work (what's working and what's not, whether I need to make changes to my writing schedule, how I'm feeling about the work), sketch scenes, think about the work's structure, puzzle through challenges I'm facing, and think through possible solutions. Like Grafton, I habitually reread my process journal and I reread it completely before I finish my work to ensure I've captured everything important.

Here are a few examples from my *Crazy in the Kitchen* process journal.

In a July 24, 2002, entry, I plan writing about my grandfather's history. "I'll . . . deal with my grandfather . . . working with his parents, or with his father, I know, on a farm . . . his coming to the US. . . . I'll deal with the padrone system, how it was illegal, how it was a form of indentured servitude, . . . his cooking on the railroad, his scavenging on the railroad, and killing little animals, like squirrels, etc."

In an August 20, 2002, entry, I think about my writing schedule. "And the upshot of taking the four days off is that I can't figure out how to get back into the book. . . . I am at the stage of the book where I have to touch it every day; then I know automatically what I have to do."

In a September 18, 2002, entry, I think about organization. "From having no bloody clue about what I was doing, I now have ideas galore, the result of following my instincts this morning and reading Auster's *The Invention of Solitude* (1982), going on my walk, reading Luigi Barzini, *The Italians* (1939)." And then I describe my plan for a book in three parts.

Keeping a journal is invaluable. It records our process and it's an important historical document. (I wrote an account of Virginia Woolf's composition of *The Voyage Out* based upon her journals.) If anyone asks how we wrote a work, we don't have to rely on faulty memory, we can turn to our process journal and describe a work's composition. Keeping a process journal helps us understand that our writing is important work. We value it enough to plan, reflect, and evaluate our work.

A process journal is an invaluable record of our work patterns, our feelings about our work, our responses to ourselves as writers, and our strategies for dealing with difficulties and challenges. Whenever I'm stuck writing, like Grafton, I turn to an earlier journal and read about my experience at roughly the same stage. I learn that I habitually think about abandoning a project just before I see how the book should be organized; this helps me reengage with my current work more confidently. I learn that completing a prior book was hard for me and discover that a successful strategy was deciding the time had come to write a final draft. I'm surprised to learn that hard days outnumbered wonderful days, giving me courage to return to work when it's difficult. I learn that what I remember as a sudden insight evolved gradually; I can let myself wait as I write my current work.

Our process journals are where we engage in the nonjudgmental, reflective witnessing of our work. Here, we work at defining ourselves as active, engaged, responsible, patient writers.

14

Patience, Humility, and Respect

Some time ago, I went to see a Shūkōkai karate training session and promotion test. (My husband and our son Justin, who teaches karate, practice the style.) After training for several days, students from around the world, who wanted to advance from one degree to the next, gathered for a strenuous test to determine whether they were ready. I was there to see my son's promotion test. He was thirty-seven years old, a second-degree black belt, going for his third, and had been training for more than fifteen years.

After a day of hard training, the promotion test begins. The world chief instructors sit facing you. They relay the Japanese names of the skills they want to see performed—a specific punch; a combination of punches and kicks; two katas (moves mimicking battles with invisible opponents). The chief instructors scrutinize each student's technique. To move from one degree to the next, you've been training for a minimum of four years.

Students stand at attention and wait as the world chief instructors discuss each person's performance. Then they're called out of line to hear an analysis of their technique. Their instructor has reported on their training, dedication, and improvement.

They ask how long you've been training; how many days a week you train; when you were last promoted. You move back to your place in line. You don't yet know if you've been promoted.

I sat and watched as fifty or more brown and black belts went through their training and promotion tests. I heard how long each person had trained, the number of hours each week they'd studied.

I reflected upon how little patience I had when I began writing, upon how often I wanted to complete a project quickly. How often I wanted to be finished with a page. How often I approached my desk not with patience, humility, and respect for my work (all traits I'd witnessed) but with a desire that comes over me all too often: to get the damned thing finished, the sooner the better. Aiming for the finish line, rather than focusing on the practice. That attitude won't get you your black belt in karate; if the instructors realize you're in it for the belt only, you're told to discontinue your study.

There was one particular moment that impressed me. There was a woman up for her next degree black belt. She stood before the world chief instructors, responding to their questions. She'd been practicing for twelve years; it was four years since her last promotion; she attended class three to four times a week; she worked on her technique daily at home; she attended training sessions; she participated in tournaments.

I thought about what it might be like if we writers were only permitted to write a new book every four years—the time required for promotion from one degree to the next, and even then, promotion isn't assured. Would we become more humble? Would we take all the time we needed to learn a new technique—interior monologue, say, or dialogue? Would we give up the obsession to finish quickly and focus, instead, on the process? Would we understand the time it takes to complete a work? If we knew the work would take that long, would our work be less stressful, would we settle into the slowness and steadiness of the process? Would our writing practice be uncompromised by haste, the pressure of the marketplace, or the desire to be in print, and the sooner the better?

And what if we thought, not of each individual work but focused, instead, on our writing life as a continuum, with the completion of each project viewed as another important step in a lifetime of practice?

The analogy of writing to karate of course breaks down. Shūkōkai karate students have instructors; they're practicing an ancient art with required moves; there's no innovation here, although there's room for individuality. Unlike karate students, writers must initiate their own practice and apprenticeship; they must rely primarily upon themselves; they must invent their own style.

But viewing writing as practice rather than accomplishment can be a valuable shift in perspective. Instead of thinking, "I want to become a writer as quickly as I can," we can try this: "I will dedicate as much time as I must to learn my craft."

My son passed his test. We celebrated. He's now a third-degree black belt. But he was reminded he must continue to practice, or his belt will be taken back.

Justin mused about the years of practice ahead of him before he can be promoted again. He knows he can move through the process of acquiring the next set of skills slowly and meditatively.

After I returned home, I began looking for examples of the traits of patience, humility, and respect that I'd seen in the writers whose lives I study.

Patience. Michael Chabon, taking five years to complete his eighth novel, *Telegraph Avenue*, while working on the novel from ten o'clock at night until two or three in the morning, five days a week. Donna Tartt, taking ten years to write *The Little Friend* (2002)—"I can't think of anything worse than having to turn out a book a year," she said. Tartt's earliest notes for her next novel, *The Goldfinch* (2013), set in New York City, Las Vegas, and Amsterdam, were written twenty years ago, in 1993, while she was in Amsterdam; she described how long it took for her central character, Toby, to come into focus because he's a listener, a very difficult character to write; but it wasn't until Tartt took a trip to Las Vegas, when she was three years into writing the novel, that she found the third setting for the work that underscores the relationship between art and dirty money and chance and luck—important themes in *The Goldfinch*.

Humility. Colum McCann, on being interviewed after winning the National Book Award for *Let the Great World Spin* (2009), describing how the difficulty of juggling the novel's several voices many critics praised was "just part of the job"; how doing a lot of editing is "par for the course"; how deleting sections he'd worked hard on was necessary because he "wanted the book to be organic and . . . flow." McCann, saying that he now has no trouble revealing he doesn't know what he's doing, that "most of the time, I'm flying on a wing and a prayer."

Respect. Maxine Hong Kingston, admitting that when she started writing *China Men* (1980), she feared she wouldn't have enough sympathy for the manual laborers she was describing, so she learned to "use a ballpeen hammer and an axe" to see what the body feels like when it does hard work so that she could re-create these experiences respectfully.

In Japan, a person who embodies the ideal of the patient, relentless pursuit of perfection (which nonetheless can never be achieved) in a chosen art or craft is referred to as *shokunin*, a title that is not awarded lightly or often. Justin's first teacher, Sensei Kimura, might be referred to as *shokunin*. Once, when a student lost an important tournament and chastised himself, Sensei

Kimura admonished him: "Tournament is not important; devotion to practice is important." Those words are worth remembering as we embark upon our writing lives. Or, as Maxine Hong Kingston advises her students, "It's all process. Don't even think of product."

15

Learning How to Learn

Ira Glass, creator, host, and producer of *This American Life*, has spoken eloquently of how we can learn to become story-tellers. When he began, Glass wished he'd known that those of us who want to write, want to write because we "have good taste"; we're avid readers; we know what a good piece of writing looks like. Yet when we begin, in the earliest stages of our apprenticeships, what we produce won't be "that great," and because we know what constitutes a good work, we realize our work isn't very good, and that's "a disappointment."

Many beginning writers, Glass says, "never get past that phase"; it's when many quit, but shouldn't. The secret that would have helped him is that when we begin, we'll have to go through years of working while knowing that our work isn't as good as we want it to be. That's the reality of a writer's apprenticeship. Getting to the point when we produce satisfying work takes patience, and it takes a long time. Everybody who eventually succeeds in becoming a writer "goes through that."

The most important way to learn how to learn our craft, Glass says, is to do "a huge volume of work," putting "yourself on a dead-line, so that every week or every month you know you're going to finish one story." You don't think about writing a good story; you think only about finishing one. Although thinking about a deadline might seem antithetical to the process of slow writing, having a self-chosen deadline doesn't mean we need to rush the process, and deciding when we want to complete a work might provide the necessary creative energy we need.

Literary history is filled with tales about how published writers penned several unsuccessful works before the first work that launched their careers. These so-called failed apprenticeship works were necessary; they taught their creators how to work; they taught them what didn't work and what did; they taught them how to fail, and so taught them how to succeed.

Peter Carey, author of *The Chemistry of Tears* (2012), never published his second novel. When he reread it, he understood why the publisher didn't like it because he didn't like it either. He was already working on another novel, "a wildly difficult, odd book about a bureaucratic investigation into a man's life." After he finished it, Carey said, "It was rather loveless—like dragging your tongue over a gray blanket."

He'd begun writing each new novel "with high hopes." But when he finished, he knew "there was something mistaken, misshapen, wrong in their DNA." Learning how to write a misshapen work, though, eventually taught him how to write a superbly crafted piece of fiction. He'd learned, through writing convoluted, complex works (the novel about the bureaucratic investigation reproduced "sixty-five newspaper photographs of car accidents"), to try, instead, to work in "a simpler form."

Even though he'd written two novels that he knew didn't work, Carey didn't give up. He turned to writing a story a week. By now, something had changed, and he knew he was "finally a writer." What helped him was his constant reading. In reading

Jorge Luis Borges, Carey learned that "it might be possible to re-invent the world in just a few pages." He decided, instead of building "grand palaces" of fiction, to build "little sheds and huts" of stories. In time, he collected and published those stories, then wrote another book of stories, and then turned to writing his novel *Bliss* (1981), about a bourgeois man "who thinks he's died and gone to hell and hasn't." All his work in the short form of the story paid off.

Colum McCann, author of *TransAtlantic*, tells his students in the MFA Program in Fiction at Hunter College that he "can't teach them anything at all." As Carey's experience demonstrates, McCann asserts that becoming a writer is "all about desire, stamina, and perseverance."

Writers, in effect, must teach themselves how to become writers. This is both terrifying and exhilarating. As Jo Ann Beard, author of *The Boys of My Youth* (1998), has written, "Writing is about doing something new." That's why each writer, even those who attend formal writing programs, must teach themselves how to learn and what they need to learn.

Beard's early work, like Carey's, wasn't successful. Her first story was "set in a post-apocalyptic Iowa City, about having to put your dogs to sleep"; other characters were King Tut and cavemen. Her second story was about "a very wealthy little girl who poisons her grandparents . . . it had lions in it." In describing these apprenticeship works, Beard said, "You can understand that I didn't publish for a long while."

Still, Beard believes that having her work rejected helped her find her way. It's important for writers to know that "nobody can help you, it's your path, your valley of the shadow, and you have to walk it alone." And even after completing successful works, Beard says we must understand that we'll "always be just starting out."

Beard's suggestion for beginning writers is to learn what it means to be an artist (Beard recommends watching documentaries like *Alice Neel*), to immerse ourselves "in literature, and in the constant practice of writing."

My son Jason is a jazz bass guitar aficionado. He's learned how to play the instrument, researched the history of guitar making, listened to recordings of jazz greats, attended performances, interviewed some of the most accomplished bass guitarists in the United Sates, made friends with many performers, collected guitars, learned about the woods used in handmade guitars, met and interviewed the finest makers of handmade jazz guitars in the United States, gotten involved with a community organization called Jazz House Kids. He's currently learning how to make a guitar by hand and studying with a famous jazz guitarist. He works long days but still practices daily, awakening before his wife and their children to give himself the gift of playing music, and he's begun to compose. Recently, he's been struggling with learning improvisation, the heart and soul of jazz.

Jason says he learned how to learn from my father, whose formal education stopped at the end of eighth grade but who continued to teach himself many disciplines—working in stained glass was one—throughout his life. When I asked Jason how we writers could learn how to learn the craft of writing as he learned about jazz bass guitars, Jason described the principles of his self-created, self-directed apprenticeship.

Practice daily. Expect to fail for a long time. Be patient. Read widely in your field and learn about antecedents and contemporaries so you're not working in a vacuum. Seek out the finest examples and learn from them. Find out how other people in other fields create and make a habit of learning something you can apply to your work or your process from each encounter. Seek out and talk to writers. Learn how books are made—learn about publishing and self-publishing. Learn how long it takes to become proficient, how long it takes to write a book and get it published, so you don't have false expectations. If you choose to, and can afford to, find the best teachers and listen when they critique your work, though this isn't essential—many successful writers never had formal training in their craft. Join a community of practitioners and give back—pass on what you know. And finally, echoing Ira Glass, don't give up too soon.

16.

Labor and Management

For me, one of the hardest parts of being a writer is supervising my work: figuring out when or when not to write, deciding what to do each day, setting goals, or shifting direction. If we work for someone else, we have a job description; we report to a superior; someone judges our performance. Every job does demand that we work independently, budget our time, and decide how to accomplish our work. But we know, say, we have two weeks' vacation, that we begin work at nine, finish at five, though we might be on call.

As writers, though, we're both labor *and* management. We work. But we also must supervise our work. We must decide when to work, when to take off, what to write, when to revise, when a work is finished, when it needs further revision. There's no one to tell us when to start, stop, finish, move on, although it's important for us to consider the advice of writing partners, members of our writing groups, and our agents and editors.

There was a time when I paid more attention to writing (labor) than to supervising my work (management). Writing pages, I could always do. But the writing life was difficult for me. I worked impulsively, too little or too much. I had no plan. At the end of a day, I didn't feel satisfied because I'd had no goals; I was always "in" the work. I didn't take time to plan, organize my days, or evaluate my performance. I never knew when or whether to take time off. Oh, I finished books. But writing felt like I was stuck in swampy ground. For a time, I thought I'd stop writing because it was becoming overwhelming.

I've found many writers excel at either labor or management. I've known writers who only write; they have thousands of pages (none, perhaps, printed out), but they've never reread, revised, or organized them or planned how to turn them into a book. They confuse being a writer with just writing. And I've known writers who only manage their work; they generate new projects ceaselessly, reorganize their work spaces continually, learn new word-processing programs, work and rework the few pages they've written without moving on. They confuse being a writer with organizing and judging their work. The first writer is stuck in the labor role; the second, in the management. It takes courage and self-scrutiny to determine how we can both write and manage our writing lives. And discipline to teach ourselves the skills we lack.

I learned how to function both as labor and management by studying John Steinbeck's *Journal of a Novel: The "East of Eden" Letters* (1969) and *Working Days: The Journals of "The Grapes of Wrath"* (1989). Reading each novel alongside each journal taught me how to function as a serious writer.

In Steinbeck's April 9, 1951, entry, written as he composed *East of Eden*, he evaluates his desk's new surface, determines how to keep his pencil drafts from smudging, figures when it's best to do his laundry, plans his week's work, determines to try to write somewhat more, assesses his energy level, discusses his fear of interruptions derailing his work, pledges maintaining his focus to complete the novel by managing his work in his journal.

Near the entry's end, Steinbeck plans his day's work: he'll return to a scene with his character Cathy, vowing he'll "take as much time" as he needs; he reminds himself to develop his theme of evil. After his workday, he summarizes what he's written, plans the next day's work—"where Adam meets his future wife"—and wonders whether, within the week, he can "get them to the Salinas Valley."

Here we see Steinbeck deliberately managing his work before he begins the labor of writing. He evaluates his tools—his desk and pencils—shapes his day, sketches the new scene, deals with his emotions, summarizes and evaluates his progress, and figures how to move his work forward. And Steinbeck engaged in this process each day.

I've learned that Anthony Trollope, author of forty-seven novels, among them, *Barchester Towers* (1857), employed a similar process. "When I have commenced a new book," Trollope wrote, "I have always prepared a diary, divided into weeks, and carried it on for the period which I have allowed myself for the completion of the work." Into this diary, Trollope recorded his progress so that if he slacked off, "the record of that idleness has been there, staring me in the face, and demanding of me increased labor."

Imitating Steinbeck, I began to take time early in the day to manage my writing, and writing—and my life—immediately became more satisfying. I knew when I'd write and when I wouldn't. I contemplated what to do, one slow step at a time. I reflected upon my work, making decisions about my habits and goals as well as all those choices a writer must make about a work in progress: what to do next, how to revise, how to structure a work, how to finish. I found I worked with greater clarity and focus. And I could enjoy my time away from the desk because I had established boundaries for my work time, I knew where I was in the process and where I was headed.

At the beginning of the day, my "manager" decides when and how long I'll write and what I'll work on. My "laborer" writes. And then, at the end of the day, my "manager" returns to assess not my work but my process and decides what to do the next day.

Like Steinbeck, I also use my process journal to record my feelings about my work. And I've generated a set of questions about my work in progress that I write about regularly based upon what Steinbeck discussed and also upon those posed in Anthony Robbins's *Awaken the Giant Within* (1991): What am I happy about in my writing or my process? What am I excited about? Proud of? Grateful for? Enjoying most? Committed to? What do I love about my work? What will my work give an audience? What have I learned? What have I done that has added to the quality of my writing or writing life? What have I accomplished? What am I looking forward to?

Just taking one question and writing for a few minutes each day can afford us insight into our writing lives and our works in progress. This practice is a guaranteed mood lifter for me. It helps me realize I love the work of writing and that I've pondered what I'm doing and why I'm doing it. It helps me feel more in control of my work.

Once we become conscious that writing is hard because we have to learn both how to write and supervise our work, the process becomes, if not easier, then more manageable and more productive. The split in tasks is defined. We pay attention to both; we neglect neither. The best writing, I believe, comes when we focus upon both the management and labor sides of the writing coin.

17

Game Plan

I just finished organizing a twelve-week plan for my writing so I'll know what I'll be doing come September. I now do this four times a year: in mid-August for September through November, in mid-November for December through February, in mid-February for March through May, in mid-May for June through August. I started doing it after meeting a writer who convinced me I needed to take time to plan and think about what I'd be writing over a swathe of time. This writer told me she begins by making, and continually revising, five-year plans, one-year plans, then twelve-week plans. She begins with her five-year plan and works back from her long-range goals to figure what she can accomplish in a year, then works back from her year's goals to think about what she can accomplish in just twelve weeks' time.

I love the freedom of being a writer, of having no one tell me what to do. I enjoy working on what I myself have chosen. Still, I believe there are advantages to long-range planning and thinking about our work over time, even—and especially—during our writing apprenticeships.

The most inspiriting writer's game plan I know is the one Henry Miller developed in May 1927, before he'd published a single novel, when he was learning how to be a writer. He sat at his typewriter in his office at the parks commission in Queens where he worked, and wrote a detailed plan for what he next wanted to write—a novel about his life with his second wife, June, that had begun with such promise but was now all but over. He worked for eighteen uninterrupted hours and outlined a road map for what would become much of his life's work.

He'd begin with an account of the day he met June; he'd finish with the day she left him for France with her lover, Jean. He outlined chapters dealing with leaving his first wife, his and June's trying to make a living selling candy, his dismal work at Western Union, June's affairs. He wrote a catalog of "events and crises"; he made a list of manuscripts and letters he could use. When he finished, he had thirty-two closely typed pages labeled "June." Miller had, in effect, outlined a plan for all the autobiographical novels he'd write in his lifetime: *Tropic of Cancer, Tropic of Capricorn* (1939), *Sexus* (1949), *Plexus* (1953), and *Nexus* (1959)—all were conceived, plotted, and planned during that brief period. Miller referred to that outline from 1927 through 1959, when he completed *Nexus*, his last novel about June. Miller's example teaches us it's worthwhile to make a grand scheme early in our writing lives.

When I read Virginia Woolf's diaries, I noticed that, early in the year, she'd think about what she wanted to work on for the next several months. These plans became her writing programs, and she revised them continuously. On January 13, 1932, for example, in the midst of assessing her novel, *The Waves* (1931), she contemplated the fact that she would soon turn fifty, and that she hoped for another twenty productive years. She thought about the books she wanted to write before she died. "And I want to write another 4 novels," she wrote. "Waves, I mean; & the Tap on the Door [*Three Guineas*]; & to go through English literature, . . . like some industrious insect, eating its way from book to book, from Chaucer to Lawrence. This is a programme, considering my slowness . . . to last out my 20 years, if I have them."

On January 5, 1933, Woolf described her current program to finish *Flush* (1933), her autobiography of Elizabeth Barrett Browning's dog, and to begin planning her novel *The Pargiters*, which became *The Years* (1937); she imagined it as "a curiously uneven time sequence—a series of great balloons, linked by straight narrow passages of narrative." On April 6, 1933, she revisited that plan; she needed a break from *The Pargiters* and decided to "bury it for a month . . . & write on Goldsmith & c [an essay]." Then "dash it off in June July August September." And she did complete a draft in September as planned.

At the beginning of 1935, she planned her next program, assigning dates for the works' completion: "But now I want to write On being despised [*Three Guineas*]. . . . And I must finish Ordinary People [*The Years*]: and then there's Roger [her biography of Roger Fry]."

Early in my writing life, I wrote day by writing day without thinking too far ahead. I often felt frustrated because I took on whatever projects came my way and had no overarching plan. I hadn't taken time to think about what I wanted to write. Speaking with that writer who wrote detailed plans, and learning that writers like Miller and Woolf did the same, urged me to begin doing so, too.

I'm nearing the end of two books. But I've planned to put one book—the book about my father—aside to finish this book about slow writing. I have a draft in hand, and a quarter of the book revised. I must revise the remainder of the book and then prepare the final manuscript. I'll also read contemporary novels set during World War II to prepare me for returning to the father book. Throughout this time, I'll jot down ideas toward its completion.

I've written a specific set of tasks and estimated how long it will take me to accomplish my goals. I've plotted my work on a calendar so I know it'll be possible to finish revising within four months' time. I'll be working three hours a day, four or five days a week, and my plan is realistic. But I can revisit it anytime, and pare it down or add items to my list if I move through my plan more quickly.

Until I sat down to write my twelve-week game plan, I was feeling overwhelmed. I was working on two books simultaneously; I'd finally found the voice for the beginning of the father book, and I was revising the writing book, too. Until I began to plan, I didn't realize I couldn't work on both books simultaneously. Like Woolf, I learned I needed to put one book aside temporarily.

Writing my plan took less than twenty minutes, but I gained a sense of relief, purpose, energy, satisfaction, and quiet confidence. Now I'm driving my work; my work isn't driving me. I've typed up my plan and put it in a manila folder on my desk so I can refer to it daily. Now I can take a few weeks off, but I'm looking forward to September to begin work.

I've discovered that, for me, focusing on a twelve-week time frame, as Brian P. Moran and Michael Lennington suggest in *The 12 Week Year* (2013), helps me create a greater "sense of clarity regarding what is important, and a sense of urgency each day to do what is necessary." Whether we're apprenticeship writers, like Henry Miller, or writers who've worked for a long time, like Virginia Woolf, consistently writing and revising a game plan is an enormously useful tool to help us decide what to do the next time we sit down to work. A game plan holds us accountable; it makes the possible—Henry Miller's writing a series of novels about June, Virginia Woolf's completing a number of novels during her remaining years, my revising my writing book—probable.

18

No Excuses

I once had dinner with a writer friend, a hardworking woman I've known for years. She's had times when she's wondered whether she'd get another contract, and times when publishers have wanted her to write three books, pronto. She's been writing through all the years I've known her, and she's in a field where you have to hustle to get work, where only well-known people receive attention. The last book she published finally got the recognition she's deserved—it's been a bestseller for many months.

Through the ups and downs, she's done her work. She hasn't waited for the right opportunity or for her health challenges to diminish. She's honored her art and written every day, no matter what.

We talked about a mutual acquaintance, a woman who wants a stellar writing career but doesn't have one. She's found scores of excuses to keep away from her desk, to stop her from beginning again: she doesn't write because a book she wrote didn't get the attention it deserved; because the publishing industry isn't what it used to be; because editors aren't worth anything anymore. And because she doesn't show up, nothing gets written. And because nothing gets written, her writing career is on hold. Still, she keeps blaming everyone but herself for her lack of fulfillment as a writer.

Like my successful writer friend, I prefer to demythologize writing and frame writing as a kind of work that we do no matter what. Sometimes would-be writers let themselves off the hook: they're not inspired; they don't know what to write; they don't feel well; their work won't be acclaimed. But Ian McEwan, author of *Atonement*, approaches his writing as if it were a job. He's "at work by nine-thirty every morning." He learned his work ethic from his father who "never missed a day's work in forty-eight years."

There are two books I keep on my bookshelf to remind myself that if we want to be writers, we write no matter what.

The first is Nawal El Saadawi's *Memoirs from the Women's Prison* (1983). El Saadawi is an important Egyptian feminist, medical doctor, writer, and perhaps most well known for her campaign against genital mutilation. She's championed women's rights in Egypt throughout her life, was imprisoned in 1981 for "crimes against the State," and was incarcerated until after Anwar Sadat's assassination.

In her afterword to the American edition of her memoir, El Saadawi describes how she first started writing her graphic description of the conditions inside the prison housing women who'd been incarcerated for political reasons while she herself was an inmate. At first, because she was denied paper and pen, El Saadawi would sit "on the ground, leaning against one wall . . . and write in my memory. . . . By night I would reread from memory, reviewing my writing, adding sections and deleting others, as if I were putting pen to paper."

But then she found herself unable to remember all she was "writing," so she got hold of "a stubby black eyebrow pencil" and "a small roll of old and tattered toilet paper" from a prostitute who smuggled them to her from the next cell and she used them as her tools. El Saadawi didn't tell herself she'd wait until she was released to write. She wrote under these difficult conditions because she wanted to capture the immediacy of life inside prison and reflect upon what she observed—the hell on earth of the mothers' cell crammed with hundreds of women and hundreds of children, the women fighting each other for space, food, and water—and because she knew no one else would write it. She knew she could have been severely punished for writing. But she never complained that the conditions under which she worked were too difficult or dangerous. Even under such horrifying circumstances, she did her work, and she saw it as a "victory over the overwhelming and arbitrary might of the unjust, oppressive ruling authority that had put me behind those steel bars solely because I write."

I was with El Saadawi in Barcelona when she called her husband in Egypt and learned she couldn't come home because it would be too dangerous. Still, she told me she wouldn't stop her work, and she wouldn't stop writing.

The other book I keep near me for inspiration is E. B. Sledge's *With the Old Breed at Peleliu and Okinawa* (1981), a firsthand account of what it was like to be a young marine during World War II during these famous battles. (Sledge's memoir was used as the basis for an HBO series, *The Pacific*.)

The armed forces forbade soldiers to write accounts of the war while serving, but despite the threat of court-martial, Sledge wrote down what he experienced and hid his notes in a copy of the New Testament. Because he was a member of the 1st Marine Division, 3rd Battalion, 5th Marines, Sledge participated in and witnessed some of the most horrific fighting of the war. His account has been called one of the five most important books about twentieth-century battles. Imagine what it must have been like to be a marine, penning your account of what you've lived through, knowing you might be punished for doing so.

Although Sledge kept his wartime notes, he didn't begin writing his book as soon as the war ended. Sledge had a difficult time adjusting to civilian life, as do so many war veterans. Sledge was a victim of a severe case of post-traumatic stress disorder before our society understood what that entailed. But after the war, it was considered unmanly to admit to having been deeply affected by combat. His wife believed it would help him recover if he wrote an account of what he'd experienced, and she urged him to do so, telling him his account would be invaluable and must be shared.

Sledge learned that writing about what he'd lived through helped him immeasurably, even though it meant revisiting the horror of his experiences. Turning his random notes into a coherent account helped Sledge make sense of the war. He learned that he could retell what happened without reliving it. And so we have *With the Old Breed* to teach us what a generation of men in combat experienced.

Sometimes I think the act of writing is far too accessible for us. We take the freedom to express ourselves for granted. We forget that writers like El Saadawi have been persecuted—and are still persecuted—for their work, yet they continue writing. We forget the struggle of our forebears to make literacy available to us—the hedge schools established in the eighteenth century in Ireland for Catholic children in defiance of penal laws, for example. And so I believe it's necessary as we begin work to remind ourselves that people living under very difficult conditions have nonetheless found the time and energy to write.

I use these two books as reminders. It's difficult—if not im-possible—to make excuses to keep myself away from my desk with models of writers who penned their narratives—no matter what—on my bookshelf beside me.

19

Writing Rehab

After I got the stress fracture in my left foot that I mention in my introduction, it took six weeks before I could begin to walk again. I'd been off my feet, and with the pain gone, my doctor said it was time for me to relearn to walk. Yes, in six weeks I'd forgotten how to walk. Not completely. But my gait was off; my hands didn't know what to do; the bottoms of my feet were tender. At first, I staggered and weaved. It would take me far longer, and it would be far harder than I'd imagined to relearn a process I'd taken for granted.

Stephen King, in describing the physical therapy he underwent after his near fatal accident in 1999—a van driven by a man he described as a character he himself might have created hit him while he was taking his daily walk—remarked that PT stands for "Pain and Torture." In describing his rehabilitation and reentering work in *On Writing* (2000), the nonfiction book he'd begun before the accident, he links the challenges he faced during recovery with those he faced as a writer who hadn't written in a while. Not that the conditions were equivalent by any means. But just as the process of rehabilitating his body was, of necessity, long, slow, and difficult, so, too, was the process of beginning to write fluently again.

Just before King was injured, he'd decided to return to composing *On Writing*. The manuscript had been giving him trouble. He'd completed describing how he began writing but he hadn't yet begun a key section answering questions about craft that had been posed to him. He wasn't sure "how to continue" or if he should. He'd started work in late 1997, stopped in early 1998, and some eighteen months later, the book was only half-finished. Though writing fiction continued to be enjoyable, "every word of the nonfiction book was a kind of torture." To ease back into work, King "listed all the questions I wanted to answer, all the points I wanted to address"—important advice if we've been away from writing for a time.

King wrote four new pages of the book. Then he was struck by the van.

As he was rehabilitating his body, King remarked that he "didn't *want* to go back to work." He was in pain; he couldn't imagine sitting at his desk "for long"; and the book "seemed more daunting than ever."

King realized it would be difficult to get back into the groove of writing, and that he would have to be patient. His first impulse was not to work. But then he thought that maybe writing "would help me again" as it had during earlier times when he'd experienced great difficulty.

I once spoke with a writer who hadn't written in several years. She'd put down a novel and then decided to begin work on it again. "It won't be that hard," she said. "After all, I've written before." Unlike King, she didn't recognize that if we stop writing, it might help us realize that beginning again will be difficult. Writing is like any other art, any other skill. We have to practice to keep in shape. And beginning anew requires us to be patient with ourselves.

Writing is a physical act. Sitting at a desk and moving pen

across paper or typing takes focus, concentration, stamina, and physical effort. Making sense takes time. If we're away from writing for long, we'll need to resharpen our skills. It will take time for us to get back in writing shape. We can be realistic and begin slowly—we can't expect our writing to be fluent if we haven't worked in a long time. But we shouldn't be fatalistic either—"I'll never write well again."

Because it takes long to get back into writing shape, many writers I know believe that writing daily, or, if not daily, not less than five days a week, is essential to keep in shape. If we're not writing an essay, a poem, a play, or a book, we can keep a notebook. We can write about the books we're reading. We can record and reflect upon our daily life. We can dream the books we want to write.

Along the way to our writing recovery, there will be setbacks, and we might become angry, discouraged, or exasperated. Progress is never linear, though we often expect it to be. We think that if we begin writing after a long hiatus, we should see daily progress. But that's not the way it goes. We make progress for a while. Then we regress. Then we make progress again. The trick is to keep at it steadily, even when it's difficult, as it was for King after his injury, even if it seems we're not getting anywhere. We'll see progress in time. But we can't expect to every day.

What if King gave up trying to relearn how to walk because it was difficult? Or rather, not difficult, but excruciating? (He relates a marvelous moment about how, when he was learning to walk again, he and another patient, an eighty-year-old woman named Alice, cheered each other on. One day he told her that her slip was showing. "'Your *ass* is showing, sonnyboy,'" she responded.)

Getting back to writing is hard. So what. King had to relearn how to walk; he had to relearn how to work. That's life. To expect that we can stop writing and then start again any time we want without some "writing rehab" is to engage in an act of hubris. We can, instead, be humble about it, let ourselves start slowly, and build our writing muscle bit by bit, day by day, and admit to ourselves that it might be difficult at times, but never more difficult than what King experienced. One day our writing will sing and we'll be lost in our world of words, just as one day King began walking again, just as one day King started writing again.

On his first day back at work, King worked an hour and forty minutes. When he finished, he was in excruciating pain, "dripping with sweat and almost too exhausted to sit up straight." Those first five hundred words were "uniquely terrifying—it was as if I'd never written anything before them in my life" to this writer who's published more than fifty novels and some two hundred short stories. His work that day wasn't inspired; his "old tricks seemed to have deserted" him. But King kept at it with "stubborn determination."

If it was hard for King, it'll be hard for us. But, as King says, the "scariest moment is always just before you start." After that, "things can only get better." King continued to write, though some days, writing was "a pretty grim slog," though on other days, as he became reaccustomed to working, he had "that sense of having found the right words and put them in a line."

King concludes that, for him, writing is about enriching his readers' lives but also about "enriching your own life." Writing is "about getting up, getting well, and getting over. Getting happy, okay? Getting happy."

20

A Writer's Notebook

I've written about the advantages of keeping a process journal. But there's another kind of journal—Joan Didion calls it a notebook—that's important for writers, too. Into her notebook, Didion writes descriptions of people she observes, random observations (the sign on a coat in a museum), facts she's learned (the tons of soot that fell on New York in 1964), recipes (one, for sauerkraut). Didion doesn't necessarily draw from this notebook in her work. But she believes it's important for her as a writer to remember what she's experienced, and the only way to do that is to keep a written record.

In her essay "On Keeping a Notebook," Didion describes what her notebook isn't. It isn't "an accurate factual record" because our recollection of an event might be vastly different from someone else's. It isn't to "dutifully record a day's events" because that task inevitably becomes boring, and such a record conveys little or no meaning. Nor should we necessarily expect that we might one day open our notebooks and find "a forgotten account" of an event we can pluck for our work.

Instead, Didion believes the notebook's value lies in its record of *"How it felt to be me"* at a particular time. This, she says, is the notebook's truth. Although we might imagine using it to fix our impressions of others, instead, "*Remember what it was to be me*: that is always the point" of the notebook. Part of a writer's education is "to keep on nodding terms with the people we used to be, whether we find them attractive company or not." Reading our notebooks helps us to keep in touch with those past selves, and a record of "How it felt to be me" can be extraordinarily useful in writing memoir, creating fictional characters, or writing poetry.

I keep just such a notebook and so I have a record of a particularly difficult time in my life—the months during which my mother was in the locked psychiatric ward of a hospital and my sister killed herself. Patricia Foster, who was editing *Sister to Sister* (1995), invited me to contribute an essay to that volume. I suggested writing a piece called "My Sister's Suicide" and she agreed.

I knew this would be difficult even though almost ten years had passed. In my earliest drafts, I wrote about how much I missed my sister; how hard it was not to have someone to talk to about our shared past; speculations about why she did it (an undiagnosed mental illness? drugs? a history of abuse I didn't know about?). Any early rendering of a piece like this is bound to need much reworking, for it takes time to penetrate the more obvious layers of such an event's meaning. I knew this. I knew I had to keep at it. But I didn't know how to get beyond the most trite and meaningless description of my sister's death.

I'd begun the piece without checking my notebook because I wanted the work to be about my *memory* of the event. Then, one day, when I was sick of rereading language I knew was insipid, I decided to go back to my notebook to read about "How it felt to be me" back then so I could authentically represent my immediate reaction to her death. And there it was: a description of sentiments I didn't remember, and once I reread them, found it difficult to admit I'd had. But these, I knew, were necessary to explore if I were to write an authentic narrative.

"Jill killed herself at the end of January," I'd written. "The feeling I have, of having escaped. . . . Sadness, certainly. But also . . . a sense of freedom, almost of euphoria, that I was no longer responsible for her, and that I had been responsible for her for so very, very long, as long as I can remember."

That entry, and several others, captured something I'm not proud of, something my memory erased, but something that invited me to write "real" about my experience—my parents' making me responsible for my sister when I was just a girl because of my mother's mental illness. Without that record, I might have written a knee-jerk essay about the loss of a beloved sister. Instead, I was forced to write something more complex about my reaction to her death in light of our family history because my notebook made me remember who I was then. There, too, I found an image comparing myself to a hermit crab carrying too heavy a burden for its small size that related precisely how I'd felt at the time.

When I teach writing, I invite students to keep a notebook like Didion's. They can write about whatever they choose. But I suggest that this single act will make them take themselves seriously as writers, and having a written record of their experiences will be valuable, both as they are writing a piece and in the future. For those who already keep notebooks, I suggest reading them as Didion does: to remember how it felt to be who we were at an earlier time.

Didion remarks on the fact that we change over time but that we forget the people we were: "I have already lost touch with a couple of people I used to be," she says. Without a notebook record, these selves are lost to us. For a writer, "keeping in touch" with our past selves is helpful. Who were we when we tried to pen our first story? Who were we when we completed our first long work? How did we feel when we moved from one place to another? When we fell into or out of love? When someone we loved betrayed us? When someone we loved died? All this, we can't possibly remember, though we imagine that we can. All this, a notebook captures for us. As Didion reminds us, "We forget all too soon the things we thought we could never forget." The notebook is a kind of buried treasure that we might one day use, as I did in writing an account of my sister's suicide, to transform what we find into scenes, commentary, descriptions, or reflections in our work.

"But isn't writing in a notebook a waste of time?" I've been asked, as if it keeps us from the "real" work of writing which should proceed apace, as if there's a cost-benefit analysis we can apply to the time we spend keeping notebooks. No writing, to me, is a waste of time and every word a writer pens is potentially useful.

When we sit at the computer, we might find, as I did, that we write safe prose. We might elide the controversial because we imagine someone reading our work. This can put a straitjacket on our prose. I once worked with a writer who was brilliant in her notebook but ordinary and safe on the page. I suggested that she use her notebook as the basis for her work and abandon the draft she wrote at the computer. Dipping into our notebooks as we write to find accounts, not of past events but of who we were when those events occurred, can help us keep it real in our work.

21.

The Creative Act

I recently met a beginning writer, working on a late draft of a memoir, who asked me, "What do seasoned writers do when they work?" Learning how a writer creates is difficult, if not impossible, for we can't penetrate the consciousness of a person in the moment-to-moment alchemy of creation. What happens during the creative act is virtually inaccessible.

Still, I believe it's important we learn as much as we can about how writers work by reading interviews describing writers' processes. The *Paris Review* interviews, *12 Short Stories and Their Making*, *The Story Behind the Story*, *The Believer Book of Writers Talking to Writers*, and *The Writer's Notebook II* are valuable tools for studying the creative act.

Learning that Christopher Beha, author of *What Happened to Sophie Wilder* (2012), studied each of his sentences, "moving its parts around, . . . struggling to achieve balance and shapeliness," can help us figure out how to work like a published writer. Learning that Beha continually asks himself, "What do I need this sentence to *do*?" and "what role the sentence plays in its scene, the scene in its story" provides a model for us to use. If these questions can't be answered, then Beha—and we—will know we have a creative problem that must be solved.

I told my writer friend about these sources but warned him about how difficult it is to describe the writing process as it unfolds. Still, he asked me if I'd take five minutes of a writing day and pay close attention to what I was doing, and then tell him. We realized this might affect my work. But I agreed, though I feared there'd be little to share and that I couldn't both work and observe my process.

I suggested he do the same thing so we could compare notes. I warned him that knowing what I did wouldn't tell him anything about another writer's process, nor how I work at other times, nor how he might decide to work. Still, I believed if he studied his process and became conscious of how he worked, and compared it with that of other writers, he might learn something valuable.

The day I watched myself work, I was beginning the sixth revision of a chapter of my book about my parents' lives during World War II. I was recounting what my father told me about my parents' decision about the timing of their marriage and the chapter would reveal the difficult choices lovers had to make as the United States headed toward war.

I planned a simple revision of the first paragraph. I wrote "reread" onto my next-to-do list. As I reread, I realized I didn't like the opening and decided to search for one more suitable elsewhere in the chapter that would put the reader in the midst of the action, and I did that. Next, I decided to revise the new beginning.

I noticed that I reread everything I'd written, making changes as I progressed throughout the paragraph. And after I made a change, I'd reread everything again, and make other changes, so I reread, revised, reread, revised, reread, and so on.

After five minutes, I was still working on that first paragraph. (At the end of my two-hour work period, I again reread that first paragraph and realized it needed still more work.)

During the revision, I spontaneously introduced a fast-forward about the impending war and also a metaphor—that the great engine of war was grinding onward toward their lives. The metaphor was rough and needed work, but I thought the fast-forward was promising and decided to keep it, because reminding readers of the war's inevitability from the beginning worked better than confining the narrative to the moment when my parents were discussing the date of their wedding. The "engine of war" came spontaneously as my metaphors do, late in the process. As I worked, I evaluated what I produced rather than judging it: "Is this working?" "Is this better than what I had before?" "How can I make this work?" "What does the reader need to know?"

A few days later, my friend and I compared notes; and he decided that, in the future, he might consider thinking about what he wanted to write; rereading his work in progress; and moving more slowly through the work, revising as he went along.

We discussed how a writer can use two different writer heads alternately: the writing writer who produces language, and the revising writer who checks to see if it works and amends it if it doesn't. I described how, when I revised the beginning, I made structural changes, such as finding a new opening; trying some material in parentheses, then without as well as linguistic changes—working with repetition, substituting a sharper word for a vague one. I reported how I changed the structure of one sentence describing when my mother wanted to marry to parallel that of the sentence describing when my father did. Although I was calling this the sixth draft, in this pass I'd revised the wording perhaps fifteen times.

We discussed, too, about how, at some point, we might think about what a *reader* needs to know to understand the narrative: it took me some time to begin to fill in the historical blanks—I had to keep in mind that this was a wartime romance but that the reader wouldn't know the United States wasn't yet engaged in fighting.

This process might not represent my process in general. Nor could it be viewed as emblematic of what we were calling the creative act. Still, after our conversation, my friend said he'd try rereading as he worked, that he'd try to start playing with the work, and that he'd start checking what was on the page against the impression he wanted to create—Beha's "What do I need this sentence to *do*?"

Yes, we writers have to find our own way. But this writer said hearing how a seasoned writer worked was helpful. He liked knowing many drafts were necessary and how slowly the work progressed because it permitted him to be realistic about how long it would take him to complete a work. He'd imagined writing got easier after you'd written a few books and thought that, by now, I should be able to write a book straight through. I told him that it didn't get any easier, though I suspected I'd complete the work. But every writer is a beginning writer, and every work teaches you how to write it, but not the next one.

22

Support for Our Work

Support is essential to the fruition of creative work. Howard Gardner in *Creating Minds* asserts that the people he studied who made advances in their work had a "significant support system" including both "affective support . . . and cognitive support from someone who could understand the nature of the breakthrough." Instead of the model of the writer as a solitary individual working alone, we can substitute another, more useful model: that of writers actively seeking and finding support and creating communities in which each member helps the others create their finest works.

We needn't—perhaps shouldn't—wait until we're immersed in our first full-length project to find that support. Peter Carey, awarded the Booker Prize twice (for *Oscar and Lucinda* and *True History of the Kelly Gang*) initially believed he wanted to be a zoologist, but he failed his university exams and had to find work. He got a job writing advertising copy. One of his colleagues, Barry Oakley, had been an English teacher. Carey learned that he, and other people he worked with, were writing every day. (It was, he said, a most unusual place.) That advertising agency became Carey's first invaluable writing community. He'd stumbled into a community where "people were writing and talking about books" and supporting one another's efforts to write their own works.

Not knowing how difficult it would be to write a novel, Carey told himself "If they can do it, I can do it," and he began "writing all the time, every night and every weekend." A portion of his first novel was published in an anthology. Without the support of Oakley and his colleagues, Carey might never have begun his illustrious career.

Literary history teaches us that enormously successful writers are often members of a cohort of creative people who, as they mature in their field, help one another achieve success. The work of each member of the group gains more notice than if each had worked in isolation.

I never would have written my first memoir unless Sara Ruddick, who'd edited *Working It Out* (1977), asked me to write a piece for *Between Women*, a collection of essays she was editing. Before then I'd been a literary scholar. But Ruddick asked me to write personally about why a woman raised in a working-class family chose to work on Virginia Woolf. I was afraid and unsure, but Ruddick encouraged me and guided me through the process. In time, Ruddick invited me to join her in editing the book, and through her I met many writers in her circle. I never would have written memoir without the support of this community of writers.

So how do we find that affective and cognitive support we need as we begin our writing life? Sometimes, like Carey, we can stumble into it. But more often than not, we must seek it out. And these helpful relationships take time and effort to cultivate.

The first step is recognizing we need support. The second step is thinking about how we can find an existing writing community to join or create one if it doesn't exist. And, throughout, we must learn to distinguish between support and sabotage and avoid the latter assiduously.

I believe it's essential for us to ask for support from those nearest us. That means having a conversation in which we relate our desire to write seriously, describe how we plan to achieve our goal (writing, like Carey, perhaps, nights and weekends), discuss the help we'll need, and ask whether we can count on support. And then we can find one other writer or group of writers who understands what we want to do and who are willing to support our work through meetings, ongoing conversations, or other means.

Virginia Woolf's loving friendship with Vita Sackville-West enriched the work of both writers. Woolf was the first friend Sackville-West had who was a committed writer, and Woolf helped Sackville-West push her talent to the utmost. Together, they discussed books, and Woolf helped Sackville-West draw up a list of "solid reading" to improve her style. After meeting Woolf, Sackville-West wrote the most highly skilled works of her career: *The Edwardians* (1930), *All Passion Spent* (1931), and *Family History* (1932). As Gardner maintains, writers need supporters who understand what they want to do but haven't yet accomplished.

From Sackville-West, Woolf learned to recognize the breadth of her accomplishments, not because of her character faults but because of her strengths. Sackville-West insisted that Woolf understand her own worth. Woolf also learned that she could earn more money writing than she had, and put a small sum aside for pleasure—household furnishings; paintings; indoor plumbing; new clothing; and, eventually, an automobile. From Sackville-West, Woolf learned to be less obsessive about her art and to take more time for relaxation, travel, and excursions to enrich her work. She subsequently spent time bowling, doing needlepoint, knitting, bread baking, and listening to music.

We live in a culture obsessed by competition. So if we view the writing life as a struggle to get to the top, we might do everything we can to best other writers. Or we might imagine that the competition is too stiff for us to contribute a significant work. But instead, we can frame our writing life as a project we embark upon together with a group of other supportive writers, trusting that our writing and our lives and theirs will improve because of these significant relationships, just as Woolf's and Sackville-West's did.

I never would have become a writer, never would have continued writing, without the support from my writing community. We edited books and we published our friends. Our friends edited books and they published us. We introduced our writer friends to editors and publishers we knew. And they introduced our work to publishers they knew. We read their manuscripts and offered constructive criticism and they read ours. We reviewed them and they reviewed us. In less than a decade, many of us had published our first important work. But none of us could have done it alone. We depended upon one another, and I continue to be blessed by belonging to a generous community of writers.

So here're our challenges: How can we find the help we need to support our work? And in what constructive ways can we help a writer friend? Can we share child care? Create a writing group or a reading group? Read works in progress empathetically? Help find a venue for a reading? Help figure out how to get the work noticed? Think together about establishing writing routines? Support one another emotionally and intellectually through difficult writing times? Listen to what they hope to achieve in their works and help them find ways to realize their goals?

I believe that our own work will flourish if we find the support we need, but also if we consistently help other writers throughout our writing lives. And not only because we can then count on a coterie of people to give us help when we need it, but also because if we're not generous to others, we can't possibly be generous to ourselves.

23

Radical Work Takes Time

Part of our apprenticeship as writers involves learning how long it takes to complete an inventive work of art. Before we begin our own lengthy works, it's instructive, humbling, and necessary to learn that a renowned painter like Henri Matisse and an accomplished writer like Jeffrey Eugenides sometimes took nine years or more to refine their visions.

Modern technology has unveiled the changes Matisse made to *Bathers by the River* from 1909 to 1916, the time it took him to complete this landmark work. Each layer of paint revealed that Matisse's work became stronger and bolder with time. In his early attempts, Matisse rendered the women's bodies with a fluid line. Through time, he made them "increasingly rigid and abstract," even iconic. The final work is a "far more radical" painting; Matisse's shift in point of view took years.

Jeffrey Eugenides is known for the audacity of his fictional vision. Each of his three novels—*The Virgin Suicides* (1993), the Pulitzer Prize–winning *Middlesex* (2002), and *The Marriage Plot* (2011)—differ greatly. *The Virgin Suicides* deals with the deaths of the five Lisbon sisters, inhabitants of Gross Pointe, Michigan, told in the first-person plural through the voices of the girls' would-be lovers years after their collective tragedy. *Middlesex* deals with the epic narrative of the immigrant family history of the hermaphrodite, Cal Stephanides, told from his point of view. *The Marriage Plot* narrates the intertwining lives of three Brown University students during their senior year and thereafter and discusses semiotics, manic depression, and a religious conversion. To achieve each work's singularity of vision, Eugenides labors for many years to craft them.

Eugenides doesn't want to repeat himself, so he relies on a "slow, methodical" process to craft each work "sentence by sentence." Sometimes just a few sentences take him long to perfect.

Eugenides constantly revises his work. "That's why I don't publish books very often," he says. Still he works every day, seven days a week, from about ten in the morning until dinnertime, in a "not-very-nice office bedroom," composing on a computer and making handwritten corrections after he prints out his work each month or so. To lead this dedicated writer's life, Eugenides has made sacrifices, but only of "things I can get along without."

Some days he's productive; some days he's not. But over time, his initial vision shifts and changes. When his novels are finished, they're a far more complex vision of the events that he originally imagined.

Eugenides is "obsessively secretive" about his work because he wants to represent his own untrammeled vision: "If I can still make the book better on my own, I'm not eager to show it to anyone" because then he might be tempted to tone down its more radical aspects. For Eugenides, the "idea that a writer is a born genius . . . is mostly a myth. . . . You have to work at your originality."

Each novel is begun without much preparation. Eugenides doesn't know "what the book is about beforehand"; his is an exploratory process. When he begins worrying that he doesn't know what he's doing, he makes "a fuzzy outline," and thinks about plot and structure. Throughout the years, he continually revises his vision because he's always "discover[ing] things and hav[ing] ideas of how it might work out." It takes time to learn what his books are about. But because they surprise him, they also surprise the reader.

In observing my own process, I've noticed that the earliest versions of my works are constrained and safe. I employ narrative solutions that have worked before. My characters are one-sided. My settings are sketchy and ambiguous. My narratives are linear. What happens to my characters isn't rooted in their history or culture. But I've learned that, dissatisfied though I may be, it's essential to continue working, for it's only near the end of the process that I develop my singular voice.

Like most writers, I don't know what I'm doing at the beginning, and I'm unsure and afraid. Uncertain work, fearful work is often safe, constrained, and timid—that's my work through several early drafts. But that's normal for my process, and for many writers I know.

During, say, an eleventh draft, I begin to see what I'm doing. And I become tired of my project and often this, and not courage, is what allows me to drop my guard. This is when working slowly and persistently pays off. So one day I experiment with a crazy kind of order, a few parentheses with wild material inside, a flashforward and flashback in the same paragraph, a shift in tenses (past to present to past within a page), an image that just appears, or a title. These changes start happening quickly and I wonder why it's taken so long and why it's been so hard until now. But it's because it does take long to break into a new vision of our work. Why should it take less time than it took Matisse or Eugenides?

These are golden moments when the work we do shifts gears. When I was composing *Vertigo*, late in the process, I stumbled into

using a young child's voice, like nothing else in the narrative, to relate how a relative abused me. My initial impulse was to discard the
section. But I decided to let the piece stand and it was the beginning of a thrilling and frightening giant leap into unfamiliar writing territory. It meant abandoning a traditional narrative and
developing something new and unexpected.

Many writers I know stop or retreat just when their work is
about to become very, very interesting. For Matisse, this didn't
happen until the seventh year of his work, although you could see
incremental changes in that direction before. It takes a leap of faith
to witness the most radical aspects of our works in progress hidden within their more conventional trappings and develop them.
It takes patience and courage to change that work in progress into
something unexpected and altogether new. How much easier to
say "That's good enough," rather than "I'm not there yet."

How long are we willing to wait to develop our most singular
work? Or rather, how long are we willing to work? Are we stopping
short of when our work begins to sing its true song? I suspect many
of us do, and that's unfortunate. If it took Matisse seven years, or
Eugenides, nine, why do we expect important work from ourselves
in, say, a year or even two? If we let ourselves work, as Matisse and
Eugenides did, long enough until our work surprises us, startles us,
or even scares us, we, too, might create a singular, authentic, powerful work of art.

Part Three

CHALLENGES AND SUCCESSES

Introduction

How many of us willingly accept failure, even look forward to it, as an inevitable part of a creative life? Mary Karr, author of *The Liars' Club*, is afraid of failure. Yet she keeps Samuel Beckett's motto "Fail better" posted above her desk. She asks herself what she'd write if she "weren't afraid."

Karr related that she was devastated when she had to abandon a "how-to-book about prayer." She realized her pages "were duller than a rubber knife." When she understood she couldn't write a spiritual book for a secular audience, she moped around "in scuzzy clothes," ate "Indian food," cried, and listened "to Beethoven really loud." She then called her former teacher Robert Hass, who told her any bad book has "some good sentences in it," and Karr went back to work.

What looks like failure is often just a way station on the road to success.

Michael Chabon began writing *Fountain City* (1995) after the immense success of his first novel, *The Mysteries of Pittsburgh*. For five years and fifteen hundred pages, Chabon struggled to discover his novel's subject amid its various plotlines: "a gargantuan Florida real estate deal . . . French cooking, and the crazy and ongoing dream of rebuilding the Great Temple in Jerusalem" set in both Paris and the fictional Fountain City. The novel was about loss. But Chabon wanted it to be about love, too. Still, Chabon "could never get those two halves to stick together convincingly." With his editor's help, Chabon tried one last time to fix the novel but decided it couldn't be done. He mourned its loss, dreaming of "all the other wonderful books" he could have written.

After Chabon abandoned *Fountain City*, his wife, Ayelet Waldman, told him she'd be unavailable for six weeks, as she needed to prepare for the bar exam. Chabon decided to take that time to think about what he wanted to write next. He imagined a scene in which "a straight-laced, troubled young man . . . was standing on a backyard lawn at night, holding a tiny winking Derringer to his temple, while on the porch of the nearby house a shaggy pot-smoking, much older man . . . watched him and tried to decide if what he was seeing was real or not."

He opened a new file, "called it X," and quickly found the older man's voice and continued to work without telling anyone. By the end of six weeks, he had "117 pages of a novel called *Wonder Boys*." When Waldman passed her exam, Chabon had completed two-thirds of a first draft. Six weeks later, he finished the draft and mailed it to his agent.

Chabon drew upon his experience writing a failed novel to create Grady Tripp, a writer who's struggled for five years to complete a novel called *Wonder Boys*: "I worked for hours, [on the] worm-ridden hole of an ending I'd already tried three times before. This would oblige me to go back through the previous two-thousand-odd pages to flatten out and marginalize one of the present main characters and to eliminate another entirely."

Chabon used all the frustration, disappointment, sorrow, and despair he experienced in writing *Fountain City* to create an archetypal portrait of a writer struggling mightily to complete a work he knows is a failure and suspects he must abandon. In one scene, Grady takes pages of the manuscript, fashions them into a little boat, "set[s] this unlikely craft in the gutter," and watches it drift away. After this ceremonial letting go, his head is clear: "I wasn't happy—I'd poured too many years of my life . . . into that book not to part with it in utter sorrow," he says. "Still, I felt light."

Was *Fountain City* a failure? Another writer might have abandoned fiction. But Chabon transformed his experience into another—immensely successful—work of art. He couldn't have written such a convincing portrait of a failed writer unless he himself had experienced it. He returned to *Fountain City* to try to learn why it failed, and began annotating it; he mentioned his project to David Eggers, founder of *McSweeney's*; *Fountain City* (2010), with its annotations, has been published by *McSweeney's* because Chabon hopes it will be useful for "fans of ruination."

If we believe that creativity is—or should be—success after success, we've got it wrong. Setbacks in the work occur often; what some people call failure occurs often. But it's what we do *after* that counts.

A setback often forces us into a necessary paradigm shift about the nature of our work that wouldn't otherwise have occurred. Chabon shifted his focus to the pain of abandoning a work of art and the vagaries of the creative process. Frustration is often necessary to fuel creative solutions to seemingly insoluble problems. Seeming failure is often necessary to push our work into unexpected terrain.

John Steinbeck wanted *East of Eden* to be his magnum opus, a novel describing his family's history in the Salinas Valley. He didn't know whether he was "good enough or gifted enough" to complete the work. Still, in the journal he kept while composing the novel, he planned the novel, and how he needed to live while working to successfully complete the book. He concluded the only way to succeed would be to slow down his process.

Steinbeck wanted to be relaxed; he couldn't rush: "I have always the tendency to hurry and I don't want to this time," he wrote. "I know this is going very slowly," he stated, "but I want it that way." To write a good book, he had to "forget even that I want it to be good." As he worked, he decided "it should not have any intention save only to be written."

Steinbeck's journal documents his successful formula for completing a work. The only way for a writer to be successful is for a writer to resist the "indiscipline of overwork," he learned, to move the book along "little by little," and to "do the best" we can each day.

24

Failure in the Middle

In working with writers, I've learned it's not talent that gets books written, it's hard, slow, steady work. But it's not only hard work—almost every student I've taught works hard. It's learning to understand that the process of writing isn't linear but filled with peaks and valleys; that sometimes we don't know what we're doing but we need to work anyway; that we must stay with the process through uncertainty, indecision, anxiety, and feeling our work is failing; that we must have tenacity when we feel like walking away from a project.

My most important job is helping writers endure the tough stages of the process. And I've learned that often the toughest stage comes just before the biggest breakthroughs. But that's when many writers decide their work is a failure and put it down. Sometimes they think because the work is a failure, *they're* failures and not meant to be writers.

The short story writer and memoirist Tobias Wolff, author of *This Boy's Life* (1989), described how, when writing a long work, "a kind of anxious wonder sets in as to whether or not you'll really finish it, whether it will be any good, whether all this time will have been wasted—and we all hate to waste our time." Wolff feels this way every time; completing one successful work doesn't mean he has more courage or conviction when he writes the next. "Everything I've written . . . has seemed to me, at one point or another, something I probably ought to abandon. Even the best things I've written have seemed to me at some point very unlikely to be worth the effort I had already put into them. But I know I have to push through." Wolff completes every work he begins: "For me, it's more important to keep the discipline of finishing things than to be assured at every moment that it's worth doing."

Chip Heath and Dan Heath's *Switch* (2010) states that if we want to reach our full potential, we need to cultivate "a growth mind-set." According to Harvard professor Rosabeth Moss Kanter, "Everything can look like a failure in the middle." At the beginning of a project, we feel hope; at the end, we might feel confident. But in between "there is a negative emotional valley labeled 'insight,'" according to Tim Brown, CEO of IDEO. During this phase, it's easy to become downhearted because it's immensely difficult to figure out what to do next.

It's hard to take a mountain of manuscripts we've written—starts, false starts, finished work, half-completed work, fine work—and turn it into a book. Brown insists it'll be easier to weather that trough in the creative arc if we anticipate, even expect, failure in the middle of the process. Brown encourages people to *"seek out failure"* because it's the only way for genuine growth to occur. Without failure, our work stagnates. Without failure, we're not frustrated enough to seek new solutions to the challenges we're confronting.

For me, too, the toughest part of the writing process comes in the middle. Middle. Muddle. That's how it's always been, although I forget from one book to the next. I start a book, excited. I go to the desk eagerly, write page after page, scene after scene. I don't yet know what the book is about, but at the beginning, I don't need to.

At this early stage, anything goes. Is it any wonder that writers often put down one work that's frustrating and begin another?

The energy of beginning can last days, months, or years, depending on the size of the project. And then we have all these pages. They're good enough to work with, good enough to revise. And revising might be fun, too, because we discover there's so much more to say. But then there's that moment when we realize that a mass of pages, no matter how good they are, no matter how good they might become, don't constitute a book. A book is different *in kind*, not *in degree*, from a mass of pages.

This is the dreaded middle. "What's the book about?" we ask ourselves, although we thought we knew when we started. There doesn't seem to be a through line, a narrative arc, a satisfactory structure. We don't know what we're doing or where we're going. And this feels like failure. It's the "insight stage" when we might stop working.

As the authors of *Switch* write, most of us haven't been taught what the growth process looks like and feels like. We don't know that the *dreaded middle*—when the work looks like a failure, when we feel like a failure—is a necessary stage that no creative person can avoid. If we know it's coming, if we understand it's inevitable, we might be more prepared for it and less likely to walk away from our projects.

I once taught a student—one of the best I've ever had—who became a brilliant writer only after she learned this lesson about her process. She'd begin a work with gusto. Write a few drafts that another writer might find acceptable. But then, in the middle of her process, she'd become confused and start muddling everything up. She'd move pieces around. Take out one significant narrative line and introduce another that didn't seem to fit. It seemed she was destroying what she'd created. But she was reaching for something unexpected, something quirky, something that united two or three seemingly unrelated narrative arcs.

The middle stage was difficult for her. She often thought of giving up or returning to the simpler, clearer incarnations of her work rather than dealing with the seeming mess she'd created. But in that mess was the kernel of a new way of understanding her material. And when she realized this—often after she said she was ready to chuck the whole thing—the piece came together seemingly without effort, though both of us understood the enormous amount of work that had gone into completing the project.

Michael Chabon has described how difficult it was for him to move through the middle period of writing *Telegraph Avenue*, centered on a used-record store near his home in Berkeley, California. "I got two years into the novel . . ." Chabon said, "and felt like it was an utter flop. I wanted to put it aside but my wife talked me out of it. She said she cared too much about these characters and wanted to find out what became of them." Chabon began again, "keeping the characters but reinventing the story completely and leaving behind almost every element" of the original version. This wasn't a new experience for Chabon. "It happens with every book now, I hate to say"; it happened, too, when Chabon wrote *The Amazing Adventures of Kavalier & Clay* (2000) and *The Yiddish Policemen's Union* (2007).

Nonetheless, Chabon persevered "thanks to my wife." Her role, he says, is "to lash me to the tiller and keep me there long enough to get through the bad patches."

25

Doubt

Doubting always seems to accompany the act of writing. Doubting whether our work is worthwhile. Doubting whether we have the requisite skill.

Nicole Krauss, author of *Great House* (2010), writes "without any sense of where the writing will take me." But instead of uncertainty derailing her, she "commit[s] to this doubt, this uncertainty." As she drafted the novel, Krauss used the doubt inherent in her process as a subject so that *Great House* became a novel about "what it is . . . to commit to our lives, all the while being uncertain about so many things."

Other writers have dealt with doubt by thinking deeply about the purpose of art and its function in society and writing essays about their beliefs so that, when they composed, they had a clearer sense of why they were writing. They'd taken time to understand why writing mattered, and this sustained them throughout difficult periods.

Though Virginia Woolf sometimes doubted herself, she thought about the function of the novel, and this gave her a sense of purpose and a set of standards against which to judge her work. She'd taken time to understand why the novel was important; she knew why writing her work was important.

In works like *A Room of One's Own*, *Three Guineas* (1938), "The Art of Fiction," and "The Leaning Tower," she discussed her beliefs about fiction's importance, developing complex insights about the role of literature. In *A Room of One's Own*, Woolf asked, "What conditions are necessary for the creation of works of art?" She wrote that "the relation of human being to human being" and the human being to society was the subject of her art. She believed it was necessary for people from all classes to write, not just the elite and privileged. For this to happen, society must become more equitable. In *Mrs. Dalloway*, she created the character of Septimus Smith, a workingman who might have been, but never became, a poet, illuminating this idea.

Because women's relationships to men had been the subject of fiction for so long, Woolf wanted, instead, to describe women's relationships to one another. Works like *Mrs. Dalloway*, *To the Lighthouse*, and *Orlando*, reveal this concern. She also wanted to describe the interior life: "Above all," she wrote, "you must illumine your own soul with its profundities and its shallows, and its vanities and its generosities, and say . . . what is your relation to the everchanging and turning world." She developed her own idiosyncratic version of the multiple point of view novel to do this.

D. H. Lawrence also reflected upon his purpose in writing the novel and described why he believed what he was doing was significant. Even when his works were criticized, even when *The Rainbow* (1915) was banned and burned, when *Lady Chatterley's Lover* (1928) was censored, when he knew no one would publish his work, Lawrence had erected a sturdy touchstone against which to judge his works' value. He evaluated his work according to *his* standards; he disavowed the notion that others had the right to judge his work.

In essays like "Surgery for the Novel—or a Bomb," "Art and Morality," "Morality and the Novel," and "Why the Novel Matters," he articulated his philosophy of the function of fiction. He believed the novel was a supremely important didactic tool that could—and should—be used to change society. "Let us learn from the novel," Lawrence wrote in "Why the Novel Matters." "Turn truly, honourably to the novel, and see wherein you are man alive or dead man in life. . . . You may eat your dinner as man alive, or as a mere masticating corpse."

Lawrence was sure his work was important and he was messianic in believing that his work would help change society's attitudes about materialism, sex, and love. He reviled his critics, cursing them in flamboyant language, calling them insects, beetles, or hedgehogs. He had his fears, too. He thought that after *Lady Chatterley's Lover* was published, he'd be regarded merely as a specialist in sexual matters. But his sense of mission—and perhaps an expectation that he would die young—fueled Lawrence's writing.

Lawrence thought deeply about the relationship between men and women and the function of marriage and expressed his beliefs in essays like "Love," "We Need One Another," and "Women Are So Cocksure." His philosophy about the centrality of love permeates his novel *The Rainbow*, which challenged the prevailing belief of sacrificing one's personal destiny to a nation's. In *The Rainbow*, Lawrence described the core experience of human existence as a kind of difficult-to-achieve heterosexual love, shuttling between the merging of two separate identities and a compelling need for privacy. The novel describes its characters' attempts to achieve this union with every subtle shift of feeling scrupulously represented.

In writing a mission statement for his work, Lawrence articulated his own goals, his own standard for success. He knew how each novel fit into his grand plan. He wasn't just writing fiction, he was writing fiction that criticized his society to change it, to help men and women live vital lives.

Krauss used the doubt she experienced as a subject in her work. Both Woolf and Lawrence show that one way to deal with doubt is to think about our writing in terms of the function of art in society.

We can—we do—doubt the worth of our work. But riding the horse of self-doubt can waste the psychic energy we need to do our work. We can own our doubt without letting it disable us. How would we react if a book of ours was condemned, banned, and burned? Would we carry on, as Lawrence did, because we know what we're doing and commit ourselves to writing despite censure, or to find ways around censorship? Or would we let society's censure about the worth of our work disable us?

Maybe we all need to take time to think about our work's significance and write a mission statement. Maybe if we do, we'll understand more clearly why we've committed ourselves to a writing life. Maybe doing this will give us—as it gave Woolf and Lawrence—the motivation to continue working.

When my students doubt whether their work is worthwhile, I ask them to think about what their unique contribution might be and where their work fits into their beliefs about the function of art. I ask them to write a miniversion of a mission statement like Woolf's and Lawrence's. Then I ask them to imagine what would happen if all potential writers stopped writing because they doubted their work was worthwhile. Do any of us want a world without books, like *Great House*, that a writer's uncertainty might have derailed? Every book that has changed their lives has likely been written by a writer who wondered, just as they do, whether their work was worthwhile.

26

Writing as Collaboration

When I go to author readings, I often hear people ask questions about writers' work habits, their sources of inspiration, or how long it took to complete their works. But I've never heard anyone ask, "How much editorial input did you have? How much did you change your work based upon editorial suggestions?" And I think this is one of the most important questions we can ask published writers.

I've noticed that beginning writers sometimes treat their works in progress as if they're sacrosanct, as if they can't—and shouldn't—be changed based upon a mentor's reading. "It's my work," they say. "This is the way I want it."

This stand assumes that writers are the best possible judges of their work, and this might sometimes be true. But according to this view of the process, writers won't revise their works based even upon what a very well-qualified person suggests. These writers might be willing to make cosmetic changes. But they stick to their own sense about the narrative arc, the work's voice, its point of view, its order. This may be the way some published writers behave, but it's not the way the ones I know do.

When a writer I'm working with refuses to budge on something

I've indicated needs revision, I suggest they read the correspondence between F. Scott Fitzgerald and his editor, Maxwell Perkins, about *The Great Gatsby* (1925), and that they compare the published version of *Gatsby* with the earlier version, *Trimalchio*, to understand how a great writer makes changes based upon editorial input.

Although Perkins praised *Trimalchio*, he pointed out three major problems with the manuscript. Two chapters—VI and VII—weren't working. Gatsby's character was "somewhat vague"; Perkins thought Fitzgerald needed to sharpen his portrait. Perkins believed the reader needed to understand how Gatsby became so wealthy. Finally, although Perkins liked the title (referring to a character in the *Satyricon*), the Scribner's editors didn't.

According to James L. W. West III, after receiving Perkins's criticism, Fitzgerald "undertook a complicated rewriting and restructuring of the novel." He rewrote chapters VI and VII; he introduced information about Gatsby's past earlier in the narrative; he alluded to how Gatsby had acquired his wealth. He also "polished the prose extensively" and introduced new material—the most memorable being the "description of Jay Gatsby's smile in Chapter III."

Fitzgerald had changed the title many times before: *Among the Ash Heaps and Millionaires, On the Road to West Egg, Gold-hatted Gatsby*. After first agreeing to change the title to *The Great Gatsby*, Fitzgerald suggested, instead, other titles, *Under the Red, White, and Blue*, for example. But Perkins insisted the novel be published as *The Great Gatsby*.

Published writers don't often share what the publication process is like. We don't often describe how many changes we've made based upon an editor's input. We don't often admit that our manuscripts required a complete overhaul. Many published works become, in effect, collaborative efforts before publication. I know of one famous writer who, at the end of a project, is installed in a hotel while he and his editor work on complete rewrites. This writer—not his editor—gets credit for the work's brilliance despite the fact that what he submitted only approximated the published work.

Writers complete their work. Editors evaluate their manuscripts. Then author, editor, assistant editor, and copy editor join forces to turn manuscripts into the best books possible. Writers might believe their work is completed when they submit. But we learn, sometimes with chagrin, sometimes with gratitude, that there's far more work to do. We've been so close to the book by the time we're finished that we sometimes lose perspective and need an objective eye to let us know what needs revision.

At this stage, in my experience, there's a lot of give-and-take, some negotiation, perhaps even a few arguments. But none of my books and none of my friends' books has been published without considerable changes. So, if seasoned writers take editorial advice, and beginning writers seem less willing, I think one reason is because beginning writers don't know how many changes published writers must make to their work because of editorial input.

After meeting with their editors, I've often heard well-known writers say, "I have to rewrite the whole thing," or "I have to rethink the way I present the central character," or "I realize the structure of the book isn't working." These writers listen and make fundamental, large-scale changes in works they've labored over for years. What they thought was the end of the process was, in fact, the beginning of yet another round of work.

Mary Gordon is one beginning novelist who took a mentor's advice and profited thereby. Gordon's first novel, *Final Payments* (1978), underwent many revisions before it was published, "the most significant of which—going from third- to first-person—was suggested by Elizabeth Hardwick, Gordon's former teacher at

Barnard." *Final Payments* became an utterly different work when it was told in the voice of Isabel Moore, a thirty-year-old woman who's given up her life to care for her father. The novel became a sensation, selling over a million copies in paperback.

Here are some changes I've made based upon editorial input.

Virginia Woolf (1989): My editor insisted I write an introduction, situating Virginia Woolf's sexual abuse in the context of Victorian England. That entailed an enormous amount of research. But I wasn't then only writing about one girl's experience but about an entire society's mores.

Vertigo: My editor's letter requesting changes was ten single-spaced pages. I had to rewrite how I dealt with my depression. I had to write a preface, which took me an entire summer and was perhaps the most difficult writing I've ever done. I had to rearrange the chapters' order, which meant revising the whole book. And I'd thought I was finished.

Adultery (2000): The editor wanted me to take a late chapter and make it the first chapter so the book would begin with a punch, and begin differently from my other memoirs. This meant revising the whole book.

Crazy in the Kitchen: My editor insisted I delete a chapter too similar in subject matter and tone to *Vertigo*. Deleting that chapter meant a revision of other chapters.

On Moving (2009): My penultimate draft was a hundred thousand words. The editor decided the book should be forty thousand words. I didn't like the version an editor presented me with. So I cut the manuscript to sixty thousand words myself, deleting much personal material.

Norman Rush calls his wife, Elsa Rush, "'a partner in the process'" of writing, helping him at every stage with support and concrete advice. They often discuss the function of the novel. Elsa believes readers enjoy works that "'move right along and things happen.'" Rush's novels are noted for pages-long diatribes by his characters and for pages-long internal monologues. Though Elsa says that Rush is the boss of what he writes, when Rush wanted to include a 154-line poem in *Mortals*, Elsa told him he was "'self-destructive and insane'" and he removed all but "14 lines across 2 stanzas."

Seasoned writers hear what needs to be reworked, and they revise. They don't cling unthinkingly to the version of the work they've completed. They listen to expert advice and, more often than not, take it. And their published works are far better for it.

Would *The Great Gatsby* have been such a success had it been called, instead, *Among the Ash Heaps and Millionaires?*

27

Creative Problem Solving

In describing how he composed *Atonement*, Ian McEwan stated that the novel "grew out of many months of sketches and doodling." Then one morning he wrote "six hundred words or so describing a young woman entering a drawing room with some wild flowers in her hand, searching for a vase," and "aware of a young man outside gardening whom she wishes both to see and avoid."

He knew he had "at last started a novel."

But beyond that, he "knew nothing." "Slowly," McEwan said, "I pieced together a chapter," the one in which "Cecilia and Robbie go to the fountain, the vase breaks, she strips off and plunges into the water to retrieve the pieces, she walks away from him without a word."

But then McEwan "stopped, and for six weeks or so I pondered." He was faced with a range of creative problems he had to solve. Who was the woman? Who was the young man? What was their relationship? When did this event take place? Where did it take place?

After that hiatus, McEwan began working again, and wrote the chapter about "Briony attempting to put on a play with her cousins." When he completed that chapter, he began to understand what the work was about. The "whole household was emerging"; he sensed that he'd eventually be writing about "Dunkirk and St. Thomas's hospital"; he realized that Briony was writing the chapters and that "she was going to commit a terrible error, and that writing . . . throughout her life would be her form of atonement."

McEwan's remarks illustrate how a successful writer sometimes begins without knowing the work's subject. McEwan spent some time sketching. He then wrote a scene requiring him to solve many creative problems. As he imagined the solution to each, the work began to come into focus. McEwan's process is worth recalling as we encounter our own set of challenges.

At the beginning of a project, I often know something about the work. The first stage is exciting: I anticipate the work awaiting me; I look forward to the surprises accompanying the process; I'm happy I have a project to work on.

But I'm also often unclear about what I'm doing for some time. Then something happens that's promising but takes me in a different direction. I've generated a creative problem that I must solve. Will I stick with my original plan? Will I head down that unfamiliar road where the work seems to be going?

To solve this creative problem, I might write a bit in the new direction. And then return to my original scheme. (McEwan swapped his first two chapters and rewrote them several times before he realized the novel should begin with Briony.)

As we seek solutions to our creative problems, we might feel unsettled because we're unsure of what to do. But we keep working through this uncertainty until, somehow, we know—as McEwan did—what the solution is. But we might not know it for some time, and we can't force a resolution too quickly.

Creative solutions often take us into unexpected territory—the introduction of Briony's narrative, for example—and often these

swerves take us into exciting solutions we hadn't anticipated—
Briony as narrator, for example—and push our work in an altogether different direction. Had McEwan rigidly adhered to the
first narrative that emerged—the woman and the young man at the
fountain—and if he hadn't understood the potential in Briony's
narrative, he might have written a less complex but still successful
novel about love, class, and war. But in solving the problem of combining both narratives, McEwan introduced another layer of meaning, about the impact of knowing you've irrevocably destroyed
other people's lives.

In writing *Crazy in the Kitchen,* I knew I wanted to tackle the
issue of my family's relationship to food. I wanted to write my
story, my parents' and grandparents' stories, too. But I knew I
didn't want to tell the story in a linear way. I didn't want to begin
with my grandparents' lives in the south of Italy and end with how
my life was affected by what theirs had been like.

I started with a narrative about how I made bread with one
of my grandmothers. With each successive piece, I moved further back in time. I described the effect of my grandparents' difficult lives upon my parents and me, before I wrote about the
history of the south. (You can see this effect-before-cause structure in Paul Auster's memoir, *The Invention of Solitude,* where
he describes the effect of his grandmother's murdering his
grandfather upon his father before he tells the reader about that
event.)

At one point, to my surprise, I began using an authoritative historical voice to narrate the history of famine in the south of Italy
and the mistreatment of farm laborers that forced my grandfather to emigrate to America—the *why* of our family history. But
this voice was far too different from my other, more personal,
narratives.

One solution I entertained that I soon dismissed was to let that jarring voice stay; I was relating information I hadn't known until I did research for the book, so the narrative felt contrived. Then I tried to find a more personal voice to relate this history, but I couldn't find a voice to write about what I hadn't known.

Then one day, after I'd wrestled with this creative problem for months, I saw that I could relate the history of the south using an "I" narrator telling the reader what I *hadn't known* about my grandfather's life—"I didn't know that . . ." I realized the simplest solution was to write a litany that went on for pages of all of the things I didn't know about my grandparents' past. ("I didn't know that farmworkers who ate every day were considered wealthy. . . . I didn't know that many people in Puglia died of thirst.")

My creative problem—how to tell the history of the south of Italy—was resolved, but it had taken a long time. Throughout, I asked, "What if I do this?" "What if I do that?" I tried several potential solutions to the problem I'd created. But then after I learned how to tell the history of the south, I had to decide where the chapter belonged in the narrative.

If we remind ourselves that writing is nothing more than creative problem solving, we'll be more likely to tolerate the confusion every writer faces. And we have to learn to tolerate the anxiety that accompanies our confusion. But one way we can derail our process is to resolve confusion too quickly. (An excellent resource to help us through this process is Eric Maisel's *Fearless Creating* [1995].)

I had to wait until I'd written every piece to solve the problem of where that historical essay belonged. I decided I wanted it to be the "turn" of the book, so I placed it in the middle. Once I decided that, I then faced the next challenge of ordering the other chapters.

Clarity will come when we encounter a creative problem, but there's no predicting when we'll arrive at a solution And, according to Maisel, confusion seems to fuel the creative problem-solving process. We can choose to trust that we'll find the answer if we keep working. Completing a work involves learning how to wait because the solution to our creative problems can't be forced.

28.

Rejection Letters

I recently met with a friend who told me about someone she knew who'd written a memoir. This writer submitted the work to an important agent and received a rejection letter telling him the writing was terrific, but he couldn't represent the book because he didn't think there was a large enough market for it. My friend told me that because of this one rejection letter, this writer was reconsidering whether the memoir was worth publishing. But Robert M. Pirsig, author of *Zen and the Art of Motorcycle Maintenance* (1974), persisted despite 121 rejections of his manuscript! Agents and editors often act as if they can predict the future. Their job is to sell books, not write them. They study the marketplace, and they make judgments, often not about whether the work is good but upon whether it's marketable. But sometimes a book that was rejected several times finally finds a publisher and becomes a word-of-mouth sensation.

The website One Hundred Famous Rejections can give hope to every writer whose work has been turned down.

J. K. Rowling's *Harry Potter and the Philosopher's Stone* (1997), the first volume of the Harry Potter series, was turned down by twelve presses then bought by Bloomsbury in London because its CEO's daughter loved it. It started small. It ended up being bigger than big. (The novel was published as *Harry Potter and the Sorcerer's Stone* [1999] in the United States.)

Many publishers rejected Chinua Achebe's *Things Fall Apart* (1958) because editors believed a book written by an African writer wouldn't sell. But then an editor at Heinemann in London reviewed it and believed it was the best book he'd read in ages. He insisted the press buy the book; it was published in a small print run of two thousand copies; it has since won awards and sold more than eight million copies throughout the world.

One rejection letter for F. Scott Fitzgerald's *The Great Gatsby* said, "You'd have a decent book if you'd get rid of that Gatsby character."

William Golding's *Lord of the Flies* (1954) was rejected twenty-one times. One letter read that it was "an absurd and uninteresting fantasy which was rubbish and dull." He won the Nobel Prize in literature in 1983.

One rejection letter means nothing. Several rejections mean nothing. A rejection letter is only saying "I don't want to work with you." Some generous editors offer worthwhile advice that a serious writer should consider. But other editors pen a variation on the themes of "I didn't like it," "I can't figure out how to sell it," "We don't handle books like this."

The problem with rejection letters is that they sound authoritative. And therein lies the challenge for us writers. Writers often lose heart and decide to stop work and abandon their projects. They mistakenly hear "The work is no good," rather than "I don't want to represent or publish this work." Or writers might decide to change the work markedly because of an editor's rejection letter, moving the work away from their own vision to try to make it match an editor's.

Writing to please a potential agent or editor—and I know writers who have—is the kiss of death for a writer who's trying to develop an authentic voice, who's trying to write a deep and soulful work. Although throughout the process we'll perhaps work collaboratively with a writing partner, or perhaps even an agent or editor, ultimately it seems best to ensure that the work is authentically our own. "Whether a publisher likes this or not, I'm committed to writing this work as best I can," I believe, is the best policy for a writer. I've known writers who've spent months changing wonderful books in reaction to an agent's criticism, only to have the same agents reject the books again. It takes courage for us to refine our own ideas about our work. We writers can all too easily be led down someone else's primrose path.

Elizabeth Gilbert, author of *Eat, Pray, Love* (2006), has said she can't "understand why people work so hard to create something beautiful, but then refuse to share it with anyone, for fear of criticism." She advises writers to send their work to agents and editors "as much as possible." And when the rejection letters come back, to "take a deep breath and try again." Gilbert believes it's the writer's job to complete the work; it's the agent's and editor's job to decide whether the work is good enough to be published. "Your only job is to write your heart out," she says, "and let destiny take care of the rest."

Jo Ann Beard, author of *The Boys of My Youth*, approached rejection and seeming failure in a positive manner. "I guess I first thought of myself as a writer when I got a rejection slip," she said. "That was a defining moment—meeting such a worthy adversary." Beginning writers, she observed, need to use rejection letters as opportunities to rethink the direction of their work.

I've known writers who've sent out their work when they've known it's far from ready hoping that an agent or editor will be struck by its potential. I believe this is never a good idea. Not only does doing this waste an agent's or editor's time, it invites rejection.

It's a hard time for writers. Fewer publishers are willing to take chances. Writers are held accountable for their sales records, but publishers often don't take responsibility for not having sold a fine book well. It's a good time for writers, too. There are still fine editors willing to support a writer's work; small publishers and university presses have innovative series; and, self-publishing is an option. (Virginia Woolf, for example, published every book from *Jacob's Room* on through her Hogarth Press. She didn't have to deal with editors, although her husband, Leonard Woolf, always read her work. And so she wrote her experimental works exactly as she chose to.)

During my writing life, I've received hundreds of rejection letters: "I can't see us publishing this book. It's not anything like what we publish"; "The writer treats the subject differently from the way the subject has been treated before and so I can't see how we can market this"; "The writing is wonderful, but we can't figure out how to publish this"; "It's a hard market and I'm not sure we could find readers for this book"; "It's not a good fit for our list"; "The book is about ordinary people leading quiet lives; we like books about extraordinary people overcoming great obstacles"; "The book falls between two stools."

These are the letters we read and file. And then we plan how to move on, whether we need to make changes in the manuscript, and how to get our work read by someone else. We refine our vision, perhaps. We revise, even, to reflect our own sensibility and not someone else's, and surely not to reflect what we think the marketplace wants from us.

Stephen King began collecting rejection letters before he was fourteen—he'd been writing and submitting his work to magazines from an early age. He "pounded a nail into the wall" in his room, and collected his rejection slips on it. "By the time I was fourteen . . ." he wrote, "the nail in my wall would no longer support the weight of the rejection slips impaled upon it. I replaced the nail with a spike and went on writing."

King's response—impale the rejection letter on a spike and keep writing—is worth remembering.

29

Hailstorms

A few years ago, my husband and I were staying at a castle in Tuscany. This was a rustic place with few creature comforts—no heat, no air-conditioning, uneven ancient floors, generations of spiders, sagging furniture. And it was ten miles down a clay track, in splendid isolation on a bluff overlooking a river in the valley below. It was not for the fainthearted, so for most of our stay, we were the only people there.

The castle was protected by a gate, a dry moat, and battlements and surrounded by meadows, woods, an olive grove, and the owners' vineyards. It was where I wanted to be after working on a book I couldn't get right. It wasn't my first; it wouldn't be my last. I knew I had to put this experience behind me and move on. Still, I needed this time away. I'd been living with this book for too long.

The family who owned the castle was hardworking. They had to keep up an enormous, ancient, historically significant structure; tend to the accommodations; run the dining room. The mother and one brother cooked. The other brother took orders and served supper. The father fixed things, and there were many things to fix. The family, with helpers from nearby villages, worked in the vineyard and made wine, gathered olives and trucked them to a local press.

One evening, as we were getting ready to order supper—a dish made from local pork, listed as Groundmother's Stew on the menu, which puzzled us and made us laugh (we soon realized they meant "Grandmother's Stew") there was a terrible rainstorm, accompanied by thunderous hail. When the storm was over, two inches of hail had fallen. The storm was beautiful, I thought, as I watched through the dining room windows.

We were safe and warm, inside a stout castle. We'd soon be well fed. Our rooms were a few paces away. As we awaited our meal, we didn't realize what the hailstorm had done to the vineyard.

And then we did.

It was almost summer, and, on our languorous walks around the property, we'd seen tiny grapes growing on the vines. We knew that in autumn they'd be harvested for the year's vintage. The evening before, we'd drunk a robust rustic red wine from the vineyard that paired so well with the simple, soulful food the family served.

A fifteen-minute hailstorm. The year's grape harvest ruined. This year, there would be no wine. And there would be no income for the family from this year's vintage.

Yet even as the hail fell, one brother took our order for supper, and his mother and brother cooked in the kitchen. We saw him glancing out the window, yet he seemed not to respond to the fact that the grapes were being pummeled by hail.

After supper, we talked. I didn't want to intrude on what I assumed to be his great sorrow at the grapes' destruction. But I wanted to offer sympathy. I knew I couldn't possibly understand what the event meant to his family. But I believed it would be wrong not to acknowledge what had happened.

"I'm sorry about the hail," I said.

"It happens," he said.

"What will you do?" I asked.

"Get back to work," he responded, "and fix what was damaged. This is our life's work. The vines will survive. Next year there will be more grapes. Next year there will be another harvest."

You complete a book, submit it to its editor. The editor leaves the press. The editor replacing him can't understand why her predecessor bought it—it's too much like one she's edited. She ignores it. If it fails, she loses nothing. Yet the book took many years of your life.

You publish a controversial biography. A relative of the subject trashes the book in a major newspaper. The subject's family pressures newspapers not to publish extracts of the book or to review it.

You publish a novel. It receives excellent reviews but doesn't sell well. Your publisher cancels your contract for your next work.

You switch genres. Try a novel. It's almost accepted for publication many times. Once, an editor asks for revisions, which take you six months, but then the editor doesn't buy it. Five years have passed. It's likely this book won't find a publisher.

You win a major award and show up at a reading. But there are no books available. You learn the publisher has accidentally shredded every copy of your book. And they don't plan on reprinting.

I've known writers—I'm one of them—who've reacted to inevitable setbacks like these with less dignity and grace than the Italian family responded when a year's livelihood vanished.

The novelist Colum McCann, author of *TransAtlantic*, has survived a number of metaphorical hailstorms. After he published *Zoli* (2006), his novel about "Gypsies and Romany culture in Europe," a part of him judged the work to be a failure. He "wanted to bounce back fast," so he began an epic novel "about New York City on the verge of bankruptcy and an America scarred by Vietnam and Watergate." But he abandoned it after writing two hundred pages because it didn't meet his standards. Deciding to set the work aside was "a fresh wound" that hurt McCann every time he thought about it.

Although McCann felt the pain of having to abandon work, he stated that, for him, "these virtues that you know as desire, stamina, perseverance—they are the key things" for a writer to cultivate: the ability to get back to work when all is not well. McCann has said that, as he writes, "a lot of time I feel like I am drowning. One step forward, two steps back, and then a sudden plunge off the cliff."

McCann believes it's important for writers to realize that every work of art is a failure because you "can never achieve what you truly want to achieve. The thing you dreamt on the riverbank is never the thing you achieve when you are back at the writing table." Paradoxically, embracing the likelihood of failure, as McCann does, can free us to do our best work. When McCann realized that the many strands of *TransAtlantic* (the aviators Alcock and Brown crossing the Atlantic in 1919; Frederick Douglass touring Ireland in 1845; George Mitchell trying to broker a peace accord in Ireland in the 1990s) were held together by the character Lily (a maid in the home where Douglass stayed who's inspired by him to emigrate to the United States), he felt he "had achieved a sort of music."

Encounter a hailstorm in your work. Get back to work. Fix what you can. Trust that there will be another year, that there will be another book. The writer will survive. A writing life will continue despite the hailstorms. A life's work is, after all, a life of work.

30

Turning the Corner

There comes a time in every project when we know we've turned a corner. Before that moment, everything was opaque, confusing, and difficult. We wondered whether what we're writing is worth anything. We worry that we'll never finish. We have a lot of good material, but we don't know what to do with it. We might have an inkling of how the piece or book will come together, but we're not sure it's right, and we're reluctant to try to implement the plans we've germinated.

We're working every day, but the work seems to be going nowhere. We circle around and around our subject, writing good material, and then writing material that seems not to fit—material we suspect we'll never use but that we need to write anyway. And this phase of the process continues. Sometimes for weeks; sometimes for months; sometimes, even, for years.

At times we think we should abandon the project, abandon writing. The book seems to be taking over our life. We think about it all the time, but thinking about it isn't solving our problems. We get downhearted and worry we'll never find the solution to the immense creative challenges we're facing. We write one possible outline and then another and then another. We organize our work into neat piles. We begin thinking we just might be able to make a book out of our hundreds (or thousands) of pages, some of which, we have to admit, are wonderful, some of which work, some of which we'll have to abandon, some of which have potential but must be revised.

Then, one day—and who knows when or why or how—we know the book will happen. We may not know exactly what the chapters will look like, or even whether there will be chapters—we might decide to opt for a continuous narrative instead. But one day we begin trusting that we have the right stuff to finish the book.

Most writers reach this moment. Beginning writers who haven't yet might find it hard to trust that if they just keep working, that time will come. This is miracle time, magic time, the move from opacity to clarity. And we can't force this moment—the arrival of clarity—to happen; this moment takes its own sweet time. We have to show up at the desk day after day, week after week, year after year for that splendid moment to arrive.

Often, that moment comes after we've put the book down for a time, after we've been dragged away on a holiday we didn't want to take. We get away from the project for a while, visit a new place, let our mind rest, and when we return to the desk, there it is—the solution to the book.

That's what's happened to me every time I've written a piece or a book. It's happened to each of my students. That moment when we turn the corner on our work, when we know we'll finish our work, when we have a felt sense of what needs to be done, although we might not be able to articulate the steps to the end of the project. When students ask me when it will happen, I say, "Who knows? Just keep working." When students ask me how they'll know when it's happened, I say, "Don't worry, you'll know." Just like when my husband told our son that he'd know when he fell in love, and wanted to know *how* he'd know, and my husband said, "Don't worry, you'll know," which again didn't satisfy him, but then, after he fell in love, my son understood what my husband had meant.

Zadie Smith, author of *White Teeth* (2000), has described what the middle of writing a novel feels like for her, that moment when she's turned the corner on the work. "The middle of the novel is a state of mind," she says. "Strange things happen in it. Time collapses. You sit down to write at 9 A.M., you blink, the evening news is on and four thousand words are written, more words than you wrote in three long months, a year ago. Something has changed."

Before that moment, problems might seem insoluble. But then, Smith states, "Incredibly knotty problems of structure now resolve themselves with inspired ease. See that one paragraph? It only needs to be moved, and the whole chapter falls into place! Why didn't you see that before?"

If we keep at it, the moment that Smith says "renders everything possible" will come. And we'll know when it does. But before that time, our job as writers is to learn to live with uncertainty and to trust that if we keep working, what seemed problematic will resolve itself. Michael Chabon, when interviewed about writing *Telegraph Avenue*, said he feels "completely stymied" every time he writes a novel, yet the lesson he's learned "is that you do come out the other side with a clear understanding of what you're doing."

That's a stage of the writing process that I love and that I yearn for before it happens. Who wouldn't love that stage of seeming ease? And it's a stage I don't like to rush, though I sometimes have the impulse to drive the book forward faster than before. For who, after spending a few years on a project, doesn't want to be finished, doesn't want to move on to something else? And that's one of the conundrums of the creative process. We become completely immersed in our work; we reach a stage where we want it to be finished; and when it's finished, we rarely think about it again because we've moved on to working on something else.

I'm at that stage right now, and I'm loving it. Every day I look at earlier drafts of this book about my parents' lives during World War II, and I know what to cut, what to expand, and how to change the voice. I don't "know" all these things, really. I seem to be working automatically, instinctively after having been so thoughtful about this book for so long. And I have no idea how I know, I just do. I have no idea about why I know now and didn't know last week, last year. Every day the work inches forward, but now I know there's an end in sight, although I don't know when it will be. I remind myself that, at this stage, it's essential that I don't overwork, that I retain my energy, and that I finish well.

To me, this stage feels better than any other phase of writing, better, even, than that exciting time at the beginning of a project. It feels better than when I'm finished, better than when the book gets accepted at a press, far better than when a book comes out.

You've worked for a long time to get it right, and now it seems to be coming together. But you're still in process; you have a good stretch of work ahead of you, and the possibility of that work feels wonderful; but you know you're heading toward the finish line.

And we should celebrate this moment, when we turn the corner on our work. Because it's been hard earned.

31

Practice Deciding

When I was a teenager, my mother took me on one of our infrequent shopping trips, and I picked out a form-fitting turquoise wool sheath. This would be my only dressy dress until I outgrew it. My mother looked at it and asked, "Are you sure you want it?" The moment she asked, I couldn't decide whether I wanted it or not. I stopped loving it and wondered whether I even liked it.

Once I started writing, my difficulty making decisions plagued me. Do I write this article or that? Do I begin this book or that? Do I take this chapter and split it in two? What chapter should come first? What event should come first in that chapter? Should I eliminate this word? Add that image? End the book this way? Or that?

Should I write today? Take a weekend off? Work in the morning or in the afternoon? Am I using being sick as an excuse to not write?

Sound familiar? Sound exhausting?

Writing can be wonderful. Those of us who didn't get to make choices when we were young get to make scores of them every day. But writing can be hellish because we have so many decisions to make, and many of us haven't practiced making them. Barry

Schwartz's *The Paradox of Choice* describes how having too many choices can be paralyzing. And writers have a seemingly infinite number of choices to make.

I've been reading D. H. Lawrence's *Sea and Sardinia* (1921), which he planned as soon as he began his journey to Sardinia. Once he arrived, he began writing; he described what he experienced, where he visited, what the Sardinians were like. He didn't ask himself "Should I write about Sardinia?" He just decided to write, and he did. With Lawrence, there was no equivocation between the time he made a decision to write and when he began to work. It was never "Is writing a book about Sardinia the right thing to do?" Instead, it was "I'll go to Sardinia and write about it." Reading Lawrence's life stunned me into realizing how much time and energy I've wasted equivocating and what a huge emotional drain it's been.

Lawrence didn't seem to spend much time making choices—even difficult ones, like leaving England without any money and becoming an expatriate. He just acted, which sometimes got him into trouble. While he was writing *Women in Love* (1920), he never asked himself whether mocking Ottoline Morrell would get him sued. While he was composing *Lady Chatterley's Lover*, he never wondered whether his work would be censored if he wrote explicitly sexual material. He wrote what he chose, and took the consequences.

He could be, and often was, overly smug and self-assured. He was often elated and excited. But he was just as often angry and miserable. Still, it was important for me to understand from his example that learning how to make decisions might help my writing practice.

So, how did I become a writer who's comfortable making scores of complicated choices each day of my writing life? I simply decided to practice deciding. And one key principle helped me more than any other: in writing, it doesn't matter what you choose to do, it only matters that you choose to do something.

I've seen students waste precious writing time because they can't decide whether to write about, say, their mother or their father; they want to wait until the subject seems right. I tell them, "Just choose. Once you make a choice, possibilities you haven't yet imagined will reveal themselves."

I've witnessed students hampered by their incapacity to decide what should come first, or what should come last in a memoir. I say, "Try it one way. Try it the other way. Think about the advantages of each. Then decide." I've learned that as you practice making decisions over time, you begin to have a stronger sense of what needs to be done.

But I've learned, too, that deciding becomes easier in my work if I focus on just one writing task at a time.

Let's say I decide to begin a new personal essay. I let myself write anything I want for a while. I decide not to think about whether my work is worthwhile.

I decide it's time to draft a full-length version of the work based on my scribbles. I decide not to think about whether the piece is working.

I decide it's time to deepen the piece, to develop the characters. I decide not to think about how to organize the work.

I decide it's time to organize the piece. I decide not to carefully edit on this round.

I decide it's time to line edit the piece, to work on it word by word, sentence by sentence, paragraph by paragraph, chapter by chapter. I decide this will be the last revision before I show the work to someone.

Antonya Nelson's essay "Short Story: A Process of Revision" provides an insightful paradigm to help us decide what to do throughout the process of composing and revising one piece of work. (Nelson used it in a fiction workshop.) During each draft, we attend only "to the requirements laid out for that draft"; we revise "with a single objective each time."

The first decision, says Nelson, is to choose what to write about—an event that we understand is "a story." We then write a five-hundred-word account of the event.

The second decision is the point of view of the narrative. In fiction, Nelson suggests a third-person narrator. In memoir, it would be an "I" narrator—but it could be the "I" during the time of the narrative, or the adult "I" who understands that event more fully. We then write a one-thousand-word account using that point of view. (Each subsequent draft increases by five hundred words.)

The third decision is "to put some sort of *clock* on the story": a road trip, an hour, a day, a weekend, a summer. Do we want to include only the time frame of that event? Or what came before and/or after? We revise, again, inserting this focus.

The fourth decision is to identify "the props and objects" to use in the narrative: this is the "detail-making draft." We revise, again, including them. In a scene where my father comes home from World War II, for example, it would be important for me to include the parachute silk he brought me as a present and my mother's horrified reaction—what I didn't then know was that my father had taken it from a dead pilot.

The fifth decision is to think about the protagonist's age in the narrative, to imagine a time line suited to the protagonist and a life-altering event. Once chosen, we revise, again, including these.

The next decisions involve introducing a world event to deepen the narrative; thinking about how to use oppositional forces in the narrative; creating a narrative arc; and trying, perhaps, something out of the ordinary.

This oversimplifies both Nelson's and my processes. But deciding what we're going to do on each round and also deciding what we're *not going to do* helps us immeasurably. We writers seem to have more difficulty making decisions if we try to do too much on one round. And we seem to work more decisively if we focus on only one thing at a time.

32

Successful Outcomes

A few years ago, I read David Allen's *Getting Things Done*. Two of Allen's suggestions have changed my writing practice. The first is determining what the successful outcome will be of any project we undertake. We often just start working, imagining that by simply writing, we'll one day finish our books. But Allen says determining our intended "successful outcome" before we begin, and as we work, will make our work more purposeful and successful. Although many writers—and I'm one of them—often plunge in and let the material take them where it will, having even a general idea of our desired outcome—a story cycle about my childhood in Hoboken, for example—will help us focus.

To illustrate, a successful outcome for my current memoir might read: "An eighty-thousand-word book about my father's experiences before, during, and after his service in World War II, and their effect upon him and our family." Writing down this intention may seem obvious. But when I ask writers to state the outcome of their work, many haven't thought about it and few can state it succinctly.

It's also helpful to determine the successful outcome for each section of our projects: "Completed Prologue, introducing major themes and characters," for example. And it's also important to write down successful outcomes for each day's work. (I keep a note-book on my desk for that purpose.)

Here are a few of my daily entries:

6 *April*: Completed draft of PT dream sequence.
4 *May*: A draft of "Lifeboat," incorporating readers' suggestions where appropriate.
10 *May*: Revised Prologue, incorporating PT dream sequence.

Allen suggests we write down our outcomes so we can refer to them and help us focus. He also suggests we state them as if we've completed them.

I try to be realistic about what I can accomplish in one day; I prefer to work slowly and methodically. When we begin, the work might proceed slowly; as we revise and near completion, we might work more quickly.

When I work like this, I don't feel overwhelmed, and I feel less confused. I know my daily writing sessions are moving my work closer to completion; I don't feel I'm circling round and round and going nowhere. Even at the beginning stages, I know where I'm headed as I draft material I will probably one day incorporate into my finished book. Most important, I know what my book is about.

Still this doesn't mean we need to be rigid; our work will often take an unexpected turn that will enrich it. But if we have *some* sense of where we're headed, we'll feel far more purposeful each writing day. This is one of Allen's crucial points—not only do we have to do our work, we have to think about the direction our work is heading and about what we want its outcome to be. And, yes, we might need to revise our successful outcome throughout the process.

Another of Allen's suggestions I use is identifying the very next action we should take to move our projects in the direction of our intended successful outcome. Once we've decided upon a successful outcome for the day's work, Allen suggests writing down the very next action to take—the "next to do"—to move the project along. We work on that single task before determining the next, and so forth.

The next to do permits me to focus. Without having a next-to-do task, my mind races. But if I finish one next to do, and then I write the next, and I work on that, my work feels purposeful. Some days, there might be only one; other days, several. But I write only one at a time. (This structure needn't cramp our creativity. One next to do I often use is to write freely on a given subject for half an hour to see where that writing takes me.)

I'll illustrate from a roughly two-and-a-half-hour writing session, interrupted by one long break. I wrote down one "successful outcome" and twelve next to dos, but I only wrote one down at a time, after I completed each task. Remember the next to do is the single next action that will move the project along to its "successful outcome."

21 May: Successful Outcome. "Flushing Out the Enemy" material [a narrative about my father's flashback to combat] "married" with second version. Potential epilogue material removed.

Next to Do:

1. Continue retyping "Flushing," incorporating yesterday's handwritten revisions. [This takes an hour.]
2. Find overlapping material. [Ten minutes.]
3. Integrate the two, keeping best wording. [Twenty minutes.]

4. Print new version. [A few minutes.]

5. Write down word total. [I update this daily; a few minutes.]

6. Assemble material for possible epilogue from deleted material and print. [Fifteen minutes.]

7. Read other epilogue material—4th pass against 5th pass—to ensure all changes incorporated. [Ten minutes.]

8. Read new possible epilogue and revise by hand. [Half an hour.]

9. Incorporate changes into document on computer. [Fifteen minutes.]

10. Print epilogue.

11. Enter totals.

12. File old versions; file new version; back up.

If I'd written down all twelve items as goals, I suspect I would've accomplished little. I might have jumped from one task to another or felt overwhelmed. But I got a great deal of work done by focusing on only one simple, doable task at a time.

Some writers believe we should move through our work organically, without writing down goals or thinking about aims. But an interview with Joan Didion, author of *The Year of Magical Thinking* (2005) and *Blue Nights* (2011), describes how she thinks about what she wants to achieve in a given work.

When writing *Play It as It Lays* (1970), Didion decided she "wanted to make it all first person." But she learned she couldn't maintain that point of view, so she revised her aim, "playing with a close third person"—"very close to the mind of the character." Then she decided to try juxtaposing "first and third."

At the end of each day, Didion steps back from her work, considers it, and decides what to do next.

"I need an hour alone before dinner, with a drink, to go over what I've done that day. I can't do it late in the afternoon because I'm too close to it," she said. "So I spend this hour taking things out and putting other things in. Then I start the next day by redoing all of what I did the day before, following these evening notes. . . . If I don't have the hour, and start the next day with just some bad pages and nowhere to go, I'm in low spirits."

Didion knows that at the end of each day, the single next thing she'll do is step back from her work and review it. Then the next thing she'll do is revise and take notes on what needs to be done next. The following day, she'll use the notes from the evening before and revise the previous day's pages. She moves her book along, one step at a time, while avoiding the "low spirits" that might derail her work. Because she thinks about the successful outcome of her work, Didion has a self-defined set of criteria against which to judge each day's work.

33

Ship's Log

I've been doing research about the aircraft carrier my father served on during the late 1930s, prior to World War II. I learned that each takeoff, landing, flight, accident, repair, event (ceremonies, parades, changes of command, orders received) was recorded in the ship's log. This was required so there was a record available for accountability but also for historians. Because of the ship's log, I can re-create my father's days aboard that carrier.

Ernest Hemingway kept something like a ship's log. In interviewing him, George Plimpton learned that Hemingway kept track "of his daily progress—'so as not to kid myself'—on a large chart made out of the side of a cardboard packing case and set up against the wall under the nose of a mounted gazelle head." On the chart, Hemingway recorded his "daily output": "450, 575, 462, 1250, back to 512," the high number reflecting days Hemingway worked longer so he could spend the next day "fishing on the Gulf Stream."

We writers so often make lists of what we have to do, but we don't often record what we've accomplished—our "done" list, the equivalent of a ship's log. How often do we think about our writing day, reflect upon what we've accomplished, congratulate ourselves for work well done, and make a record that we can refer to in order to help us document how a book was written?

I recently spoke with a writer friend who's been chastising herself for not having accomplished much. Then one day she and her writer husband revisited the work of the past several months, and she was startled to discover that she'd reviewed and revised scores of her poems, made a significant decision about the book's order, detached several poems from the collection to turn them into a chapbook, submitted the chapbook to the press that had published her work before, submitted her work to a community of writers for review. She's also been working on a biography of a famous poet; she's helped scores of writers with their works in progress; she's read her husband's novel manuscript and made detailed suggestions for revision; she's discussed a collection of essays she's edited with a publisher.

But until my friend wrote everything down, she'd been telling herself she wasn't productive and that she'd been wasting her time. This eroded her sense of self-worth, although there was no reason for her to feel this way.

My friend does far more than write. So if she were to write down her accomplishments as a partner, teacher, friend, householder, reader, and so on, her "done" list would be extremely long. And perhaps if she'd recorded these items at the end of each day, she would have spared herself the self-flagellation.

Why bother spending a few moments each day recording what we've done?

If you're anything like my friend or like me, your perception of what you accomplish is faulty. We don't often record our accomplishments. But honoring what we've done (whether it's writing a few pages, washing a sink full of dishes, sitting in silence to gain perspective on a challenge) helps us value our work and value ourselves.

Unless we keep an accurate ship's log, we might not hold ourselves accountable—as Hemingway did. And having such a log is essential if we claim our work space, equipment, and travel as tax deductions: we can easily document how long it took us to write a book.

Leonard Woolf kept the equivalent of a ship's log which became the basis for his five-volume autobiography. Because of his detailed entries, he could, for example, document his meeting on January 28, 1939, with Sigmund Freud, whom the Hogarth Press published, and their discussion about the Nazis. He could relate that on his drive from Cantal to Dieppe in France in his Singer automobile, his tires blew out "an average every 25 miles" and that he made friends with a French family who helped him repair a tire.

Virginia Woolf also kept a version of a ship's log in her diary so literary scholars can chart when she conceptualized a work, when she was at work on a book, when she revised, what her goals were for her works in progress, when she believed she was finished. And because these entries are dated, we can coordinate her writing with historical events as I have in the introduction to this book, when I described how she created a working-class character in *To the Lighthouse* when England was experiencing a massive strike and Woolf realized how dependent society is upon the working classes.

I keep a ship's log of my writing that permits me to look back and recall the progress of one of my essays or books. I know, for example, that I spent two hours revising an essay for this book, that I rethought its organization, that I read interviews with Norman Rush about his writing process. I often reread my log so I can remind myself of the hills and valleys of the creative process. No matter how accurate I think my memory is, I often misremember how I wrote a particular book. I seem to think it was harder or easier than it was. Rereading my log during a difficult stage of a current project—often when I'm urging myself to work too quickly or beating myself up for my slow progress—reminds me of how slowly my work progressed before.

When I've been interviewed about how I wrote my memoir *Vertigo*, for example, I could describe the work's progress accurately. I know that on February 16, 1994, I was revising the chapter about my sister's suicide to figure out how to incorporate it into the memoir. I know that on March 29, 1994, I read Jay Martin's *Who Am I This Time?* (1988) and it helped me understand why Alfred Hitchcock's movie *Vertigo* (1958) was so important to me when I was a teenager, because I wrote some ideas into my log on this date about my personal connection to the movie that I subsequently used in the memoir—that the character played by Jimmy Stewart was obsessed with the character played by Kim Novak and that I had to think about my relationship with a particular boy. I know it took me until June 11, 1994, to actually begin work on the piece called "Vertigo" about that movie.

By referring to this log, I can re-create my process of working on this book. And now, when I'm in the midst of writing another memoir, reading the log helps me remember that although I thought *Vertigo* was an easy book to write, my log shows, instead, that it was slow going, that it was hard work, that it took a long time to write, that I agonized over its order, just as with the memoir I'm writing now. I learned, for example, that "Vertigo," the piece about the movie, took me over a year to perfect. And it was a piece I erroneously believed came quickly.

I've found that keeping such a record is an important way of honoring my work. It's not easy for a woman like me with origins in the working class to value the work of writing. My mother, for example, didn't consider writing as work. She felt free to interrupt me whenever I was writing and wasn't proud of the writing I did. So I must do all I can to value my accomplishments, to remind myself that, indeed, my writing is work, and that I work hard at writing.

34

What Worked and Why

Mark Williams, John Teasdale, Zindel Segal, and Jon Kabat-Zinn's *The Mindful Way Through Depression* describes an experiment called The Mouse in the Maze, the results of which can help us with our writing. Two groups of students were shown a cartoon mouse, trapped in a maze. Each group was shown a different version. One depicted a piece of Swiss cheese at the maze's exit, the other, an owl hovering to seize the mouse.

The maze took a few minutes to solve. Later, the students were tested to determine their current state of creativity. "Those who had helped their mouse avoid the owl turned in scores that were fifty percent lower than the scores of students who helped their mouse find the cheese. The state of mind elicited by attending to the owl had resulted in a lingering sense of caution, avoidance, and vigilance for things going wrong. This mind-state in turn weakened creativity, closed down options, and reduced the students' flexibility in responding to the next task."

Imagining that the owl would capture the cartoon mouse significantly diminished the students' creative responses. But imagining that the cartoon mouse would get the cheese significantly boosted the other group's creative responses. According to *The Mindful Way,* the experiment suggests that if we approach any task—our writ- ing, say—with "qualities of interest, curiosity, warmth, and good- will" we can counter "effects of aversion and avoidance," and choose more creative strategies. But this takes awareness, and conscious, deliberate work.

Now imagine two scenarios in our writing lives. In the first, we go to our desk, and tell ourselves, before we've written a word, that we don't want to be writing and that we're likely to encounter insur- mountable problems. In the second, we pause for a moment to cul- tivate a state of "interest, curiosity, warmth, and goodwill" toward what might emerge during our writing session, to imagine a positive outcome of our day's work and the surprises in store for us. We imagine the sense of fulfillment we'll feel when we're finished for the day. If we deliberately cultivate the idea that all will be well as we work, as the authors of *The Mindful Way* report, it will likely en- hance our creative capacity.

Martin Seligman, one of the founders of the positive psychol- ogy movement and author of *Flourish* (2011), suggests we keep a what-went-well-today-and-why diary. Seligman states that this simple practice tends to lower depression and increase satisfaction— the results have been documented. The technique also increases self-discipline and grit, essential qualities for writers.

The what-went-well diary focuses on the positive; it invites us to learn about our own effectiveness and provides us with informa- tion we can use to plan our future behavior. If we understand what went well today, and why it went well, we'll be more likely to engage in activities that will yield positive results in the future.

We can apply Seligman's technique not only to our daily lives but also to our writing. What if, at the end of our writing day, we deliberated and then wrote about what went well with our writing today, and why? If we do this consistently, we'll have an invaluable record of what works for us and why what we did worked, rather than the altogether more common litany of complaints about what isn't working, and goodness knows why.

I've just finished writing a chapter of my book about my parents' meeting and marriage during World War II; I still have a few more chapters to write. When I spent time writing what went well as I wrote this chapter and why, I learned that organizing my notes into a time line of worldwide events helped—I didn't have to refer to hundreds of pages of notes to check dates. I learned that inserting events from my parents' lives helped—I could plot their lives against historical events. I learned that culling family photographs into one photograph album helped—I could see what my parents looked like, and because the photos were dated, I could determine when events (like their honeymoon) had taken place. I learned that working in the morning for two or three hours on this project helped—it was good for me to stop when I still had something to say. I learned I worked best when I'd had a good night's sleep, done thirty minutes of aerobic exercise, turned off my phone, and didn't check e-mail. I learned I needed twenty days to complete the chapter; I learned I needed seven days to organize my materials before beginning the revision. I learned it was best to work without showing the chapters to anyone and without talking about it. I learned the proposal I'd written for the chapter acted as a guide for my writing.

After I wrote what worked and why for a few days, I started feeling better about this book in progress. I learned that I really know what I'm doing and know how I work best. I learned that, for me, the writing process is far less haphazard and far more studied and planned than I'd imagined. I learned how to organize my work for the next chapter based upon what worked for me while I was writing this one.

Rick Bass, author of thirty-one works of fiction and nonfiction, including, most recently, *All the Land to Hold Us* (2013), has described what he does "when a story isn't working as well as it could be—or when it isn't working at all." He says that when we face this situation as writers, we have two choices—"to endure and accept the failure or to try something different." Because accepting failure isn't an option for Bass, he's learned, from past experience, that when he encounters tangles in his work, what works for him "is to try to stay calm and go back to basics, to try to show, in gestures, images, and descriptions as simple as possible, what it is you're trying to convey, and not to try to do it all at once, but break it down into pieces."

When the work is confusing, and Bass can't figure out what he's trying to communicate, he tells himself, "Try to say it straight. . . ." After "frustrating attempts" at untangling a snarl of language, Bass has learned to step back and ask himself, "What is the one thing, the main thought, the simplest thought?" Next, Bass tries to "speak the thought out loud, as if in conversation." Then he writes down the sentence he's uttered aloud as a "placeholder" and then he "proceed[s] anew."

The reason this works, Bass says, is that he's learned that he often asks "words to do too much work" in his prose. His prose becomes incomprehensible not because of a "muddled brain" but because he's trying to relate something that's "too complicated to be captured or expressed in a single sentence."

Bass has taken the time to reflect upon what has worked well for him and why it has. His tried-and-true formula empowers him to dig into a draft that isn't yet working because he's learned what he needs to do to make a draft work. The benefit of this strategy, he says, is that "your body and mind will relax"; "your body and mind will seek tenaciously to solve the problem. . . ." Rather than telling himself he's failed, Bass looks at his muddled prose as a challenge that he can solve because he can rely on his proven strategy to "Say it straight."

Part Four

WRITERS AT REST

Introduction

Maxine Hong Kingston took seven years to write both *The Woman Warrior* (1976) and *China Men*. Then she took a very necessary break from writing. "You go into the subconscious by not writing," she said, "and then you make it normal consciousness by writing." Periods of not writing are as important to Kingston's process as the times when she's working: those times permit her to "get far into the subconscious," the source of some of the stories she relates.

Sometimes writers misconstrue their need to take time away from their work as "writer's block." At a reading of *Home* (2012) that Toni Morrison gave at Princeton University, a schoolchild asked her how she avoids writer's block. Morrison said, "I don't avoid it. If something happens, and I can't do it, I respect the block." When writers don't take time off and try to write through a so-called block, she added, the work feels forced, and "it shows."

Carolyn See in *Making a Literary Life* (2002) describes her schedule. She writes five days a week, uses Saturdays for chores and housekeeping, and reserves Sundays as a day of rest. See's success depends upon gaining distance from her work with the minivacation she takes each week. Knowing that weekends are devoted to keeping her life in order and recharging her creative energy helps her focus during the weekdays she sets aside for work.

For relaxation, Amy Hempel, author of the collections *Reasons to Live* (1985), *At the Gates of the Animal Kingdom* (1990), and *Tumble Home* (1997), needs time away from her desk so she can return to her work refreshed and able to maintain the intense concentration the short story form requires. She walks her dogs and takes them to the park. She loves movies, and attends them often—she has a friend who accompanies her to see the latest Korean horror film. A typical day for Hempel "includes around two hours of *writing* writing, about six miles of dog walking (which also counts as writing), a lot of time on e-mail, a movie, some forensics shows, and CNN to see what I missed."

A substantial amount of research indicates that most of us would benefit from regularly scheduled relaxation. In a culture that values productivity and views leisure suspiciously, it's harder to take rest breaks than in one that views time away from work as necessary for the human spirit. Researchers at the Institute of Leisure Studies at the University of Deusto, Spain, have concluded that leisure is essential for creativity: it's important for rest, replenishment, diversion, personal development, and spirituality. If we spend time away from writing, we'll find our work more satisfying, we'll find we're more inspired when we return to work, we'll recover more quickly from fatigue from bouts of hard work, and we'll be able to more easily determine what needs doing.

At the end of June 1938, after completing what he was referring to as Book One of *The Grapes of Wrath* (1939), John Steinbeck realized how fatigued he was from the intense work of completing that section. "It would be good to have a few days off," he wrote. "I think I'll take them. . . . Why should I rush?" During his break, he saw friends, enjoyed their conversation, and had a high-spirited time dancing madly. During his four days off, Steinbeck conceptualized much of the rest of the novel.

Zadie Smith, author of *NW*, believes that after writing a draft of a long work, we need a long break before we begin editing. We shouldn't try to convince ourselves that working constantly is good for us, or good for the work. She urges writers to stop work, put their projects *"in a drawer,"* and let time pass—a "year or more [off] is ideal—but even three months will do"—before revising. And Ray Bradbury in *Zen in the Art of Writing* warns us not to work too hard: "Those who try hardest," he writes, "scare it [the Muse] off into the woods. Those who turn their backs and saunter along, whistling softly between their teeth, hear it treading quietly behind them, lured by a carefully acquired disdain."

Once I understood how essential leisure is to the creative process, I instituted a few practices that help me strike a balance between writing and the rest of my life. I never work after supper (time for relaxation and family); I almost never work Saturdays (household errands, time for family and friends); I never work Sundays (time for spiritual and emotional renewal). I take a few hours once a week to do something pleasurable—visit a gourmet store, a knitting shop, a museum, a garden; see a movie. My husband and I, sometimes with our family, take two holidays a year. Reluctant as I may be to leave my work, I've returned refreshed and with scores of new ideas.

While Junot Díaz, author of the story collection *This Is How You Lose Her* (2012), was recovering from back surgery, he accepted the fact that he couldn't write (under the best of circumstances, Díaz takes a long time to write his books). Instead, he said, "I read like crazy while I was laid up; reading for me is proof against anything, but especially pain." Krys Lee's *Drifting House* (2012), a novel about the Korean immigrant experience; Tania James's *Aerogrammes*

(2012), stories by the author of *Atlas of Unknowns* (2009); and Ramón Saldívar's *The Borderlands of Culture* (2006), about Américo Paredes's work, in particular, gave him solace.

There will be times when, like Díaz, we can't write—periods when health challenges, family issues, or emergencies make writing impossible. Then we're entitled to take an extended leave from our writing. But there will also be times when, like Kingston, Smith, or Morrison, we may decide it's best for us to step away from our work before returning to our projects. And, like See and Hempel, it's important for us to understand when, during the week, or during a day, we need to do other things. Learning when not to work is as essential for writers as knowing when we must.

35

Dreaming and Daydreaming

Naomi Epel's *Writers Dreaming* (1993) presents her interviews with twenty-six writers who spoke about the relationship between dreaming, daydreaming, and their creative lives. Each of these writers declared that they continually drew upon their dreams or daydreams as they composed.

Some writers, like Charles Johnson, author of the National Book Award–winning *Middle Passage* (1990), about the final voyage of an illegal slave ship, dreamed the solution to a challenge. Johnson sensed that a scene where slaves were about to be herded into the hold of a slave ship lacked an essential component. Before Johnson revised this section, he decided to take a nap: "As soon as my head hit the pillow, I started to drift off into that marginal place that you enter between wakefulness and dreams." During that liminal state, Johnson imagined Yankee sailors hauling a crate out of the jungle. "What's in this crate?" he wondered. A "kind of cryptic, encoded dream image" of a god came to him.

Johnson had been working on the novel for four and a half years when that god became a crucial element in the narrative. He'd sensed he needed a central symbol that would deepen its meaning. When he daydreamed that image, the solution came to him. But it took a month and a half of work for Johnson to discover how to use that god to initiate the freed slave, Rutherford Calhoun, into "enlightenment and illumination."

Bharati Mukherjee, author of *Wife* (1975) and *Jasmine* (1989), dreams the endings of her novels. During her first drafts, she doesn't know what will happen to her characters. While working on *Wife*, her novel about a young immigrant wife's difficult adjustment to New York City, Mukherjee decided the narrative would conclude with the wife's becoming depressed or killing herself, the only reasonable outcome for such a "pliant, good, obedient Indian wife." But in a dream, Mukherjee witnessed her character deciding to kill her husband. Upon awakening, she told her husband, "The guy's going to die!" This dream drastically altered the conclusion, and the meaning, of *Wife*. Mukherjee asserts, "Art really is quite often anticipated by or resolved by dreams."

Gloria Naylor, author of *The Women of Brewster Place* (1983), *Linden Hills* (1985), and *Mama Day* (1988), uses daydreaming to resolve problems in her work. When she's stuck, she "play[s] [the problem] out in my mind to get myself past that bump some way." In writing *Linden Hills*, a retelling of Dante's *Inferno*, Naylor couldn't decide how to move two boys who didn't belong there into a really posh neighborhood. "That's when I lay down and invented the idea of a policeman com[ing] and stop[ping] them." Then she imagined another character sending her husband on an errand, who then leads the boys down into that hellish place. "That's an example of daydreaming a solution," Naylor said.

Naylor's novels often begin with her seeing images. "You know which images are important," she observed, "because they hit you so powerfully." The initial image inspiring *Brewster Place*, about the lives of a group of women in a rotting tenement, was "the rocking of women"—"Mattie rocking Ciel." Naylor wrote that scene, but she put it away because she didn't understand its meaning. But she continued writing because she wanted to understand who Mattie was.

The initial image for Naylor's *Mama Day* was that of a "woman carrying a dead baby through the woods." The image came to Naylor as she was sitting on a sofa in a studio apartment while she was living in Washington, D.C. She knew the woman was keening, and she heard the lines, "Go home, Bernice. Go home and bury your child." Naylor says that after images come to her, she feels her "characters are waiting" for her to unravel the meaning of their story.

William Styron described how "the whole concept of *Sophie's Choice*" (1979) was "the result . . . of a kind of waking vision which occurred when I woke up one spring morning in the mid-seventies" when he was working on another, difficult book. After he awakened, Styron had a "lingering vision," a "merging from the dream to a conscious vision and memory of this girl named Sophie."

Sophie Zawistowska was based upon a woman Styron knew, whom he first saw entering a boarding house in Flatbush, wearing a summer dress with "her arm bared and the tattoo visible." The image of Sophie that returned to Styron was so powerful that he knew he'd have to abandon the novel he was working on and write about Sophie. He walked to his studio, and "wrote down the first words just as they are in the book." From the beginning of the novel to its conclusion, Styron wrote *Sophie's Choice* without hesitation. "You could say that the whole concept of the book was, if not the product of a dream itself, the product of some resonance that a dream had given me." In time, he imagined the tragic choice she was forced to make at Auschwitz, her life in Brooklyn with her dangerous lover, Nathan Landau, and the novelist's narrator, Stingo.

Styron believed that writing the novel was "an absolute necessity."

He realized that it had to end at Auschwitz "with [Sophie] sacrific-ing her children." When Styron had that first apparition of Sophie, he realized he was "onto something that for me was absolutely es-sential to deliver myself of." His job became rendering the narra-tive in a way that moved his audience as much as he himself had been moved by his initial image of Sophie.

Dreaming and daydreaming are essential features of the creative process. They're not distractions from our work but necessary to it. Don't many of our projects, like those of these writers, begin this way? While we're engaged in a routine task, an idea for an essay, a book, a line, or a scene we need to write springs to consciousness. Or we're in that liminal zone between sleeping and waking and a startling image comes to us about our work that changes its course. Or we awaken in the middle of the night knowing that what we'd planned to do won't work. As the experiences of these writers sug-gest, we can help our work by paying careful attention to these thoughts and images.

But I've learned many beginning writers don't capture these ideas by writing them down, and they don't act on their dreams or daydreams. Unlike seasoned writers, they haven't yet learned that dreams and daydreams provide inspiration and important informa-tion about our work. We might not know how this information will fit into a narrative in progress, as Johnson initially didn't, but if we write it down, it won't be lost; it will be there for us when we need it. But many writers treat these inspirational moments as ephemera rather than as rock solid knowledge of what we need. We can sub-vert our creative process by dismissing these thoughts and visions as meaningless, rather than taking them seriously. I like to look at them as presents that come unbidden that might not be given to us again.

The most productive writers and creative people I know realize that dreaming and daydreaming are important parts of how writers work. We might not know, now, what to do with the images our dreams or daydreams provide, but one day, if we continue to try to unravel their meaning, as Naylor's process illustrates, we will.

36

Dumbstruck

I was a writer who thought I'd write, no matter what. I wrote the introduction to a collection of Irish stories, lying on a sofa after I shattered a bone in my leg. I wrote about my father for my memoir *Vertigo* while I cared for him as he recovered from open-heart surgery. I wrote the day after my sister died; I wrote as my mother was dying and as my father was dying after spending hours by their bedsides. I wrote after I got Lyme disease, though I knew I had to recover to turn those pages into a book.

I thought I'd write after I was diagnosed with cancer. And I did, for a few hours. Six pages entitled "The Cancer Book" about the fine day I had before my diagnosis while, unbeknownst to me, that tumor was growing; about how I learned I had cancer. And that's all I wrote for a very long time. A writing life, put on hold.

Did I really believe I could write after an operation, during complications, chemotherapy, and a prolonged recovery? I suppose I did.

But all I wanted to do was take walks when I could (slow ones, short ones). Watch children playing. Be with my family. Try to cook. Read. Take naps and baths. Knit, some. Watch movies. I didn't want to—couldn't—write my books. I'd been arrogant to think I could write, no matter what.

But I wrote in my journal, as often as I could, for about twenty minutes, just for myself. I tried to keep my spirits up. I described my pain, anger, and sorrow. I assessed what didn't help me and what did—establishing a routine (a cancer survival guide suggested this). I later learned that Matthew J. Loscalzo, executive director of Supportive Care Medicine for City of Hope, suggests that the "key to dealing with grief . . . is getting the executive function of the brain active"—"the part . . . that controls emotions, organizes issues, and solves problems." One way of "fueling the executive function" is writing—but not immediately after a trauma. Although writing might not lessen grief, it can help us feel more in control.

During my recovery, a writer friend was diagnosed with cancer. Her friend (even before expressing sorrow) suggested she take notes so she could write a book. My friend was considering whether she'd want to. I told her that I'd thought I, too, might write but found that I couldn't, and that I didn't want to. (I chose not to share with her how debilitating treatment was for me; she'd find out soon enough.) But I observed that people seemed to expect me to turn that experience into a book.

I thought about those times I'd unthinkingly told someone going through a difficult time that they should consider writing about it. But I now believe it's unfeeling to say this to someone who's suffering or who's grieving. You get cancer; write about it. Your father dies; write about it. Your child is gravely ill; write about it. Your spouse dies; write about it. It's almost as if the value of a writer's experience is determined by whether it can be turned into copy, almost as if people who don't write expect us to write about everything we experience even if we want to remain—at least publicly—silent. In his memoir *A Whole New Life* (1982) Reynolds Price recounts how he was diagnosed with cancer of the spinal cord in 1984 when he was writing *Kate Vaiden* (1986). The treatment—surgery and radiation—left Price "paralyzed from the waist down." For five months after the treatment, Price "just couldn't do anything but sit in a chair and gaze out the window or at the ceiling. . . ." He couldn't read; he couldn't write; but he drew, "as he had in his childhood." This period was "a normal reactive depression"; but it was also "a very real kind of spiritual hunkering down. . . ."

During this time, a friend asked if Price would accept a commission to write a play for student actors. He accepted, and began to write again. After completing the play, he "very rapidly finished *Kate Vaiden*." After his cancer, Price became more prolific than he'd ever been.

After Julian Barnes's wife, Pat Kavanagh, died, it took Barnes "several years to express his grief in writing." He wrote "hundreds of thousands of [words] in a diary." But to compose a public document, Barnes "needed to find the right form." The first two sections of *Levels of Life* (2013) are about ballooning; the third, a fifty-page essay, is about his descent into "darkness and despair" over the death of his wife. In it, "the classic consolations offered to the bereaved are considered and repudiated: that suffering makes you stronger; that things get easier . . . that the two of you will be reunited. . . ." He describes contemplating suicide, but decided that because "he is his wife's chief rememberer," he'd be killing her again if he killed himself.

Joyce Carol Oates, who's written about her response to her husband's death in her memoir *A Widow's Story* (2011), observed that Barnes asked the question "How do you turn catastrophe into art?" in *A History of the World in 10½ Chapters* (1989). Barnes's response, Oates writes, veers between "the desire to speak and a stoic reticence in the effort of what Barnes calls 'grief-work.'"

After I was diagnosed with cancer, for the first time in my writing life, I experienced a similar yet far from stoic reticence. The writing in my journal didn't allay my feelings, didn't put them into perspective, didn't allow me to achieve distance from them—all the things I'd always believed writing could do for me. I learned that there are experiences that can't be easily put into words, or, rather, there are experiences for which the written word can be only an inadequate simulacrum to describe what occurred.

And so, I've chosen to keep this one subject to myself. It's not something I want to write about, not something I want to talk about, not something I want to remember. I don't want to go back to that time; I don't want to go back over that experience. I'd thought that I could handle any subject. And, yes, there are writers like Reynolds Price who've written valuable books about cancer—Mary Cappello's *Called Back* (2009) for example. But I know I can't.

I hope I've emerged from this experience capable of understanding that, for some writers, there are certain experiences that will be kept private, and that's all right. I won't assume (as I had in the past) that if writers choose to sidestep something important in their lives in their work, there's something wrong with them—a failure of nerve, incapacity to climb deeply into a difficult experience, an avoidance of something potentially important.

I'd promised myself I'd never write the words, "Cancer taught me. . . ." But I will say that cancer taught me I can't write about everything. And it taught me, too, that I must respect those writers who consider certain of their experiences to be private and off-limits in their work.

37

Taking a Break

When I was stumped while writing my memoir *Adultery*, my husband and I were supposed to go to Hawaii, where we'd never been. When we'd first arranged the trip, I was thrilled. But close to the time of our departure, I didn't want to go. I had a book to unravel. Leaving my work was crazy.

"Let's not go," I said one morning. "My work isn't going well, and I don't have time to fool around."

"We're going," he said. "If you get away, you'll figure it out when you get back."

My husband believes in taking time off. I do, too—theoretically. But, practically, I feel more myself when I'm working. As the psychologist Howard Gruber has said, for "the creative person, the greatest fun is the work." We've never taken a holiday without my first trying to subvert it. I don't feel well. Travel is difficult. The weather is terrible where we're going.

My parents valued education, so when I was young, the only time my parents didn't bother me was when I was doing homework. My father made me a triangular desk that fit into a space at the top of the stairs. I'd finish my assignments and then invent more homework. I'd have to read about the Civil War in the encyclopedia; I'd have to practice vocabulary; I'd have to read two additional novels.

Sitting at my desk while I was working, nobody told me what to do. My father was pleased with my industry rather than angry with me. My mother wanted me to study because, no matter how much she needed my help, she wanted me to do well in school. Sitting at my desk working helped me feel a sense of control in my chaotic household. Who knew what might happen when I left my desk? With this history, who'd ever want to leave a desk piled high with work?

And then I met and married my husband, a man with a far different sense of what life should be. He started dragging me away from my desk soon after we met, and has been doing so ever since. I was going away to relax, I'd tell myself, and this was necessary. And I hoped that wherever I went, I'd come back with a story to tell, a change in perspective, or perhaps even a new way of working, just like some of my favorite writers, like Virginia Woolf and D. H. Lawrence. If it was good for them, it had to be good for me, too.

I know many writers like me—writers who'd rather be writing than doing anything else. Writers like Marcel Proust, with their own equivalent of a cork-lined room. Writers who feel unmoored when they're anywhere but home, who don't want to leave a book in progress until it's finished, who take their work with them wherever they go. But not all writers are like this. Many have traveled often, and to far-flung places, and their work has been enriched by these sojourns, like Elizabeth Bishop, whose Brazilian poems "Squatter's Children" and "Questions of Travel" and her story "A Trip to Vigia" illustrate how necessary travel was to her art.

When I read in Howard Gardner's *Creating Minds* about how necessary travel is to foster creativity, and that I could construe my holidays as a kind of homework necessary for writing my books, I stopped resisting. In "Breakaway Minds: Howard Gruber, Interviewed by Howard Gardner" Gardner remarked that "creative people combine a zest for work and a capacity for play."

There is a shift in the way the brain works when we're in an unfamiliar setting. That shift into a different kind of awareness and alertness seems to precipitate changes in writers' works that often occur after they travel.

And so, when I was writing about Virginia Woolf, my husband and I traveled to Rodmell, where Virginia Woolf lived, and we took a walk on the Sussex South Downs as Woolf did most days. That single walk changed my perspective—and how I wrote—about Woolf. She'd been described as an ethereal creature, but I learned that she had to be robust to hike up and down those hills.

Before Woolf married (she was then Virginia Stephen), she traveled to Italy in April 1909 and kept a journal, writing detailed descriptions of the landscape, portraits of the people she met, and observations about how the English lived when they journeyed abroad. When she returned to England, she used what she'd seen and heard in writing the earlier version of her first novel *The Voyage Out*, then called *Melymbrosia*, although she changed the setting to South America.

After she married Leonard Woolf, she was often as unwilling to travel as I am. But her husband insisted: he made her take official holidays—six weeks a year away from her work, though she never stopped writing. She'd read, write in her journal, look, listen, and store away experiences for when she returned to England. She'd unlock conundrums and dream new books.

D. H. Lawrence was an outsider, as his biographer John Worthen describes. After Lawrence left England, he wandered the globe. And he was one of those writers who seemed to be at his best—less angry, more cheerful, and less hostile—when he was en route from one place to another. Without Lawrence's travels, there would have been no art; there might have been no Lawrence. He wrote about every place he visited and lived—Mexico, Ceylon, Australia, Germany, Italy, New Mexico—and turned the people he met into characters in his novels. A visit to ancient tombs in Tuscany, for example, was used in his *Etruscan Places* (1932).

My husband and I *did* take that trip to Hawaii. While we were away, we wandered into a gallery displaying works by Dale Chihuly, who transformed the art of glass blowing into realms previously unexplored. His pieces are astonishingly beautiful in their form, color, and dynamism.

When we returned home, I bought a DVD showing Chihuly at work. He was coaching those who blow glass for him—you can't do it for very many years; glass blowing is dangerous work and damages the lungs. He was telling the glass blowers to go where the glass wanted to go. "Let it go, let it go, let it go," was his message, as the glass took on one form and then another. Rather than forcing the glass into predetermined shapes, Chihuly was insisting that the glass do what glass does when it's blown. He was working *with* the material of his art rather than against it.

Go where the work wants to go. Don't resist.

I wrote that down on a card after our trip, after seeing Chihuly's works, and after seeing the DVD of Chihuly at work. And that trip, which I'd resisted, provoked me into working on *Adultery* in an entirely new way upon my return. The work found its voice, its shape, and its meaning with less effort than usual. I worked more freely, more fully, and more dangerously. The subject matter found its form. When I was at my desk, I imagined Chihuly standing behind me, saying, "Let it go, let it go, let it go."

38

Why I'm a Writer Who Cooks

Everyone who knows me knows that I cook almost every night. When I cook, I focus on something other than my writing and, paradoxically, this helps my work. As Diane Johnson, author of *The Shadow Knows* (1974), has said, "How I think about my work is indistinguishable from the way I think about my . . . cooking: here is the project I'm involved in. It is play. In this sense, all my life is spent in play."

I love good food, and the food offered by most takeout places and many restaurants (even expensive ones) doesn't always satisfy me. So I cook because I hate to have a bad meal. And when I cook, I get drawn into its pleasures, even—perhaps especially—at the end of a day's writing when I think I'm too tired.

The real reason I cook is that I *need* to cook because I spend part of the day writing, though several writers I know pride themselves on not cooking. Lots of writers say they have no interest in cooking, or have no time to cook—writing is so important and it takes so much time. And that may be fine for them, but it's not for me.

Michael Chabon has described how he learned how to cook in his essay "Art of Cake." When Chabon was ten, he read the recipe for velvet crumb cake on the back of a Bisquick box and set to work. "Cooking," he learned, "was a magical act, a feat of transformation, a way of turning the homely and familiar into something finer." Chabon had been helping his mother cook for several years by that time. After she became a lawyer and went to work full-time, he cooked for his family every night until he went to college, and he cooks for his wife and children now, too. During the years, he's found an "enduring source of . . . pleasure . . . in the kitchen."

"[W]riting is a lot like cooking," Chabon says. It requires "stubbornness and a tolerance—maybe even a taste—for last-minute collapse." Things can work out well when we cook; or they can go horribly wrong—just like when we write. "As a writer," Chabon says, "I try to write books I think I would love to read. You cook the foods you'd love to eat, you write the books you'd love to read."

I finished a chapter of the father book yesterday. Or, I should say, I finished it for now. You know how these things go. You think you're finished. You put the thing down, you reread it, and you realize what else has to be done. You know there's more to be done, but you can't do it now. You send it out to a writing partner, and she agrees there's more to be done. But every so often you have to tell yourself you're finished, at least for now, because writing a book goes on and on and on, sometimes with no seeming end point, until one day the book is finished, and you can't figure out how it happened. But in the meantime, you're stuck in the never-never land of the process of writing a book. (And a succubus it sometimes seems to be.)

But last night, after a marathon revision session (unusual for me), I came into the kitchen, cut up some tiny tomatoes I'd bought from a farm, put them into a bowl together with some minced garlic, capers, olive oil, and goat cheese. I got out a package of artisan fusilli; threw them into boiling, salted water; cooked them until they were al dente; then tossed the pasta with the sauce and a touch of pasta water. For a vegetable, I'd boiled up some tiny green beans from that same farm and tossed them with some garlic oil I'd prepared. Within half an hour, there we were, my husband and I, on the porch, eating our meal and drinking a glass of lovely Montepulciano d'Abruzzo. It was twilight. The work I still need to do, forgotten, for a while. The meal was simple, but it gave us both enormous pleasure.

That's why I'm a writer who cooks. A book can take three years, or five or ten or more. A chapter can take a few weeks, a few months, or more. The chapter I finished took months of research, a month and a half of writing, maybe more, and I know it's not finished yet. A great meal takes me half an hour, an hour to cook. In that short space of time, I start something, finish it, and enjoy what I've created. Writing is so open-ended and takes so long that cooking provides me with an antidote to all the ongoingness of the writing process that sometimes feels like forever and ever, without end.

I never enjoy writing a book the way I enjoy cooking a meal. Howard Gardner has observed that when we're creating, we're dissatisfied much of the time—this urges us to find creative solutions to our challenges. We can spend years on a work, but the moments of satisfaction are few. Once it's finished, we might feel a sense of satisfaction but no real pleasure, for we're already thinking about the next project. Pleasure, we hope, is what a reader gets from our work.

I learned this even before I wrote my first book. My mentor, Mitchell A. Leaska, had just finished writing a book. "Aren't you thrilled?" I asked. I imagined the completion of a book to be a rhapsodic time.

"I was," he answered, "for a few minutes."

The day my first book was published, I was taking out the garbage (a lot of it), and I opened the bin and thought, "Hmmm, life does go on pretty much as it did before." But cooking provides both satisfaction *and* pleasure. There's the big bang of satisfaction from cooking—you don't have to wait long to realize the fruits of your efforts. And then you have the pleasure of eating.

When I shop for vegetables, say, or when I rummage around in the fridge or cupboards for what I need, or when I slice a carrot or a pepper or an onion, I have to pay careful attention. I can't be thinking of my work, and so cooking pulls me out of that intense focus my work requires. On the days when I don't cook, my writing brain has a hard time shutting off, and I'm not very good company; I don't pay much attention to anyone or anything around me. I'm in that writing bubble every writer is familiar with.

My son Jason said that when he was a kid, and he came home from school, and I was writing, he'd stand in front of my desk and say, "Hi, Mom, I'm bleeding to death." And I'd say, "That's nice, dear. Get yourself a little snack. I'll be with you in a minute." Cooking forces me out of that interior space; it forces me into a relationship with something other than words and with the people I love. Which, after all, is what I need to do when I'm away from my desk.

39

Slow Reading

Bill Gates periodically takes a reading retreat. He chooses his books and goes somewhere or stays home. He shuts out the world and sinks long and deep into reading. This retreat is revitalizing. Getting away, and reading what he otherwise wouldn't have time for, Gates returns to work refreshed and more able to encounter new challenges. (Steven Johnson's *Where Good Ideas Come From* discusses the importance of Gates's reading vacations.) Gates regularly posts the books he's read, and comments on them; among the most recent are Steven Pinker, *The Better Angels of Our Nature* (2011), and Katherine Boo, *Behind the Beautiful Forevers* (2012). "That's for me," I thought, when I learned about Gates's reading vacations.

There's a scene in Michael Cunningham's *The Hours* (1998) in which a woman checks into a hotel to read Virginia Woolf's *Mrs. Dalloway*. She's in crisis; she's trying to be a good mother but she's unfulfilled in her traditional marriage. When I first read the novel, I was struck by her need to escape to a hotel to read without interruption.

I'd had two small children and raised them while I started writing. I'd read scores of books while I cared for them. But for years, I'd read a paragraph, then tend to a crying baby; I'd read a chapter, then organize my children to go to the park; I'd read a few pages, then peel some potatoes for supper. It was in and out of reading every time I read. I hadn't experienced that luxury of falling into reading since childhood, when I'd go to the library in summer, check out a pile of books, sit on my family's back porch, and read to my heart's content.

Henry Miller's *The Books in My Life* underscores the importance of reading for writers. Miller thought it was important for us to read slowly: "How much better and wiser it would be," he writes, "how much more instructive and enriching, if we proceeded at a snail's pace! What matter if it took a year, instead of a few days, to finish the book?" Miller took a year to read Thomas Mann's *The Magic Mountain* (1924), spending time with the novel "as with a living person, . . . I might even say."

Miller believed that the "way one reads a book is the way one reads life." That is, if we read haphazardly and inattentively, that's how we live our lives, that's how we write. Learning to read slowly and attentively can help us live more fully realized lives and can help our work.

Reading, for Miller, is a "fecundating" experience, intimately connected to the act of writing: "Drunk with ecstasy, one returns to his own work revivified." For Miller every act of writing begins with reading. Miller's reading was voracious and idiosyncratic. Although he left City College because he was forced to study Spenser's *Faerie Queene*, reading meant the world to him. He read Jean Giono, H. Rider Haggard, Marie Corelli, Greek drama, Rimbaud, Rabelais. He believed reading was "an act of creation" because unless a writer has an "enthusiastic reader . . . a book would die." By reading slowly, carefully, and with complete attention, Miller believed, we respect the writer's work and enrich our lives.

Jeffrey Eugenides, author of *The Marriage Plot*, has described how, in college, he read "the great modernists. Joyce, Proust, Faulkner." Soon he and his friends "were reading Pynchon and John Barth." His generation, he says, were "weaned on experimental writing before ever reading much of . . . nineteenth-century literature."

But when Eugenides was in his early twenties, he "read Tolstoy for the first time," and learned about a different form of narration. He learned that he preferred the "clarity of Tolstoy . . . and the vividness and lifelikeness of his characters" to the "cerebration . . . [and] the play of language" in Joyce. Taking time to read Tolstoy with care and attention eventually led Eugenides to "attempt to reconcile these two poles of literature, the experimentalism of the modernists and the narrative drive and centrality of character of the nineteenth-century realists" in his work.

A few weeks ago, I decided to take a reading retreat. I was going away to a remote location, cut off from the outside world, and I could look forward to two solid weeks of reading. I'd gotten an iPad. And although I still love to read conventional books (especially in the bathtub), I wanted to take several books away. Among the books I downloaded were Ernest Hemingway, *For Whom the Bell Tolls* (1940) and *The Sun Also Rises*; Ian McEwan, *Atonement*; Alan Paton, *Cry, the Beloved Country* (1948); Sarah Hall, *How to Paint a Dead Man* (2009).

Throughout those two weeks, I settled into a few hours of reading in the morning, a few hours in the afternoon, and an hour in the evening. I read about five hours a day, every day. There were no interruptions—no telephone, no e-mail, no Internet. I stopped reading when I wanted to, not when I had to.

By the end of the first week, I felt as if I'd found the reader in myself I'd lost many years ago. The reader who wept over a passage. Who laughed out loud. Who circled back to the beginning of a book to start it all over again. Who marveled at the brilliance of a phrase, of a sentence, of a long stretch of writing. Who sat and stared at the sky in astonishment, recalling something wondrously written. I read Hemingway as if I'd never read him before; I read Hall for the first time and was humbled by the brilliance of her work.

Sure, I itched to write. What writers don't when they're reading something skilled? But I promised myself I wouldn't write, at least not for my project. But I wrote long meandering appreciations of what I read. I noted what I wanted to remember. And, like Miller, I copied long passages into my notebook—copying, I've learned, is a superb way of slowing down reading, of noticing how a writer's sentences work.

I wish I'd had conventional books with me for the tactile pleasure of holding a book, of turning a page. But still, the time I spent reading was everything I'd hoped for, and much more. "What a privilege it is to do this," I thought. And I came home eager to reengage my work. Though reading is part of my life's work, during those two weeks, I relearned how to *really* read. To read the way we were meant to read. Slowly, carefully, with respect and attention.

Miller has written that if we fear we'll neglect our "duties by reading leisurely and thoughtfully, by cultivating [our] own thoughts," we'll neglect our "duties anyway, and for worse reasons." When I returned home, I vowed to continue to read without interruption. For if we don't read slowly and carefully, and choose, instead, a life filled only with obligations, Miller believes we'll miss the possibility of living "a new life, [filled with] new fields of adventure and exploration."

40

Fresh Air

Sue Monk Kidd, author of *The Secret Life of Bees* (2002), has observed that although she believes in working hard, she also believes her writing can suffer "from a lack of loitering." Kidd says, "I try to go out to my dock every morning and just sit there, watching the wind blow." Though she doesn't know if this routine is crucial for her writing, she thinks it might be "because the imagination needs that little bit of downtime to browse around. . . . Maybe the mind simply needs a breather, some mindless diversion."

When Virginia Woolf's work on *Jacob's Room* came to a standstill because she was sick, she wrote into her diary that going out onto the Sussex South Downs was intimately connected with her ability to write. "[W]hat wouldn't I give," she wrote, "to be coming through Firle woods, dusty & hot, with my nose turned home, every muscle tired, . . . so sane & cool, & ripe for the morrows [sic] task. How I should notice everything—the phrase for it coming the moment after & fitting like a glove; . . . so my story would begin telling itself."

Woolf knew what she needed to do to practice her art. Each day about four, she left her house and went outside. In writing

Jacob's Room, set during the Great War, she knew she was "writing against the current" and to do this well she needed to be in good shape and clear her head and lift her spirits by taking exercise outdoors. She trusted that when she was outdoors, the words she needed would come.

You can see the evidence of the time Woolf spent outdoors in her work. The walks that Jacob takes in *Jacob's Room*—one with his friend Bonamy—replicate those Woolf herself took through London. Mrs. Dalloway's famous walk in *Mrs. Dalloway* and her essay, "Street Haunting" (1930), are other examples of Woolf writing her walks into her work. Her descriptions of London, Sussex, and Cornwall are based upon years of her paying careful attention to what she saw as she walked.

When Toni Morrison was composing *Beloved* (1987) and working on the infanticide scene where "Sethe cuts the throat of the child"—an enormously difficult passage to write—she remembered "getting up from the table and walking outside for a long time—walking around the yard and coming back and revising a little bit and going back out and in and rewriting the sentence over and over again." The scene was so difficult, so fraught with emotion, and required so much authorial control that Morrison found herself "unable to sit there and would have to go away and come back." Those breaks from the work, those perambulations outside, enabled Morrison to write the scene in the understated way she desired so that the language didn't "compete with the violence itself."

Henry Miller walked the city of Paris and kept notebooks describing what he saw. He used them when writing about Paris. In *Tropic of Cancer*, you can see the artistic payoff of these walks—his descriptions of the Seine, of the various quarters. His walks also kept him alert enough and fit enough to keep working. Miller wanted to be a long-lived writer, and so he knew he had to keep active by walking, or, later in his life, by swimming when he lived in California.

My friend Christoph Keller writes about the effort it takes him to get outside in his memoir *The Best Dancer* (2003). Keller uses a wheelchair, and getting it down the steps into the street from an apartment where he lived with his wife, the poet Jan Heller Levi, took enormous coordination between them. Keller routinely roams New York City. "When I'm out and about in this city," he writes, "I am amazed simply because everywhere you look there is something to be amazed at." Keller shows us his adopted city from his vantage point; he describes the people who interact with him; he relates the impediments to his getting around; he writes about his intense love affair with New York.

"I'm stuck," I sometimes complain to my husband when I'm working on a thorny piece of writing.

"Don't just sit there. Go outside," he replies.

Writing is intense work. It's hard work. It's work I need to take a break from each day to clear my head, to broaden my perspective, and to take care of myself. If I don't, my writing suffers. Like Woolf, I'll have a case of the fidgets. I'll ruminate. I won't know what to write. I'll stare at the screen. I'll begin to believe there's nothing significant beyond the desk. And unless I breathe some fresh air each day, my work sounds as if it's been written in a hermetically sealed and stuffy room.

Thinking about how necessary this outside life was/is to me and to the writers I've mentioned reminds me that the ability to be outside alone, freely and fearlessly, cannot be taken for granted. Nawal El Saadawi's *Memoirs from the Woman's Prison* describes what it's like to be imprisoned for your political views, and wary of being outside when you're released. Keller's *The Best Dancer* recounts the thoughtless impediments our society puts in the way of those of us using wheelchairs as our only means of locomotion. Woolf describes how, for years, she took for granted the fact that she could open her door, walk out onto the Downs, or into the streets of London, and dream her books. And then, during World War II, the Luftwaffe began bombing England, and she could no longer roam her beloved Downs for fear of being hit by a bomb dropped from an airplane. That's in her diary, too. What it was like not to be able to roam freely outside and how it adversely affected her life and work.

Some writers I know think that when you're a writer, you should stay indoors at your desk and just write. It's as if time spent away from the desk will impede your progress irrevocably. There are some writers—Peter Ackroyd, author of more than fifty books, for whom life is mostly work (he writes three books simultaneously—history in the morning; biography and fiction in the afternoon) and little play (two outings a month to visit historical villages in England). But many prolific writers—Sue Monk Kidd, Virginia Woolf, Toni Morrison, Henry Miller, and Christoph Keller, among them—took/take time to go outdoors. They understood/understand that we often get our best insights when we're away from our work, while we're doing something restful like Kidd or something rhythmic like walking (Woolf) or rolling along in a wheelchair (Keller) or something to ease the intensity of the work like Morrison. A writer's work is close, intense, focused work. It's often helpful for us to get away from our desks, change our point of view, and look at the outside world.

41

Waiting for an Answer

Ian McEwan, author of *Sweet Tooth* (2012), has described how he's cultivated the habit of waiting until an idea announces itself between projects. "I know," he says, "that between books I'll simply wait and see what comes up. This is a process you can't have, and don't want, under your full conscious control." If McEwan forced the process prematurely, his work would be far less authentic, far less complex, far more stereotypical, and far more formulaic. And he might have a far more difficult time completing the book.

McEwan knows he must wait for the right subject. He often has a recurrent dream of sitting at his desk in his study, "feeling particularly well." He opens a desk drawer, and sees "a novel I finished last summer that I've completely forgotten about because I've been so busy." The imagined work is brilliant, and he recalls how hard he worked on it before putting it away. The dream attests to McEwan's trusting that he'll never run out of ideas, there will always be another novel awaiting him.

Before beginning work on *The Cement Garden* (1978), about a group of young people reacting to a terrifying environment, McEwan had "delayed writing a novel for years." He'd come back to

London from the United States in 1976, and he started thinking about writing a novel about "children trying to survive without adults," but he didn't know how to begin. "One afternoon as I was at my desk," McEwan said, "these four children, with their distinct identities, suddenly rose before my imagination." He didn't have to figure out who they were: "they appeared ready-made."

McEwan "wrote some quick notes," then slept. When he awakened, he says, "I knew that at last I had the novel I wanted to write." He worked for a year, "paring the material back" to realize his goal of writing a "brief and intense" novel.

Stephen Nachmanovitch, in *Free Play*, remarks that learning patience—waiting for solutions to unfold in their own time—is essential for the creative person. Patience, he believes, will help us "accomplish infinitely more" than if we try to force the process along: "The great scientists and scholars are not those who publish or perish at any cost, but rather those who are willing to wait until the pieces of the puzzle come together in nature's own design."

Ray Bradbury, in *Zen in the Art of Writing*, describes how he adopted the mantra, "WORK RELAXATION DON'T THINK." For Bradbury, "hard work prepares the way for the first stages of relaxation," necessary for the creative process. We can't fail unless we stop working; but we don't work simply to work, but "to find a way to release the truth that lies in all of us." To do this, we must cultivate a kind of "dynamic relaxation" during which the "body thinks for itself": "True creation occurs then and only then," says Bradbury.

Victoria Nelson's *On Writer's Block* is the most important work I've read on the role of waiting in the creative act. Making art, Nelson says, isn't always superior to *not* making art: "That belief comes out of . . . [a] production-quota mentality. . . ." Forcing ourselves to work when we don't have the answer to a challenge "via a kind of

internal Sherman's march," Nelson says, "is not always synony-
mous with artistic victory." If we force ourselves to overcome "a real
resistance," we might be "prematurely tearing the curtains away from
a delicate, half-formed something not ready for the full light of
consciousness."

Many of us try to rush the creative process. But, as McEwan's
process illustrates, and as Nelson asserts, it often takes time "for an
imaginative idea to grow to full term in the unconscious. . . ." If we
proceed "entirely by ego command," we're likely to subvert "this
mostly invisible gestation period." As writers, we need to cultivate
the twin traits of "*[s]urrendering* and *listening*" but this will be impossible unless we give up our struggle to control our artistic process, unless we cease engaging in what Nelson calls "a solipsistic
master-slave struggle for control over yourself."

Some time ago I'd finished a good enough draft (nearly ready,
I thought) of a chunk of my father book, describing how he pretended to be killing an enemy while he was playing charades
with my grandchildren, and how unnerving it was for them. But
I knew there was something missing, and I didn't know what. I
had that unsettling feeling of not having found the right way to
tell the story that often accompanies the creative process. My first
inclination was to continue working until I figured out what to
do next. But having read Nelson and others who warn against
trying to force a creative resolution, I knew that would be coun-
terproductive.

It took a long time—many months, in fact—for me to see how
to move the draft along. I realized that my voice was completely
missing from the narrative. I went back to the draft, and began inserting my reactions to my father's behavior, my recollections of his
violence when I was a child, my trying to protect my grandchildren. The narrative was now linking past events to those in the

present, and I finally became a character in the narrative when I hadn't been one before.

I've learned that we can't rush aesthetic resolutions, and that we can't force them to come when we want them to. We can ponder them; we can write about probable solutions. But an authentic resolution can't be compelled no matter how hard we work. In fact, we often find the solution when we take time off, when we're away from our desks, or when we allow sufficient time to elapse. Our work as writers will be helped, not hindered, if we learn to wait.

I now accept that when I don't know what to do in my work, I'll feel out of sorts, perhaps for some time. Part of my job as a writer is learning to live with this dissatisfaction. I try to remember that feeling unsettled is a prelude to that moment when I become aware of the solution to a creative challenge.

This often happens when I'm doing routine things—showering, laundry, straightening up the house, walking, cooking, or washing dishes; we often have to let go of trying to find the solutions to our creative challenges in order to discover them. Then, when they arrive, we must learn to recognize that we *have* found them—I've known writers who've discounted these intuitive leaps.

I'd initially planned to keep myself out of the narrative to focus on my father's story. That never felt wrong; it just never felt right. But when I heard a voice that said "You have to be in the narrative," I knew that solution was absolutely right.

Through the years, I've learned that I'm always anxious prior to a breakthrough and that I feel relieved when one occurs. When a breakthrough occurs, it's often a surprising solution inviting me into unfamiliar narrative terrain, in this case, combining two voices—my father's and mine—in one narrative. But I remind myself that I've waited a long time to arrive at this solution and that it's inviting me to try something new, to try a form I haven't tried before.

42

A New Perspective

A writer friend wrote me she was traveling to Venice. Could I suggest restaurants? Reading material? I suggested a restaurant on the main square in Burano for spaghetti *con vongole*, and a splurge lunch at the rooftop restaurant of the Danieli, overlooking the Canale di San Marco and its chaos of crisscrossing boats, where George Sand and Frédéric Chopin stayed. And I suggested she read Joseph Brodsky's *Watermark* (1992), about his annual winter retreats to Venice, and I'd read it, too.

Brodsky's memoir is a series of short meditations upon his yearly forays to Venice in winter and their effect upon Brodsky's heart, mind, and spirit. He arrives in Venice on a cold night, and steps from the station into the darkness and notices something utterly unique yet quintessentially Venetian in winter—the "smell of freezing seaweed," which fills him with "utter happiness" because it recalls the Russia of his youth.

Brodsky relates his observations about why winter there is so compelling for him and how Venice changes your perceptions about beauty and human behavior—the city is a series of stage sets and everything that occurs there seems dramatic. The sense of confinement you feel in its alleys yields to the expansiveness you feel when you emerge at the edge of the lagoon. The quality of Venetian sunsets. Winter's inevitable fog—it's often so thick that the only way to find your way back to your hotel after a brief errand is to hope the path your body cut through the fog is still visible. The interior of an ancient palazzo—rotting draperies, corridors filled with terrible paintings of unattractive ancestors, ever-present mold and mildew.

Reading *Watermark* reminded me how, when great writers travel, their way of seeing changes, and this shift in perception inevitably changes their works in progress or later works. When Brodsky traveled to Venice in winter, he began to view his experience there as a series of vignettes rather than as one continuous narrative, and that's how he composed his memoir. "If I get sidetracked [in relating my narrative]," Brodsky says, "it is because being sidetracked is literally a matter of course here...." Finding one's way in Venice inevitably means taking a wrong turn, getting lost, finding one's way again.

Watermark suggests that each time we visit a new place, our senses are bombarded with a series of disconnected observations: it's as if cause and effect don't exist because we haven't been there long enough to understand the connections among the events we witness. We're forced to live in the moment. And what we see becomes paramount: "the eye identifies not with the body it belongs to but with the object of its attention."

Brodsky traveled to Venice in winter in part because he'd read *Provincial Entertainments* (1925) by Henri de Régnier, which described the "damp, cold narrow streets through which one hurries," and this sounded like the Petersburg of Brodsky's youth. But the format of that novel was significant, too. The novel taught him "the single most crucial lesson in composition": "what makes a narrative good is not the story itself but what follows what."

And so Brodsky's *Watermark* is a series of vignettes in which the meaning of each tiny narrative reverberates against what has come before and foreshadows what comes after. He invites the reader to ponder how "what follows what" contributes to its meaning, a personal experiential account of Venice rather than a linear narrative of his journeys. *Watermark* describes Brodsky's Venice only.

Brodsky doesn't immediately tell us why he visits Venice in winter. All this backstory (about reading *Provincial Entertainments,* about how he doesn't like to see glorious monuments spoiled by scantily clad people) comes later. If Brodsky began with his life in St. Petersburg, continued with his reading *Provincial Entertainments,* his decision to visit Venice in winter, and his first and subsequent journeys, the narrative would have been different. But that linear arrangement wouldn't have revealed the "what follows what" chain of Brodsky's associations nor his *experience* of being in Venice.

Reading *Watermark* didn't make me remember Venice. Instead, it made me see and understand *Brodsky's* Venice—it shifted my perception of that city immeasurably, inviting me to understand every place exists both as a communal referent and as a deeply personal space for every person who lives or journeys there. It taught me to respect my seemingly trivial impressions of a new place—my own equivalent of Brodsky's frozen seaweed—rather than viewing it through a guidebook's eyes. It made me remember the gunshot holes in the facades of buildings throughout Provence, a reminder of the Axis retreat and the Allied advance. Before reading Brodsky, I wouldn't have thought to describe them.

The impact of place upon the formation of character is central to *Watermark.* Brodsky describes that the Venetians can only be understood with reference to Venice's geography: "Because of the scarcity of space," Brodsky observes, "people exist here in cellular proximity to one another, and life evolves with the immanent logic of gossip."

After reading *Watermark*, I realized my work about my parents' lives during World War II didn't account for the impact of their living in Hoboken, New Jersey, a prime German target during the war, and a place where you could see warships assembling for their forays to the great sea battles of the war. I knew I'd have to consider this issue when I revised, for I'd been treating Hoboken as just another city, rather than as a place where it was dangerous to live and where battleships were constant reminders of the war.

Two moments I might juxtapose. The first—my mother scurrying up to the parapet overlooking the Hudson River with her friends to watch the U.S. fleet sail up the Hudson to celebrate the 1939 World's Fair; my father (whom my mother hasn't yet met) stands in formation on the deck of the aircraft carrier *Ranger*; neither yet knows the other exists. The second—my mother pushing me in a stroller up to that same parapet years later to watch warships assembling for the next naval assault on the enemy while my father is away in the Pacific.

Reading Brodsky helped me discover an important thread of meaning that was missing from my narrative; *Watermark* invited me to think about the importance of juxtaposition—what follows what—in my narrative.

43

What's in Your Drawer?

Diana Athill, in her memoir *Somewhere Towards the End* (2008), reflects upon what it's like to be almost ninety and knowing you're nearing the end of life. It's forthright and unflinching, yet hopeful, a work worth reading for writers composing works of reflection.

Athill describes her life as an editor of V. S. Naipaul and Jean Rhys, among other famous writers. She describes how thrilled she was to discover, late in life, that she, too, could write. After she retired, she began writing a memoir, something she didn't have the courage to do earlier, although she'd squirreled away the beginnings of three books in a desk drawer.

"[L]ooking for something in a rarely opened drawer," she writes, "I happened on . . . two pages, and read them." She thought "something could be made of them after all, so the next day I put paper in my typewriter and this time it wasn't a blip, it was a whoosh!—and *Instead of a Letter* [1962], my first book, began." The work became an account of how a pilot she'd loved broke off their engagement and then died in combat. After she completed the work, she was happier than she'd ever been. But she realized it might have taken her that long to comprehend her grief and write about this crisis in her life.

I suspect most writers have a manuscript hidden in some drawer that, like Athill's scribbles, could be turned into a work of art. We might feel because we haven't worked on it for a long time that we may as well let it go. But, instead, because time has passed we might arrive at a new perspective on that long-neglected work.

Jeffrey Eugenides, author of *The Marriage Plot*, has described how, in the late nineties, while he was writing *Middlesex*, he "hit a rough patch and put the manuscript aside." During this hiatus, he started writing another book "about a rich family throwing a debutante party." Tired of the demands *Middlesex* was placing upon him, he hoped the new effort "would be less demanding" and easier to write. He toyed with it for about a month, and then realized it, too, would be a challenge. Besides, he missed working on *Middlesex*, and in the interim he'd figured out what he needed to do.

After publishing *Middlesex*, Eugenides "went back to the debutante book and worked on it for another couple years." He thought the work was adequate, but he sensed something wasn't working. "Then one day," he said, "I wrote a sentence that changed everything. . . . 'Madeleine's love troubles had begun at a time when the French theory she was reading deconstructed the very notion of love.'" After writing about Madeleine and the two men in her life, Mitchell and Leonard, Eugenides realized he was writing two books. He excised the material about the party and instead "followed Madeleine, Mitchell, and Leonard on an entirely different journey." He didn't yet know that the notion of "the marriage plot" would provide him with "a structure for the novel"; this only became evident in time.

Early in her life, before her marriage, Virginia Woolf wrote a work called *The Journal of Mistress Joan Martyn* about a historian who discovers a journal written by a woman in the fifteenth century, describing her life. Woolf chose not to publish it, but she kept it. It contains many themes Woolf would later engage—the inequity between the sexes, the unrealized desire of many women to write because of family demands, the lost examples of women's writing in England.

The Journal of Mistress Joan Martyn is an example of an unpublished work that serves as a template the author devises in a preliminary examination of the themes of future works.

I have just such a text in my drawer—"White on Black." I wrote it more than twenty years ago. When I finished—or rather, stopped—I'd composed seventy pages about my childhood. The title referred to my Italian grandmother, dressed in black, crocheting a white tablecloth resting in her lap. I wrote about my love for her, about my family during wartime, about my relationship with my mother when my father was away. I stopped because I didn't know what to do next. It wasn't an essay; it wasn't the beginning of a book. So I took it and put it in a drawer, and there it stayed for years.

When I was asked to write a memoir, I dug it out. For a while, I tried to work from it. But I realized this was the wrong approach. The work revealed the subject I wanted to tackle, but I wanted to use another voice and structure. I read it, imbibed its meaning, and put it back in the drawer. If I hadn't written that failed work, I doubt whether I could have written my first memoir, *Vertigo*. Because much time had passed, I understood what I could use—the scenes I'd sketched—but I also realized I had to begin anew.

I pulled "White on Black" out of that drawer four more times: when I was writing *Crazy in the Kitchen* and knew my grandmother would figure in the work, when I was writing *On Moving* and knew I wanted to describe where my mother and I lived while my father was in the Pacific, when I wrote an essay about my grandmother's handiwork, and when I began writing my current book about my father going to war.

What I've learned from having returned to, but never completing, "White on Black" through the years is that sometimes provisional, unsuccessful work will yield its treasures in time. I got more mileage out of this piece than I would have had I tried to force it into publishable shape before I understood what to do with that material.

Jeffrey Eugenides took work he'd put away and learned, in time, what story line to focus upon. Diana Athill learned her forgotten scribbles could be turned into powerful works. She didn't initially think her writing was worth much, so she'd hidden it away. But when she found it years later, she learned she could muster the skill to complete the work. And she did this with two other abandoned manuscripts.

It's worth looking for work we've stored away long ago, digging it out, and deciding if there's anything we can do with it. Perhaps, like "White on Black," something we've abandoned can inform a book we're currently writing. Perhaps, like Athill's bits and pieces, it can serve as inspiration to try again. Perhaps, like Eugenides's manuscript, we'll discover what to do with the work. It's up to us to decide. But I believe that it's important to honor work we've stashed away and think about its possibilities and potential. It might reveal precisely what we need to write right now.

Part Five

BUILDING A BOOK, FINISHING A BOOK

Introduction

It's important for us to understand that finishing a book has nothing to do with talent. Finishing a book requires a host of other qualities, among them, stamina. Keeping at a task for a long time when there's no reward along the way (other than the satisfaction of engaging in the writing process and watching our work develop), no public acknowledgment that our work is worth completing (for many of us), and perhaps no guaranteed financial payoff for the hundreds or even thousands of hours of work we're putting in is enormously difficult. It's daunting to contemplate the completion of a long work even for seasoned writers. For beginning writers, it might seem overwhelming. Still we can cultivate the stamina that completing a book requires; it's a skill that can be learned and that will be transformative.

I've learned what it takes to develop this skill from reading and rereading the journals John Steinbeck kept while composing *The Grapes of Wrath* and *East of Eden*. In both of these journals—one entry for each day Steinbeck worked on each of the novels—Steinbeck writes about what it took him to begin, build, and complete a work of art. I urge all my students and every beginning writer I know to read and reread these journals. They offer a manual of instruction on how to work day by day by day and how to overcome the inevitable roadblocks we encounter so that we can persevere in our work.

Even a writer as successful as Steinbeck needed to assess his process every single day of his writing life. He needed to think about what he was going to write and decide how it related to what he'd already written and what would follow. He needed to continually remind himself of the ongoing structure of his work and the themes and meanings he wanted to express. To plan how what he was writing that day fit into the scheme he'd already established and how it related to what he'd already written. To think about how to marshal the courage, strength, and stamina he needed for his work. To avoid thinking about the reception of the work, the money he'd make, and to focus, instead, on what he wanted to do each day. To think about his responsibilities to his wife and children and what he needed to do to maintain his relationships with them. To record whatever chores needed doing and how he would find time to do the woodworking and inventing that was an important part of his creative life. To think about how to create the kind of life that doing his work required. To ponder how he might need to change his writing space so it suited him better. To manage his emotions so he could go to the page each day, despite how he felt, by writing about what troubled him; to describe his doubts, his nervousness, and his fears. To remind himself that his work went best if he worked slowly and deliberately, if he refused to rush or to push himself to write more than his daily quota of two handwritten ledger pages though he might be tempted to work faster. Yet to hold himself to his self-assigned task lest he give in to what he termed his inherent laziness and to use his journal to warm up his writing muscle, and to prepare himself for the day's work.

Although Steinbeck worked slowly and deliberately, halfway

through writing *The Grapes of Wrath*, he wrote, "My work is no good, I think—I'm desperately upset about it." Still, Steinbeck carried on despite his self-doubt and a host of interruptions—among them, buying and selling a house—with his daily, disciplined work schedule.

What *does* it take to turn pages into books? What *does* it take to finish a book? I've witnessed writers complete their work, and I've witnessed others stumble along the way and stop working. I think it's important for us writers to understand that it takes a different set of skills to finish a book than it does to produce pages. Finishing a book demands that we think about a score of issues that we needn't concern ourselves about in the earliest stages of our work. It requires us to assess what we've already written to determine what's working and what's not; to revise and refine our work. It requires our willingness, in effect, to rethink what we've written as we decide how to shape our work, and to jettison what doesn't fit, and to write completely new material as required.

What do we want our work to say? What is the significance of the writing we've done? What should come first? What should come at the midpoint of our narrative? What should come last? What is our narrative's structure? How should parts of our narrative relate to one another? Have we delineated place and time sufficiently so that our readers understand where and when our narratives take place? Are the people we're writing about complex or do we have to go back through our work and deepen their portraits? Do the details of our work contribute to what we want our work to say? Have we gone through the work line by line, paragraph by paragraph, section by section? Does each sentence mean precisely what we want it to mean? Are there parts of the work that need to be discarded?

Years ago, I attended a lecture by the late historian Robin W. Winks, who spoke about his book *The Historian as Detective*. The writer, Winks said, must live with the knowledge that any book will be incomplete and imperfect. He suggested that we think of each work as an essay: an attempt to get at something and not as a definitive work.

"I work until I'm finished, not until the book's finished," Winks said. The book is never finished. And if we are to complete our books, we must learn to live with the fact that each effort will be an incomplete, imperfect attempt to codify our vision. To complete a book, we must accept that it won't be perfect. And our pages will never become books unless we take the necessary steps to complete them, imperfect as they are.

44

How Long Does It Take?

Once, a woman writer asked me, "How long does it take to write a book?" It was a disconcerting question because I couldn't answer it. It's as if we think knowing how long another writer took will tell us how long it will or should take us to finish our book. I suspected she was asking me if it was all right that she was taking a long time to finish the book she was currently writing.

I could have answered that nearly ten years passed between the publication of Jeffrey Eugenides's *Middlesex* and *The Marriage Plot*, during which he'd spent "most of every day writing." Or that Charles Johnson took six years to write *Middle Passage*: "I had a draft done after a year and it didn't work. So I went back and rewrote it for five years." Or that John Barth, author of *Lost in the Funhouse* (1968), takes "about one presidential term to write a book, about four years." Or that Elizabeth Gilbert wrote *The Signature of All Things* (2013), about a nineteenth-century woman botanist, in four months after spending "three and a half years on research alone." Or that Joan Didion composed *The Year of Magical Thinking*, her memoir about her husband's death, in three months, but had difficulty finishing because she "didn't want to let John go."

A big challenge writers face is not knowing how long a book will take, and becoming comfortable with not knowing. So much about writing is uncertain. And how long a book will take to write is just another uncertainty. Changing our attitude to time can be part of our growth process while we write a book. An inexperienced writer might decide to give up on a book that's taking a long time. But it's important for us to understand just how long it might take to complete an important work.

It took Norman Rush eight years to write his National Book Award–winning first novel, *Mating*, and ten years to write his second, *Mortals*. Rush promised his wife, Elsa, "his next novel would . . . take two years." But *Subtle Bodies* (2013), a novel about a gathering of male friends after twenty-five years, also took ten years.

As time passed, Rush "began feeling guilty" because writing the novel "was taking time out of our life when there were lots of fun things we could do if I just stopped writing." But "the never-giving-up part" is an important characteristic that has enabled Rush to complete books that take a long time.

In the midst of writing *Subtle Bodies*, Rush told Elsa, "I can't finish this book." She "got a yellow pad" and asked him to tell her where, in the narrative, he became confused. She took ten pages of notes as he answered, and told him his challenges weren't insuperable: when she asked him what needed doing, he had an answer. She thought he was tired, and suggested, "Look at it again in the morning."

Rush used the notes Elsa made, and he finished the novel.

It took Margaux Fragoso "eight years, on and off," to write her first book, the highly acclaimed memoir, *Tiger, Tiger*. Fragoso began the work after Peter Curran, a far older man with whom she'd had a sexual relationship—she met him when she was seven, lost her virginity to him at sixteen—killed himself. "I needed to examine things and figure things out," Fragoso said, "so I started writing." She composed the first draft "that summer after Peter died," while she also did a lot of reading—Arundhati Roy, Philip Roth, Dorothy Allison—to help her understand her experience. The draft wasn't "organized at all—just memories all strewn together with no particular focus." Then, in graduate school, she "started to work on carefully composing the story," but she also wrote material—about 170 pages—she eventually extracted. She often thought she should censor herself, then decided not to: "*this is the truth, . . . this is what pedophilia is.*" There were also "five or six rounds of edits in the pre-publication state."

Fragoso says it's important for beginning writers to understand how long it takes to complete a book so they don't abandon their work. She believes they might be encouraged to learn she is a working-class woman and "a high school dropout," who nonetheless resumed her education, earned a Ph.D., and composed her first book, while she was the young mother of a young child.

So much of life today occurs quickly. All this instant this and instant that makes it hard for us writers to understand that it might take a long time to write a book, and that we often can't predict how much time the work will take. It might make us expect to write our books more quickly than they can or should be written. It might make the people in our lives believe we should finish our work sooner than it's possible. It might make us feel like failures because we're taking such a long time. And it might cause us to abandon an important work, like Rush almost did.

Sometimes a book comes quickly. More often, a book takes a long time. The only way to finish is to keep working until a book is finished. Rushing through writing a book is rushing through life.

What I finally told that woman who asked me how long it takes to write a book was this: a book takes as long as it takes. And you'll enjoy writing it more if you focus on the process rather than the product. As Leonard Woolf said, "The journey not the arrival matters."

45

Over Time

As we write our books over time, and as we add new material bit by bit, our work can take on a depth and complexity that would be missing if we rushed through the process. A writer like Jeffrey Eugenides works *with* rather than *against* the fact that his books take long to write. Through the years, as he adds new material, he slowly develops the complexity of his novels.

Through the years Eugenides was composing *Middlesex*, his multigenerational saga about the life and past history of the intersexed Cal Stephanides, many "life-altering things happened"—his father died in a plane crash and his daughter was born. He wanted the novel to respond to those changes as he worked.

Initially, Eugenides wanted *Middlesex* to be "a fictional memoir of a hermaphrodite," which led him to inventing his character's Greek ancestry. But when his wife became pregnant, he became interested in "birth and fetal development"; he transformed that knowledge into discourses on Cal's genetic history. And when his father died, he became newly interested in family history; he transformed this preoccupation into a discussion of Cal's family in Greece and their emigration to the United States. When you're writing a book, Eugenides said, "everything you come across seems to fit into it."

While working on the early chapters of the novel, Eugenides read about "W. D. Fard, the founder of the Nation of Islam," reputedly a silk merchant, who established a temple in Detroit, the setting of *Middlesex*. Eugenides's—and Cal's—grandparents were "silk farmers," and Eugenides was writing the silk farming material in *Middlesex* when he stumbled upon Fard's story and decided to include him as a character.

"Fard seemed ordained to become part of *Middlesex*," Eugenides remarked—the serendipitous connection between Fard and silk farming and Detroit were too good to let go. While Eugenides works, he continually finds material he can incorporate into his novel, and, as he discovers how to include it, and how it relates to what's already there, his narrative becomes richer.

Although Eugenides has described how he achieves complexity during the long process of writing a novel, when we write shorter pieces we also can allow ourselves to incorporate material that comes our way during the time we're composing a work.

In "Old Flame," a short piece I wrote for *Ploughshares*, I began by digging out a chapter I'd deleted from *Crazy in the Kitchen* about the time I saw an old boyfriend's wife in a health food store when I was a grown woman. That led me to recalling the last time I'd seen him.

I tried to work with the wife material for several weeks and got nowhere. But then I suddenly felt compelled to write about attending a funeral, which I abandoned but which led me to write about my father's stay in a nursing home in the months before his death, very difficult material.

At this point, there was no piece, just tangled, unrelated threads of meaning. I knew that this piece would take several months, and that it would take time to figure out what it was about; and I let myself write whatever I chose for a while, trusting it would some-how come together.

I remembered that when I visited my father once, I brought an art book depicting the paintings of Michelangelo. My father lingered over Michelangelo's *Last Judgment*, and I wrote a scene describing how this painting depicting tortured sinners going to hell captivated this old man, near death. This led to my writing honestly about my difficult relationship with him, and how he'd harmed me when I was young, and how he again tried to harm me in the last weeks of his life.

Then one day, for relief, I went back to writing about the very last time I saw that old boyfriend—I was married; he was married; he was walking home past my parents' house, and I was out on my parents' lawn fighting with my kids. "What's he going to do in a piece about my father?" I wondered, but still didn't know.

And then I remembered driving to see his house one day after I'd had a particularly difficult time with my father—I'd never done it before—and I wrote about that.

Finally, I asked myself what the piece was about, and figured out (very late) why these narratives belonged together and what the narrative about that boyfriend had to do with the narrative of my father dying. I remembered how my involvement with this boy when I was a teenager helped me deal with my father's rages, and I wrote about that.

I had the title "Old Flame" from the beginning, and it helped me understand how the seemingly disparate components of the work could fit together. There were flames in Michelangelo's painting of the Last Judgment. My father was old. My boyfriend was an "old flame." And I could use that metaphor to bring the strands of meaning into alignment, to speculate on what that boyfriend had meant to me when I was enduring the worst of my father's brutality. Old flame/boyfriend; old/father; flame/hell—which my life with him often was, and how often I'd said to him, "Go to hell."

Kathryn Harrison, who edited that edition of *Ploughshares*, suggested I change the ending. The piece originally ended with my father's narrative. Harrison rightly believed ending with what that boy meant to me during the worst of my adolescence was better for the arc of the narrative—beginning with seeing him as a grown woman, ending with my being with him as a teenage girl.

Working bit by bit over time means that we're often not sure about where we're going, or what the work will look like when it's finished. I'm pleased with the way "Old Flame" turned out. But imagine if I'd been less receptive to the way the work evolved and said to myself, "Look, this has to be about your father or the boyfriend, not both." My job was trusting that the pieces I'd written fit together, and trusting that, in time, I'd understand how to construct the work.

My mentor, Mitchell A. Leaska, taught me that every completed work reverberates against its unwritten and unchosen alternatives. Imagine "Old Flame" without the boyfriend. Imagine *Middlesex* without W. D. Fard or genetics or silk farming. And in doing so, we can see how exciting it is for writers to allow layers of meaning into their works that they hadn't even imagined when they began. This is the benefit of being receptive, as Eugenides is, to whatever happens during the time that we do our work. "Slowly, as you write the book," Eugenides said, "you become aware of . . . correspondences, and then you make them cohere into a pattern" over time in the process of constructing the work.

46

Architecture and Design

When I talked about my first memoir, *Vertigo*, with my editor, Rosemary Ahern, she asked me, "What's the shape of the book? How many words do you plan to write?" Ahern had asked me to write about my Italian American working-class childhood in Hoboken, New Jersey, and the unlikely story of how I became a Virginia Woolf scholar. I'd written an essay about it. I had a list of subjects to cover, a seventy-page piece called "White on Black," and a statement of purpose. So now it was time to plan the book.

Before I started writing *Vertigo*, I picked a few memoirs off my shelf that were about the same length I intuitively wanted mine to be. I counted the words in sample pages, calculated these books were from ninety to a hundred thousand words, and decided my book would be roughly a hundred thousand words, long enough for my story.

After I determined the length of my book, I made a provisional outline. By the end of a few hours' work, I had a list of chapters and a tally of about how many words each chapter would contain. I recalled from my previous books how much detail is needed for a reader to understand a narrative, so I decided to jettison a few chapters so I could write more fully about fewer topics, taking that age-old advice that it's best to write more about less. When I thought about the narrative's structure, I decided I wanted the book to resemble a spiral—a dizzying structure that circled round and round the same material.

Stephen King has written that, although writing a book involves a certain amount of magic, we shouldn't forget that a book is also an object in the world. Hold a book in your hand, and you'll realize "words have weight" and that producing a book is as much a "matter of commitment" as it is about inspiration. King has compared the process of building a book to that of building a house. A writer builds a book "a paragraph at a time," and we can "build . . . whole mansions" if we "have the energy." Still it's important to ascertain the shape of our projects when we begin lest our work seem jerry-rigged. A work of art isn't so much written as it's constructed.

I like the comparison King makes between writing a book and building a house. Building a house requires a well-thought-out plan, although that plan can change. Although I know many writers who work without knowing much about the architecture of their books, I find that I work best when I've settled certain issues beforehand— the book's length, and its provisional structure, among them.

Years ago, when I was reading Virginia Woolf's handwritten draft of *To the Lighthouse*, I learned that, before she'd written a word, she'd thought out her design. "The plan of this book," she wrote, "is roughly that it shall consist of three parts: one, Mrs. Ramsay (?) sitting at the window: while Mr. R. walks up & down in the dusk. . . . 2) The passing of time. . . . 3) This is the voyage to the Lighthouse." Woolf also determined that the style she'd use would employ "an everyday sentence," "less emphatic & intense" than those in *Mrs. Dalloway*. Woolf wasn't yet sure about the style of the middle section, but she'd attempt "an interesting experiment . . . giving the sense of 10 years passing."

I'd written a few books without determining their structure. But that caused me tremendous anxiety, even panic. I never knew where I was in the process, how much I'd accomplished, how much more I had to write. In writing my Virginia Woolf biography, I had a provisional outline but hadn't determined my book's parameters or its structure. I discovered, to my horror, that I'd written more than three hundred pages about Woolf's sisters' childhoods before I'd even started writing about hers. Her sisters' lives *did* become a part of my narrative. But I had to stop and think about the design for the book, which I realized was about the effect of Virginia Woolf's childhood upon her work, and sweating down those three hundred pages to incorporate them into my book was agonizing and time-consuming.

Because I knew the structure of *Vertigo* beforehand, I could gauge my progress throughout the writing process. Instead of feeling lost while continuing to write an indeterminate number of words, I knew where I was. If I drafted five hundred words a day, I could write a draft in two hundred working days, or about ten months. And this plan could be flexible if I added two months to my deadline to account for illness and emergencies. This realistic plan would permit weekends off and time off during the week if necessary. And I could ascertain whether my work was meeting the criteria I'd established in terms of style and subject matter.

As I worked, I regularly calculated my progress. I always knew how much I'd written and how much more I needed to write to produce a first draft. I found it comforting to know I'd written, say, 40 percent of that draft. I'd also planned to revise that draft four or five more times so I knew I could work provisionally—I'd have future drafts to make hard choices and tidy things up.

I still decide how long a book will be, write an outline indicating how many words each chapter will contain, chart the progress of my work, determine roughly how long a draft will take, sketch my design, and determine my intentions for the project. Paradoxically, as rigid as this process seems, it permits me to write freely.

The book I'm now writing about my parents during World War II will be 80,000 to 90,000 words. I'm 37,197 words into my current draft (the penultimate, I think). I know that I'm about 41 percent finished with this draft, and that makes me happy. I know the book will be eleven or twelve chapters long; I know each chapter will be about 7,500 words. I've decided the book will begin with the last years of my father's life, then move chronologically from his enlistment in the navy through when he returns from the war.

I'm not saying that having a design, counting words, calculating how much we've done, is a cure-all. The writing process is still a mystery. But I need some idea of where I'm headed, as did Woolf. And knowing something about my book's design provides me with a profound sense of comfort. I might not know everything about a book. But this much, at least, I do know.

47

Turning Pages into Books

A former student of mine, who wanted to transform her MFA thesis—a memoir about her Indian forebears—into a book, discussed that process with an agent. During a conversation, the agent asked a number of questions my former student needed to think about to turn her pages into a book.

- What is the book? Is it memoir? Journalism? Creative nonfiction? Fiction?
- What's the voice? Personal? Authoritative? Whimsical? Irreverent? Solemn? Is there more than one voice? If there are several, how will they be handled?
- What's the structure? Is it chronological? Does it move sequentially through time? Does it begin at a high point and work by association? How many parts are there to the narrative? Does it have chapters? Or is it a book without chapters? What is the chapter breakdown? Can you synopsize the chapters?
- How long will the book be? Does the subject require a lengthy treatment (Anne Fadiman's *The Spirit Catches You and You Fall Down* [1997]—368 pages)? Or one that,

though complex, can be treated in a short book (Kathryn Harrison's *The Mother Knot*—96 pages)? Or does the work function as a collection of short pieces that are tied together by an underlying theme (Jo Ann Beard's *The Boys of My Youth*).

* What's the narrative arc? Where does it start? Where does it end? What happens to the characters in the story? What's changed? What's remained the same?

* How are the events linked by cause and effect? How and why do they unfold as they do? E. M. Forster makes the distinction between "The king died and then the queen died" and "The king died and then the queen died of grief" in *Aspects of the Novel*.

* What is the argument? What is the significance of the work?

* What are the themes/issues/questions in the work?

* What are the narrative threads and how are they linked to the theme?

* What are the central patterns of imagery? How are they related?

Often, when we work, we accumulate pages without thinking about what the meaning of our book will be. The preceding questions force us to think about how we might turn our pages into books: we can't amass pages and expect a book to miraculously appear.

Ian McEwan, author of *Enduring Love* (1998), among other novels, has described the method whereby he turns his pages into books. He often begins by writing "random scenes and sketches, whistling in the dark." When he works on these early pages, although he writes freely, not worrying about structure or chapters or order, McEwan nonetheless often has a general theme in mind. With *Enduring Love*, he "wanted to write in celebration of the rational," and he also wanted to illuminate his belief that "the ways people are similar is at least as interesting as the ways in which they vary."

After spending time writing whatever he chooses—"doodling," McEwan calls it—he begins to develop a first draft, paying careful attention to the language of each sentence, considering it a "basic unit of thought." McEwan has said, "I feel that if I don't get the sentences right in the first draft, it's going to be hard to get them right later."

Throughout composing his first draft, McEwan works slowly, and he works meticulously, pretending the "first draft is the last." This saves him difficulty when he's completing his work. He reads his work aloud, paragraph by paragraph. And then he thinks of "the chapter as an intact, independent entity with a distinct character of its own, a kind of short story"—the chapter is an "important building block" of his work and McEwan ascertains whether his chapters are meeting those criteria. Sometimes, though, when he's working on a scene, he'll work steadily "to get it down." These scenes will then "need a lot of slow revision."

What is our book about? Can we answer this question simply and directly, in no more than a sentence? If we can, fine. If we can't, then we might work aimlessly. We can revise our answer through time, of course.

When I've asked students to answer these questions, they often resist, saying they don't know the answers. I tell them they'll have to take time, at some point, to answer them and to determine the shape of their book. Students needing structure might want to think about this early; students working in a more exploratory manner might not be able to tackle this challenge until they're in the middle of the process, but surely before the final stages. Of course, as the work changes, these parameters might change. Writing down the answers to these questions, revising them until they're stated clearly, and refining them can help us understand what we're doing. They can serve as a study guide. If we take time to think about our books in progress, we won't be just writing, we'll be writing toward a well-defined outcome.

Although many writers begin working in an exploratory way, and learn about their works as they progress, at a certain point I think it's useful to step back, read our work, and make some decisions. This is difficult because we must begin to think about our work differently from when we're simply generating prose. We must begin to think about what a naive intelligent reader needs—what background must we provide for a reader to understand what's happening. We must think about the meaning of our work and its structure. We may begin the writing process, hoping our work has intrinsic value (and it always does to us), but unless we can articulate its meaning and significance clearly to someone else, our writing might be solipsistic and not meant for a general readership.

Unless we shift our attention to thinking about what we want a reader to take away from the time spent reading our work, we won't be able to clarify the obscurities within it nor will we be able to understand its importance and significance. This often happens with time. In answering these questions we can begin sculpting our pages into a work of art for an eager reader.

I've found that beginning writers who stop and think about what their narratives mean are more easily able to complete their books. This work takes time and thought. But when we've produced a hefty sheaf of pages, we can sometimes become frustrated when we realize that turning those pages into books will take us a long a time—as long, or even longer—as it took us to generate the pages themselves. But it's necessary work. And it's exciting.

48

Structuring Our Work

I routinely study the structure of the books I read. I look at the beginning, just before the midpoint, the midpoint, just before the end, and the end. I study foreshadowing, repetitions, character development, image patterns, depictions of place and time, flashbacks and flash-forwards. This practice has served me well when I compose my own books and when I discuss the possible structure of a work with a writer. Structuring our work is one of the hardest parts of completing a project. Anyone can write pages, but it takes a special skill—a learned skill—to turn pages into books.

When I'm writing a book, I work until I accumulate much of the raw material that will become the book. Then I reassess my work and make some decisions. They're not irrevocable, but they give me an anchor.

I think anew about the beginning, the place just before the middle, the middle, the place just before the end, and the end. I think about what I want to happen at these points in the narrative. This forces me to think about structure, about how a reader will experience what I've written.

Alice Adams, author of the collection *To See You Again* (1982), indicated she needed to know what she was doing when writing a short story, so she often used a formula—an ABDCE formula (action, background, development, climax, ending). It's one way of structuring a narrative and an excellent structure for a beginning writer to learn. Begin with an "action that is compelling." Discuss "who these people are . . . and what was going on before the opening of the story." Then develop their characters, describing what they desire (drama, action, and tension "grow out of that"). "[E]verything comes together in the climax, after which things are different . . . in some real way." The ending lets us know "who these people are now, what they are left with, what happened," and what the narrative meant.

When Adam Braver, author of the novel *November 22, 1963* (2008) about Kennedy's assassination, realized that a chunk of his work, "The Casket," wasn't working, he realized the linearity of his work was the problem. He wanted to transmit *the experience* of a character witnessing "the calamity and confusion taking place within the emergency room" after Kennedy had been shot.

He realized to accomplish his goal, he had to break the chronology. He took his draft, cut the pages into scenes, and reorganized them, searching for "that 'something else' that inherently connected them." After reassembling the work, he faced "narrative challenges" requiring research, revision, or rewriting. The work was "slow and meticulous." But the result was an exciting—rather than a predictable—reinterpretation of the events. The right order of a work, according to Braver, "doesn't always equate to linear narrative."

In most narratives, the beginning of the story isn't the beginning of the narrative. The beginning is that moment telling the reader everything needed to introduce the world of the narrative. A writer's obligation is to make the reader fall in love with the subject, character, setting, or writing. The first words of a narrative are a seduction. When a writer understands this, the beginning becomes more obvious. And, no, a reader can't wait for the good stuff. Study the first pages of the books you love. They'll teach you what you need to know about how to begin a book. An excellent example is Cheryl Strayed's prologue in *Wild* (2012), where the narrator, hiking alone, watches one of her boots drop into the forest below.

I've rarely composed the beginning of a work at the beginning of the process, though sometimes it happens, as when I wrote "Old Flame" for *Ploughshares* about an old boyfriend. I heard a line in my head—"I saw him once in all these years, walking up the steep hill from the bus stop, past my parents' house . . ." that I knew would be the first line. More often, though, that beginning is buried somewhere in my jumble of pages.

When I start turning my pages into books, I try to find something a little unexpected for the beginning. How does a reader become engaged in a narrative? For me, it's when I find myself in the midst of something fascinating, something unexpected, something that leaves me questioning, but something that leaves me satisfied, too. So that's what I aim for at the beginning of my books. For the first words of my biography of Virginia Woolf, I chose these words, originally buried in a chapter: "Virginia Woolf was a sexually abused child; she was an incest survivor." They immediately told the reader what the book was about.

My writing partner, Edvige Giunta, is writing a memoir about her childhood in Gela, Sicily. During today's conversation, we discussed how she could take her pages and structure them so they become a book. Edvige has decided she wants the book to have three parts. I suggested she decide what chunks would come first, second, and third. She already knew what would come close to the middle—a key scene where her grandmother tells her a story. I suggested she calculate how many words she'd already written for each section so she'd know how many more words she needed to write.

I suggested she take all the chunks of her book and organize them on her dining room table—everything for the first third of the book on one side; everything for the "turn" of the book in the middle; everything for the conclusion on the right. She wouldn't necessarily be arranging them chronologically but in circles of meaning: the history of Gela and how she learned of her family's past, her childhood and friendships, her emigration.

She couldn't do that yet, though, because her book existed only as a single long document in her computer. She had to break it into chunks, make each a separate document, and give each chunk a "tag name" so she could refer to it and locate it. (I've learned that working in one very long document, as Edvige had been doing, makes turning pages into books difficult, if not impossible.) She had to print everything out so she could see what she had, sort everything, and determine what she needed to write. She'd then be closer to ascertaining the structure of her book. And she wouldn't be working in the dark.

49

The Second Sleeve

Right now, I'm knitting a complicated Fair Isle sweater called thistle coat. I've finished the back, the fronts, and the first sleeve. I've been knitting this sweater for months. But I'm still knitting that blasted second sleeve. The shaping is complicated, and I've had to rip it out a few times. I've come close to abandoning it, but haven't. To finish it will take persistence and some skill. One of my knitting teachers told me she wished she had a dollar for all the unfinished sweaters languishing in closets missing only that second sleeve. She thinks it's because by the time knitters are working on the second sleeve they're bored and want the excitement that comes from beginning a new project; the second sleeve is nothing but a slog. Yes, it's hard to finish what we start—a sweater, a book—especially if we run into challenges near the end.

There isn't a clear analogy between finishing a sweater and finishing a book, of course. But I know many writers who've abandoned projects close to the end because they've become frustrated trying to figure out how to fix something that isn't working. And, yes, sometimes abandoning a work to start something else is wise. Still, when I have a snag in my own projects near the end, I always call Edvige Giunta, and tell her I'm thinking of abandoning the project. Edvige knows I need to think that I *can* stop work on something that's giving me trouble. And she knows that once I entertain the possibility of casting a project aside, I'll somehow figure out what I need to do next. When we get to the stage when we want to abandon our books, it might be because we've worked so hard to get where we are that we can't imagine tearing the book apart to fix something we know doesn't work and we just want to walk away. Maybe we realize we need a new ending or a new beginning. Or that we need to completely overhaul the work. Or that the structure is wrong. Or the voice. Or the point of view. Or that something central isn't working—when Donna Tartt was writing *The Secret History* (1992), she realized: "I was torturing myself unnecessarily" with a "tricky time sequence"; when she decided to tell it "very simply from beginning to end," everything in the novel "fell smoothly into place," and the solution was "just cut and paste."

Do we decide to stick it out and do the grunt work that it takes to complete the book like Tartt? Or do we throw it in a drawer, sick of it or confounded by what needs doing, eager to get on to another piece of writing? But writers who haven't completed their projects tell me the unfinished work feels like a thorn in their sides: they often think about it and it makes them feel bad.

Writers have asked me how to get through this stage. Knowing this is normal helps. Knowing that I'll get to start something new after I finish helps. It also helps to realize that if I abandon what I'm working on and start something new, I'll just get to that stage again, and then I'll have not one piece but two to untangle. When I arrive at this stage, which I've come to call "the second sleeve stage," it helps me to know that many important writers have been there, too. I've learned strategies from them. But, I've learned that most important writers face this moment and that they get to the other side and finish their books.

When Zadie Smith was composing *NW*, set in the northwest London of her youth, "describing the simultaneously tangled and divergent lives of four people in their 30s who were all born on the same housing estate," she came to a seeming impasse in writing the last section of the novel. After she gave the work to readers, "nobody liked it." Smith knew it wasn't good, but she had been working on the novel for so long that she "had a very childish, throwing-the-toys-out-of-the-pram reaction," and she contemplated abandoning the novel.

But her husband, the poet Nick Laird, said, "'Don't do that.'" Laird made her go back and rework the third part of the novel. "'We've all had to put up with you for seven years,'" Laird said. "'Something has to come out of this.'" So Smith went back to work: "The last section I rewrote entirely," she said.

When she was still writing, Alice Munro often got to the point in the composition of a story when she realized she didn't "want to work on it anymore." She would have an adverse visceral reaction to it, "a terrible reluctance to go near it," a sense that she'd have to force herself to continue.

Munro learned that a moment like that told her "something is badly wrong" with the work, and she contemplated abandoning it. And this happened with "about three quarters" of the stories Munro wrote.

At this point, Munro usually experienced "a day or two of bad depression." She let herself seriously contemplate stopping work on that troublesome story and she began to "think of something else" she could write. Munro likened this time in her work to a stage where there are problems in "a love affair: you're getting out of all the disappointment and misery [of the relationship] by going out with some new man you don't really like at all, but you haven't noticed that yet." Somehow you realize that if you go out with that other man, you'll face the same challenges, or worse ones, with him than you're experiencing with the first man, so you might as well try to figure out how to stay with him.

By emotionally distancing herself from that troublesome work and flirting with the possibility of writing another work, Munro "suddenly come[s] up with something about the story that I abandoned; I will see how to do it. But that only seems to happen after I've said, No this isn't going to work, forget it."

But the time preceding when Munro happened upon her artistic solutions was difficult. She would be "on edge and enraged"; she'd try to figure out the answer, but would just keep "running into brick walls." And this process—thinking of abandoning the work, trying to figure out how to fix it, thinking about beginning a new work—would last for some time. Then, and "quite unexpectedly," when Munro was away from her desk "in the grocery store or out for a drive" she'd know what she had to do. Perhaps she'd have to change the point of view. Perhaps she'd have to eliminate a character. Perhaps she'd have to shift the relationships of the characters in the work. "The big change, which is usually the radical change," one which might not necessarily have improved the story, Munro admitted, but one, she said, which made "it possible for me to continue to write."

50

Tied Up in Knots

While composing her acclaimed novel *Swamplandia!* (2011), Karen Russell became "convinced it was doomed." After her short story collection, *St. Lucy's Home for Girls Raised by Wolves* (2006), received so much acclaim, Russell had high expectations for herself in writing her first novel, which she had to abandon: "The goal," she said, "was no longer to write the Great American Novel. It became . . . just write a novel." Russell learned that though you feel despair, "you don't really have to respond to it. You can feel like the thing you're working on is doomed and then just keep working." She realized that it "takes time" to figure out the solution to complex writing challenges; she wished that someone would tell her what to do, but she had to figure it out herself.

Despite her doubts, Russell continued working through more drafts than she cared to admit. The resulting *Swamplandia!* was named a *New York Times* Best Book of the Year in 2011.

Have you ever gotten yourself tied up in knots as a writer? Has your work ever appeared so tangled you fear you'll never be able to unravel it? It happens to most writers. It's happened to me many times. And I believe it happens because we're ambitious, which is a good thing. We reach for the stars, we stretch our limits, we try a new design. But to complete a tangled work, we have to assess what we have, determine what's working and what's not. We might need to scale back our ambition, as Russell did. We might have to opt for a simpler design, while still reintroducing some radical elements that might well become the hallmark of our aesthetic. Or the solution might be more complicated.

When Virginia Woolf was writing *The Pargiters*, her early draft of *The Years*, she tried alternating prose interchapters about women's issues in Victorian and Edwardian England—"telling"—with fictional chapters—"showing." In writing *The Pargiters*, Woolf wanted to conjoin her talent for nonfiction and fiction into an artistic whole.

Woolf didn't find a successful formula and repeat it. *Jacob's Room, Mrs. Dalloway, To the Lighthouse*, and *The Waves*—each presented a different challenge that Woolf successfully surmounted. But Woolf determined she couldn't pull off the ambitious design of *The Pargiters*.

So, what did she do? She became despondent, but she kept working and didn't abandon the book. Though she believed the novel was a failure, she devised a solution. She extracted the fictional chapters and turned them into *The Years*. And she took her polemical essays and used them to write *Three Guineas*, her diatribe against the mistreatment of women, imperialism, and war. Woolf emerged from her tangle writing *The Pargiters* with not one but two books. Not bad, considering Woolf believed the work to be unsalvageable. And she learned from that experience. For her next novel, *Between the Acts*, Woolf opted for a simpler design with a bravura pageant enfolded into its narrative arc.

Could Woolf have pulled off her plan for *The Pargiters*? Maybe. But probably not. But coming out of this challenge with two books to her credit was an ingenious solution to a difficult problem. Still, rather than praising herself for her steadfastness, Woolf criticized herself and called *The Years* a failure.

I believe it's important to complete works. But it's also important to admit something isn't working and do something about it—bail out of it or reconfigure the design so it does work. Woolf knew that *The Pargiters* wasn't working. She found an ingenious artistic solution. Still she chastised herself for her inability to complete her book as planned. I believe, instead, that nothing along the way to a satisfactory completion is a failure. Even works put aside deliberately aren't failures. Paradoxically, they can teach us more about writing than easily written, successful attempts. They can teach us that there are limits to our ability, that sometimes we have to admit defeat, that our willingness to redirect our efforts indicates the kind of flexibility we need to develop as writers.

In my own tied-up-in-knots book, *On Moving*, I tried to combine a narrative about moving with one about my parents' lives during World War II. After several years, I realized I was in over my head. When I determined my book wasn't working, I called Christina Baker Kline, author of the bestselling *Orphan Train* (2013). She's a brilliant novelist, and a fantastic editor. "Help me figure this out," I said, when I gave her the work to read. The manuscript was as polished as I could make it, even though I knew it wasn't working and that it wasn't finished.

Kline read the work and said, "You have two books here," which I suspected. And she told me specifically what she thought I should do. Extract all the material about moving into one book and write more about famous writers' moves and their thoughts about relocating. Extract the material about my parents and save that for the other book. Write the moving book first. I took her advice and finished *On Moving* in two years; I'm working on the book about my parents now.

So what *should* we do if our work is tied up in knots? I wouldn't suggest stopping work immediately because, as Russell's experience indicates, we might be able to pull off a complex design if we keep working. But I *would* say that when we repeatedly dread going to the desk; when we feel as if we're drowning in the complexity of our own design; when we're feeling hopelessly confused beyond the normal confusion that attends the writing process; and, most important, when our writing is making us ill (as writing *The Pargiters* made Woolf ill), we might consider stopping to rethink what we should do.

And we can ask for help, as I did. We can ask a writer we respect for specific suggestions about the work. We can listen, really listen, to what we're told and reconsider our plan. We might decide to carry on. We might decide that we have two or even three books that need to be untangled. We might decide to abandon the work. But we must remember that writers who take risks, who want to grow as writers, will almost inevitably get tied up in knots. That won't happen if we continually repeat a tried-and-true formula. But to do so will mean artistic stagnation, not growth.

51

Writing Partners

Writing doesn't have to be—perhaps shouldn't be—solitary. For years, Edvige Giunta has been my writing partner. When I don't talk about my work with her, I second-guess myself; I'm afraid I'll never finish; I can't figure out what to do; I doubt the worth of my work. Having a writing partner is a blessing because I can ask for help when I need it.

These days Edvige is revising a second draft of a memoir about her youth in Gela, Sicily; I'm working on that book about my parents during World War II. We don't share pages because Edvige and I work provisionally during our respective projects' early stages. We usually don't share work until ready for publication. We want to shape our work without criticism until we consider it ready; we don't want to confuse our evolving vision.

We don't want someone to critique our work; we want a collaborator in the creative process, someone to hold us accountable. As Edvige phrased it, we want an interlocutor—someone who asks us questions about our work, our process, our challenges, and who suggests solutions when asked. When we have regular telephone conversations discussing our work, we each proceed more confidently.

Edvige tells me what she's accomplished during the past week, then describes her current writing challenges. She recently reported she'd completed a second pass of the first chapter of her memoir, and she'd previewed a heavily edited first pass of her second chapter. She'd found a chunk of writing describing Gela's geographical/historical background, essential for readers. Should this become an interchapter? Or should the material be incorporated into the first and second chapters? As we talk, we take notes so we have a record of our discussion to consult the following week.

"Enter the handwritten edits into the computer document of the second chapter," I suggested. "It'll be too hard to incorporate the historical/geographical material unless you have a clean copy. I think you need to hang out with the uncertainty of what to do with that material; you'll eventually know what to do."

Edvige and I always commit to realistic work schedules and writing plans for the coming week. Edvige said she had four hours to work on her memoir—she was teaching, editing, and had household responsibilities. She decided to start entering the handwritten changes, though she didn't know how long it would take. She agreed to postpone deciding what to do with the geographical/historical material. Meanwhile, she'd reread it.

I reported that as I was revising a section of the prologue, where my father laboriously climbs the stairs to my house near the end of his life, I stumbled into using a new voice and added flashbacks describing my early relationship with him. I'd struggled with incorporating my point of view into this book about him and hoped I might have found a way to do it. But I wanted Edvige's opinion about the work's new direction. I was excited, but also skittish, and worried this meant revising everything else I'd written to incorporate this more complex point of view.

Edvige knows I make radical changes near the end of my process. She suggested I move slowly through the prologue again, taking as long as I needed to refine this new point of view. "This just happened," she said. "But you usually shift the work dramatically in your final drafts. Don't rush the process. You knew something was missing, that you weren't yet in the narrative, so it seems like you've learned what you need to do." With Edvige's help, I decided I'd revise the prologue again, and then revise it once more before deciding how to incorporate this new point of view into subsequent chapters.

Edvige asked me about my schedule for the coming week. I told her I wanted to work two hours each day. She suggested I not try to complete the revision by the end of the week but instead simply commit to my two-hour schedule. She reminded me it was essential that I not feel pressured.

Talking specifically in this way about a work in progress proves invaluable to us both. I'm revitalized by our meetings; I know the direction my work will take; I've generated some possible solutions to my current challenges; I know my plan for the coming week is doable. Each week, Edvige and I recommit to the slow and steady process of our work.

When Jonathan Franzen couldn't find an agent for his first novel, *The Twenty-Seventh City* (1988), a satire set in St. Louis, Missouri, in 1984, he contacted Hugh Nissenson, author of *In the Reign of Peace* (1972) and the only writer Franzen knew, and asked for advice. Nissenson asked how long the book was and when Franzen told him, Nissenson responded "I can tell you right now it's two times too long. You've got to go back and cut it by half." Nissenson also said, "There's gotta be a lot of sex in it."

Franzen considered Nissenson's advice "a wonderful gift." He realized he could cut "two hundred pages." More important, he understood the "connection between my needs as a reader and what I was doing as a writer, which I had never made before." That discussion taught Franzen that if he wanted readers, the novel "needed to move" and he "had to make the cuts to make it move."

Before Franzen wrote *The Corrections*, he and David Means, author of *A Quick Kiss of Redemption and Other Stories* (1991), had telephone conversations about how they could connect with a larger audience. They wanted to move "beyond pure intellectual play into realms of . . . emotional significance." They finally agreed that fiction was an "effective way for strangers to connect across time and distance." After these conversations, Franzen decided to "write books that ordinary people . . . could connect with." *The Corrections* was an outgrowth of his conversations with Means.

Having a writing partner can help our work immeasurably. Knowing we needn't necessarily work alone if we choose not to can ease the difficulty of the process and can help us gain insight into what we need to do to our works in progress. Even if we choose to work in solitude, it still helps to have supportive writer friends who understand what we're going through.

52

Revision

When I first started teaching writing, I had a student who told me he didn't believe in revision. "First idea, best idea," he said, misquoting Jack Kerouac. He was a Kerouac fan, and whenever I suggested revisions, he'd quote passages from Kerouac's "Essentials of Spontaneous Prose" (1957). I finally suggested he do some research to see whether his hero, in fact, revised. When I was working on Virginia Woolf's manuscripts in the Berg Collection at the New York Public Library, I met a railroad conductor, a fan of Kerouac's, who was studying Kerouac's manuscripts. He told me Kerouac *did* rewrite and *did* revise and that his editor also worked on the manuscript of *On the Road* (1957) before publication.

Even so, my student wouldn't budge from his intractable stance even though his work, admittedly, continued to be unsatisfactory. I suggested he could try revising—it was an important skill for a writer to learn—and if he didn't like the result, he could always revert to the original. I told him that many writers I knew revised many times, and it was only through this process that they learned what their books were about.

My student thought that if he continued writing, he'd one day be skilled enough so that his first—and only draft—would be wonderful. "It'll never happen," I thought, but didn't say but likely should have, because I didn't know a single writer who didn't except, perhaps, certain Zen practitioners writing haiku.

Darin Strauss—author of *Chang and Eng* (2000), a novel about conjoined twins, and the memoir *Half a Life* (2010), about his experience of inadvertently killing a girl with his car when he was a teenager, among other works—in discussing whether writing can be taught, echoed Jonathan Lethem's belief that "talent was kind of meaningless." It's the writers, Strauss says, who "keep trying, keep trying," who allow themselves "to be bad" at the beginning of the process, who trust that after much hard work and countless revisions, they'll complete a work, who have the best chance of becoming writers.

Strauss observed that, of the writers he knew as a graduate student, "it wasn't the most talented people who moved on—it was the people who could take their first draft and make it a second draft." Almost every writer at a certain level can write a decent first draft. But it takes grit and determination to climb back into a work and revise and revise again and again. It takes humility, too—a willingness to say, "This isn't good enough yet; it needs more work." And a dedication to the process of doing the work, coupled with a belief that, in time, we'll likely produce a completed work.

When Paul Auster was writing his memoir *The Invention of Solitude*, his first prose work—he'd written and published poetry before—he became confused about the form the book should take. He'd written the first part of his narrative, "Portrait of an Invisible Man," in first person, about his father's lonely life, about his grandmother murdering his grandfather—a history Auster learned by chance when he was a grown man—and the effect of that act upon his father and upon him.

He'd begun the second part, "The Book of Memory," about

how he composed the work, about chance, about his years in Paris, about his reading, in the first person, too. "But there was something I didn't like about it," Auster said, although he couldn't figure out why he was dissatisfied. Still, he continued writing, until he felt he "had to stop."

Before returning to the work, before revising the second section, Auster put the book away, and "meditated for several weeks" about the challenge he was facing. He realized that "the problem was the first person" narrator he was using. In the first section, about his father, using the first person worked because Auster was "seeing him" from his point of view. But using first person for his own narrative, Auster discovered, meant "I couldn't see myself anymore." He realized that he needed to revise the work by shifting the second part to third person. Then, he could "get a certain distance from myself," which made it possible for him to see himself, which "made it possible" for him to complete the book.

Auster says that in writing his books, he is "[s]lowly blundering my way toward consciousness": he "find[s] the book in the process of doing it." He speaks of using notebooks as "a house for words, as a secret place for thought and self-examination." But when asked by an interviewer whether he works from a plan or from previous materials, he answered that he begins a novel with what he describes as "a buzz in the head." He starts, he says, "with the first sentence and then I push on until I've reached the last," working one paragraph at a time. For Auster, the paragraph is his "natural unit of composition." And he keeps working on a single paragraph, "writing and rewriting" it by hand until he's "reasonably satisfied," until he's determined "it has the right shape, the right balance, the right music." The process of completing work on a single paragraph can take Auster "a day . . . or half a day, or an hour, or three days." Once it's finished, Auster types it—"each book has a running manuscript and a typescript beside it"—and then later, he'll revise the typed page yet again.

Although he has a "sense of the trajectory of the story" from the beginning, and perhaps the first and perhaps the last sentence also, "everything keeps changing as I go along," Auster says. Each book is a surprise; none "ever turned out as I thought it would. Characters and episodes disappear; other characters and episodes develop" as Auster works.

Auster often makes "radical shifts" in his novels as he composes them. If he knew everything in advance, he says, the process "wouldn't be very interesting." Finding out what the book is about through writing and revising it, Auster has said, is "the adventure of the job."

When he was writing *The Book of Illusions*, his tenth novel, about how his protagonist, David Zimmer, dealt with his wife's and son's deaths by searching for an elusive silent-film comedian, Auster kept changing his "ideas about the story right up to the last pages." When he was writing *Mr. Vertigo*, his novel set in the late 1920s, about a rescued orphan who becomes a member of a traveling circus troupe, he initially conceived it as a "short story of thirty or forty pages." But the work "took off and seemed to acquire a life of its own," developing into a nearly three-hundred-page-long picaresque novel.

The act of revision allows writers to discover the hidden potential in their own work and to arrive at undreamed of levels of meaning. For Auster and for many other writers, revision doesn't simply refine the language on the page. It's the heart and soul of the process. And, as Auster indicates, by far the most exciting phase of composing a work.

53

The Toughest Choice

During a day's work, a writer makes hundreds, even thousands of choices. Keep this, change that, move this paragraph here, toughen up the language there, split this paragraph in two, rewrite this, chuck that. Many writers do this automatically without realizing that every choice affects the meaning of a work. Nor should we be self-conscious or it will inhibit us.

By the time we declare our work finished—or declare ourselves finished with the work—we've made a choice about every element— the characters and their presentation, the setting, the dialogue, the structure. We've considered every word and mark of punctuation. Sometimes these choices are difficult; sometimes they are nearly paralyzing. If I tell myself that making choices will become easier as my work progresses, it helps. And many of my students have noticed that when they're nearing completion, they're sure (or surer) of the choices they make.

But whatever choices we've made aren't the only ones we could have made. And this can make the end of the process difficult as we assess the effect of our choices and decide whether we need to make major changes in our work.

After Mary Karr finished a draft of *Cherry* (2000), her memoir about her adolescence in Texas, she realized she was "superimposing a forty-year-old woman's libido on a twelve-year-old girl." As it stood, Karr judged that the way she treated her sexual awakening was perverse and she realized she needed to radically change the voice of the work because she'd "misrepresented the experience" of adolescent sexuality. Karr rewrote the memoir, now focusing on what that young girl's desire *felt* like, using "lyrical language." Rewriting *Cherry* was a tough—but necessary—choice.

The final and perhaps the toughest choice a writer must make is whether to declare the work finished, or whether to revise it one—or several more—times.

Virginia Woolf worked for years on a novel she called *Melymbrosia*, about the sexual initiation of Rachel Vinrace, a young woman, who travels to South America with her aunt. She could have published it: it's a fine first effort. But she made the difficult choice to completely revise it into the version she published as *The Voyage Out*.

Melymbrosia is more overt about same sex love and more critical of imperialist politics than *The Voyage Out*. Perhaps Woolf lost her nerve and feared criticism; perhaps she justifiably feared censorship; perhaps her aesthetic had changed—the sexuality in the published version is more ambiguous than in the earlier text. *The Voyage Out* and *Melymbrosia* treat the same subject, have the same narrative arc, and deal with the same events—a central moment is Rachel's being kissed by a married man and its profound negative effect on her, perhaps because she was sexually abused by her father, which is far more obvious in *Melymbrosia*. The books are different; one is no better than the other. But Woolf made the tough choice not to publish the novel but to revise it yet again.

James Joyce's *Stephen Hero* is another earlier version of a novel that could have been published. But instead of declaring his work complete, Joyce revised that manuscript into *A Portrait of the Artist as a Young Man* (1916).

Stephen Hero is far more approachable for the general reader. In the earlier version, Stephen's mother, sister, and brother play a more prominent role, and his father, a lesser one. In *Portrait*, Joyce emphasizes the father-son relationship to strengthen the Daedalus theme in the work. And there is also a "more dramatically immediate rendition" of a love affair that is "merely hinted at" in *Portrait*. Stephen is a far different character earlier, too—he's more social, more gregarious, more a man of the people in *Stephen Hero*.

When Joyce transformed *Stephen Hero* into *Portrait*, he used Stephen to illuminate his view of "the role of the dedicated artist in our society as pre-eminently heroic." *Portrait* shows the evolution of the boy into the artist, and the sacrifices he must make along the way, among them discarding religion, to realize his destiny. This necessitated stripping away the social aspects of Stephen's nature.

The Nobel laureate William Faulkner remarked that the writer's "obligation is to get the work done the best he can do it." Yet he believed a writer should "never be satisfied" with a completed work because "[i]t never is as good as it can be done." Still, it's essential to complete a work because an incomplete work, Faulkner learned, can haunt a writer.

When Faulkner was asked how he knew when he'd arrived at the standard he'd set for himself, he replied that "objectivity in judging his work" is essential for a writer, "plus honesty and courage not to kid himself." Faulkner admitted that no work met his standards. Still, he published them, but not until he was satisfied that he couldn't improve the work.

The novel that caused Faulkner the most difficulty was *The Sound and the Fury* (1929), which he wrote "five separate times." He wanted to relate the "tragedy of two lost women: Caddy and her daughter [Dilsey]." Faulkner believed that unless he got the story right, it would "continue to anguish" him until he did.

The inspiration for the novel was an image Faulkner had "of the muddy seat of a little girl's drawers in a pear tree, where she could see through a window where her grandmother's funeral was taking place and report what was happening to her brothers on the ground below." He first wanted to write it as a short story but realized that the necessary backstory of "who they were and what they were doing and how her pants got muddy" meant he'd have to write a novel. Another image came to him, that of a "fatherless and motherless girl climbing down the drainpipe to escape from the only home she had."

Faulkner first tried telling the story from the point of view of one of the brothers, "the idiot child," because that narrator would know what happened, although he wouldn't know why. Then he tried to tell the story through the eyes of "another brother." And then, again, through the eyes of "the third brother," but when he finished, he realized the novel still wasn't working.

He rewrote it a fourth time, by making himself "the spokesman." And still, the novel wasn't working to Faulkner's satisfaction. Still, he reworked it and published it, and fifteen years later, because the story wouldn't leave him, he wrote an appendix included in *The Portable Faulkner* (1946) in a "final effort to get the story told and off my mind, so that I myself could have some peace from it."

Though *The Sound and the Fury* caused Faulkner the greatest agony, and though he "couldn't leave it alone," he still felt "tenderest toward" it, even though he "never could tell it right," though he'd "tried hard." Even so, though the challenges he faced were often difficult, Faulkner accepted them as necessary because he knew he had "complete liberty to use whatever talent I might have to its absolute top."

54

Self-Censorship

I once visited the Metropolitan Museum of Art in New York to see drawings by Agnolo Bronzino, court painter to the Duke Cosimo I de' Medici and compared Bronzino's drawings—drafts of his work—with his paintings.

Bronzino's drawing *Madonna and Child with Saint Elizabeth and Saint John* (1540) was used to prepare for the oil painting by the same name (1541–1543). In the drawing, Saint Elizabeth appears as an old embittered crone and the Madonna seems sad and preoccupied—these women react to this child's brutal future. But in the painting, Saint Elizabeth is portrayed as a congenial old woman and the Madonna's face bears a half smile. The drawing is more powerful; the painting, more decorative. Bronzino has revised his earlier, complex vision of grief into saccharine sweetness.

Bronzino's drawing *Dead Christ* (1538–1539) differs, too, from the *Pieta with Magdalen* (1538–1539). The drawing presents Christ realistically; he's strong, even in death. He appears unwounded, so he's not presented as a victim; he's filled, instead, with resilience and purpose. The painting, though, depicts a pitiful, dejected Jesus. Bronzino has revised his powerful idiosyncratic portrayal of Christ into a stereotype.

Bronzino prepared for his painting of St. Mark (1525–1528) with a drawing depicting a grotesque, sneering St. Mark with glazed eyes, disheveled hair, and clenched fist. The painting, though, has revised the drawing into a sweeter, gentler depiction of what had been fury incarnate.

Bronzino, employed by the rich and famous, blunted his idiosyncratic vision in continual acts of self-censorship. And who could blame him? Still, Bronzino never transformed his early vision into robust oil paintings. The drawings remain as testimony to what his paintings might have depicted had he not needed to please his patrons.

As we revise our work, do we expunge our quirkiness; sweeten our tough-mindedness; transform authentic, complex portraits into sugarcoated misrepresentations; delete the defiance and power in our work? If we read our early drafts or process journals against our latest revision, we can determine whether we're censoring ourselves.

I once taught a student whose writing didn't feel real, so I asked to see her earlier drafts. In them, she'd developed lucid, complex portraits of people she'd later rendered as vapid nonentities.

"What happened?" I asked.

"I don't want to upset them," she replied.

I told her only she could decide what to do. But she had to consider the consequences of artistic self-sabotage and of waiting until the people in her narrative died before writing honestly about them. Still, even as accomplished a writer as Joan Didion admitted she couldn't have written *Where I Was From* (2003), her book about California's underbelly, while her parents were alive.

The Pulitzer Prize–winning novelist Carol Shields noted that *every student* she taught worried about "the injury they might cause" to family members. She advised them "to set those fears aside and to write without being throttled by them" because "you can always go back and change details later." Shields was struck by how reluctant her students were to reveal the "darker self," the source of our authentic work.

I once had a student who showed every version of her work to her parents. She wanted to describe her father's abandonment and her mother's subsequent depression. But she circled around this material. I couldn't see these people, couldn't understand what had happened.

"Try not showing your parents your work," I suggested. But she never did, and never completed her memoir.

I wrote a no-holds-barred portrait of my father in *Vertigo* while he was alive. Contrary to what I expected, I found it easy to write about him. I ignored the possibility that he might read the book until I'd finished the manuscript. When the memoir appeared, my father found out about its publication, and my husband and I decided to meet with him and his second wife to discuss the book.

"What did you write about?" my father asked.

"Everything," I responded.

"Everything?" he asked.

Whereupon his second wife said, "You know, you were very scary, and she was just a little girl."

I suggested they not read the book. He didn't; she did. But my stepmother found my father's portrait to be fair and well balanced. And my father became something of a local hero when his friends found out about it.

"How could you write about him when he was still alive?" I was asked. "He did what he did," I replied, "and that gave me the right to describe it." Like many writers—Jeffrey Eugenides, author of *The Marriage Plot*, is one—I never let anyone read my work until it's finished so I don't risk changing a work because of an early reader's response. Eugenides has remarked that if he "can still make the book better" on his own, he's "not eager to show it to anyone." Early criticism, though well intended, might cause us to blunt what's most courageous about our work. Unlike Bronzino who censored himself with time, as I write my later drafts, I seem to find the courage to write those tough moments I wasn't ready to describe earlier.

Before attending the Bronzino exhibit at the Met, I'd glanced at the prologue to the book about my father. There's a phantasmagoric scene where I imagine taking my father's body back to the island where he served during World War II and giving him a hero's burial like those given to the indigenous peoples on that island. In the ceremony, which I'd researched, the bones of the dead are wrapped in cloth and worn by the bereaved. I'd written an imaginary scene, called "Wearing My Father's Bones." In the margin, I'd written a question mark. "Too much?" I'd asked myself. Not too much, I decided, after I came home.

55

The Finish Line

As Zadie Smith, author of *NW,* has said, "I think sometimes the best reason for writing novels is to experience those four and a half hours after you write the final word."

Years ago, when I took painting lessons, my teacher, David Boyd, took a new canvas to demonstrate something he believed it was important for us to learn. He put a stroke on the canvas, then another, then another. And as he worked, he reflected on the process and said that when we begin a work of art, anything is possible. But that with each successive stroke, the possibilities become more limited, until, by the end—the most difficult stage—we have relatively few choices because the universe of the work has been defined. Or as Nicole Krauss, author of *Great House,* centering on the history of a desk and its owners' lives, loves, and losses, has said, "The book, which for so long was something elastic, shifting to accommodate each new thought, every nuance in the writer's mood, begins to harden."

I've often thought about what it takes for a writer to finish a project. I've spoken to writers full of promise. Writers with glorious projects I can still vividly remember. Writers intent on living a creative life. But years later, nothing. Or, not nothing. A work of art that hasn't been completed. But an unfinished work not deliberately set aside is a drain on the psyche. It's like a sore on the bottom of a foot, an ulcer on a finger, a wound that won't heal. Every writer I know who has a book they want to complete but that they're not working on feels this way.

What stops writers from finishing? What keeps writers from picking up works they've set aside? A misapprehension about how long it takes or the intense kind of work that it takes to finish a book? Perhaps. Because I've found that when my students understand what finishing a book entails by reading about how published writers worked as they completed their projects, they were more likely to finish because they were prepared for the intense work that completing their projects would demand.

When Jeffrey Eugenides was finishing *The Marriage Plot*, describing the interrelated lives of students at Brown and what happens to them after graduation, although he'd worked on the novel for years, by the end of the process, he was so afraid the book was "going to be bad" that he continued working until he "fixed everything" that he could. Eugenides knew that "you can keep fixing things ad infinitum," and that there's a point when you have to stop. Still, he worked up to "the last minute" before his deadline.

Eugenides handed in an incomplete manuscript of *The Marriage Plot* to his editor, Jonathan Galassi—the last two chapters remained unwritten. Galassi determined the book was "almost there," urging Eugenides to finish in time for a fall 2011 publication date.

For the next four months, Eugenides "worked like a madman, finishing the last two chapters and revising the entire four-hundred-and-fifty-page manuscript. . . . The thing was done." To complete the book, Eugenides worked from the critiques of four trusted readers, including his wife and Galassi: "I responded to all their queries and suggestions," he said. His wife's notes alone "ran to a hundred and fifty pages." And Eugenides reworked passages that still didn't satisfy him.

When he received the page proofs, Eugenides went back to work, "this time listening only to my inner promptings," he said. He worked into the summer, staying "alone for a month in Berlin" for the most intense work. At that stage, he "inserted new transitions and polished everything." When he received the final page proofs, "there was little left to do."

Eugenides compares his work at the end stage of *The Marriage Plot* to a sprint to the finish of a long and very difficult race: "I sprinted the last mile," he said, "and held out the sacred flame, in the form of a red pencil."

Eugenides did the best he could with the book; then he handed it to trusted readers, listened to their advice, and revised. He reverted to his own instincts late in the process, and worked intensely to finish. Some writers—Eugenides is one of them—describe that working toward a deadline somehow allows them to work better and more instinctively, if not more easily, than they had before.

John Steinbeck noted that, for him, the hardest work on a book came toward the end. That was the time when it was especially important for him to marshal his energy to complete the work. On October 27, 1951, nearing the end of *East of Eden*, Steinbeck wrote, "Weariness is on me, really creeping in, and I can't give in to it." He wondered whether he was "a little nuts" and vowed to shake the mood off as soon as he could.

What was getting in Steinbeck's way was a promise to finish his book by a certain date. "I find myself trying to make it when I said I would," Steinbeck wrote, and that unnecessary, self-imposed pressure was reflected in his writing work so that he had "to throw it out." Steinbeck decided that "[t]his book is more important than the finish." He reverted to his trusty method of trying to get his quota of work done each day. For Steinbeck, a looming deadline interfered with, rather than helped, his process.

Shortly before completing the novel, when he estimated he had but two or three more days of work to do, Steinbeck said, "I wish I were finished and at the same time I am afraid to be finished." Steinbeck understood that the completion of a book was a loss, and he prepared himself, as best he could, in his journal, for its passing. He knew that he needed to try hard "to keep some kind of discipline together." And he realized that, though he was nearing the end, these pages would "probably [be] the hardest work in the whole book."

Nearing completion of *The Grapes of Wrath*, Steinbeck wrote, "But I feel very lost and lonesome. . . . I don't seem to have the knack of living any more." Steinbeck realized he had to work through this feeling or it would either impede the completion of his novel or harm him. He understood that some writers inadvertently don't finish books because they're trying to protect themselves from losing them. As Steinbeck—and many writers, including myself—near the completion of our books, and after their completion, we move into a period of mourning that might also be accompanied by elation. It's a confusing time, as Steinbeck's testimony reveals, but one that we can move through more easily if we honor those feelings and if we remind ourselves that there will be another book waiting to be written. After confessing his feelings of loss, Steinbeck returned to work, nonetheless. "This book," he attested, "has to be written."

BEGINNING AGAIN

The end of the writing process is a complicated time. We might be elated that the work is finished. We might feel empty because this project has preoccupied us for so long. We might miss the grounding routine of our daily work. We might enter a temporary state of mourning as we release the work to the world. We might experience intense anxiety and uncertainty about the work's worth. We might wonder whether we'll have the will to write again; we might worry that our ability to create might desert us. We might be eager to begin another work. Or we might find ourselves in extremely difficult emotional terrain, as John Banville, winner of the Man Booker Prize, did after completing *Mefisto* (1989), a novel discussing the price creativity exacts; after the book appeared and was ignored—"a traumatic time"—Banville spent a summer in his garden, healing. Although Banville's experience is extreme, most writers concede that finishing a project isn't always a blissful time.

Some writers need to take considerable time off between projects, or after certain projects, especially if the work required intense concentration—Maxine Hong Kingston needed to rest after she completed *The Woman Warrior* and *China Men*. After I've completed a difficult project, especially one requiring much research, like

Virginia Woolf, I need time off to clean my study and to deal with what I've neglected taking care of in my house. And then I either wait until I decide what to work on next, or I begin the next project awaiting me—like Anne Tyler and many writers, I have a collection of ideas for books.

The end of any book marks a transition in a writer's life. Part of our job as writers is to honor the work we've done, to be grateful for what the work has taught us, to learn how to let the work go so that we can move on.

When we draw near the end of a book, especially if it's commanded our attention for a long time, we might realize how much we'll miss working on this particular book, and we might want to linger in that special world we've created that's perhaps become more familiar to us than our daily lives. When I finished my novel *Casting Off,* I didn't want to let go of Maive Macnamra, the free-spirited character I'd created.

Norman Rush has a "hard time letting go of a novel." He works on his books for years—*Mating* appeared in 1991, *Mortals* in 2003—and he spends so long in the worlds he's created, he begins "to breathe the air the characters breathe."

Rush is deeply aware that the meaning of his novels' endings affect his readers. He feels an ethical obligation to the meaning his endings impart and he works hard to get them right: "I want my books to reach only the conclusions that are implicit in the trajectories of their characters." In both *Mating* and *Mortals,* Rush settled on "sad outcomes" for his characters, "but optimistic codas."

Rush takes so long wrestling with conclusions that are right for his books, that in the case of *Mortals,* his wife, Elsa, "threatened to move to Mohonk Mountain house, which is a pricey place to move," until he "let go of the manuscript."

Writing provides structure to a writer's life. When we complete a work, unless we begin a new project immediately, that structure disappears. When she was still writing, Alice Munro was asked whether she took any time off after working on a story for months, she replied, "I go pretty much right into the next one." Although she didn't do this when she had children—she had other tasks to occupy her—as she aged she became "panicked at the idea of stopping—as if, if I stopped, I could be stopped for good."

Munro didn't lack story ideas. Nor did she fear that she would someday lack "technique or skill." Instead, Munro knew that it took a tremendous effort of will for her to "maintain excitement and faith" in the writing process, and that if she didn't continually write, she feared she'd lose her will and never begin again. So she kept working, kept adhering to her strict schedule of writing "every morning, seven days a week" from eight to eleven, completing her self-assigned "quota of pages" each day "to keep this from happening."

John Banville has said that he always has to be writing, that stopping writing would be dangerous for him, and that when he finishes one work, he begins another. "I cannot not write," he said. "If I find myself with a spare forty-five minutes at the end of my working day, I will turn to adding a few sentences to something."

Banville publishes a book every three years. He's published sixteen novels in his own name, among them, *The Sea* (2005), *The Infinities* (2009), and *Ancient Light* (2012), a fictional trilogy about science, and another about art. He's published eight detective novels, using the pseudonym Benjamin Black, among them, *Vengeance* (2012) and *Holy Orders* (2013). He also reviews books for the *Guardian* and *The New York Review of Books*, among other publications.

Still, writing his Banville novels "is a constant torment." But writing his Black novels is "a frolic." Banville has found a method that works for him. Because he works in three genres—literary fiction, detective fiction, and nonfiction—each requiring a different voice, a different level of concentration, and a different style, Banville can always be writing. He can move from the excruciatingly taxing work of writing his Banville novels, to the more pleasurable work of writing his Black novels, to the more quickly completed work of journalism.

And each work calls upon a different set of literary skills. Banville has said that, "for Black, character matters, plot matters, dialogue matters to a much greater degree than they do" in his Banville books. Black's characters are "consciously crafted"; Banville's characters "sort of drift out of me."

Zadie Smith, author of *NW*, feels dissatisfied with each book she finishes. But Smith uses that feeling to impel her to begin afresh, to start work on another, completely different novel. Finishing a work, especially one you know has flaws, as all works do, Smith acknowledges, means you have "to start again, means you have space in front of you, somewhere to go." Letting a work go is far easier if we understand that the act of leaving it behind will urge the next, and different, work into existence.

We writers often have ideal works in our imagination against which we evaluate the work we've completed. Although we write the best book we can, understanding that our work can never meet our expectations can help us let go of it, and can allow us to move on to the next phase of our writing lives. If we see our writing life as a continuum, we can acknowledge that writing each book teaches us something that writing no other book can, and we can look forward to what we'll learn from the new work awaiting us.

Sources

Please note: These sources are listed in the order in which they are mentioned in the text. If a source is used more than once, the complete citation is indicated when it is first referred to. I've included detailed references to interviews with writers, a primary source for understanding how "real" writers work, so that interested readers can access the complete text and so more fully investigate a writer's process.

Many of these reflections began as essays in my blog "Writing a Life" at www.writingalife.wordpress.com. They have since been substantially revised.

Preface

Roxane Gay, "Jonah Lehrer Throws It All Away," *Salon*, July 31, 2012, http://www.salon.com/2012/07/31/jonah_lehrer_throws_it_all_away/.

"American Centaur: An Interview with John Updike," by Macy Halford, *The New Yorker*, October 28, 2009, http://www.new yorker.com/online/blogs/books/2009/10/american-centaur -an-interview-with-john-updike.html.

Introduction: The Art of Slow Writing

Andrew Harrison, *D. H. Lawrence: Sons and Lovers* (Penrith, Cornwall, UK: Humanities-Ebooks.co.uk, 2007).

Jeffrey Meyers, *D. H. Lawrence: A Biography* (New York: Alfred A. Knopf, 1990), p. 114.

Salman Rushdie, *Joseph Anton: A Memoir* (New York: Random House, 2012), pp. 49, 53.

Ted Loos (quoting Louis van Tilborgh on Van Gogh's development), "Van Gogh's Evolution, from Neophyte to Master," *The New York Times*, October 26, 2012, http://www.nytimes.com/2012/10/28/arts/artsspecial/van-gogh-and-his-paris-years-at-the-denver-art-museum.html.

Julie Bosman, "Writer's Cramp: In the E-Reader Era, a Book a Year Is Slacking," *The New York Times*, May 12, 2012, http://www.nytimes.com/2012/05/13/business/in-e-reader-age-of-writers-cramp-a-book-a-year-is-slacking.html?pagewanted=all&_r=0.

John Steinbeck, *Journal of a Novel: The "East of Eden" Letters* (New York: Viking Press, 1969), p. 139.

Adam Gopnik, *The Table Comes First: Family, France, and the Meaning of Food* (New York: Alfred A. Knopf, 2011).

Virginia Woolf, *On Being Ill* (1926; repr., Ashfield, MA: Paris Press, 2012), p. 3.

Virginia Woolf, *Virginia Woolf: To the Lighthouse* (London: Hogarth Press, 1927); *To the Lighthouse: The Original Holograph Draft*, ed. and transcribed by Susan Dick (Toronto: University of Toronto Press, 1982).

Julie Bosman, "To Use and Use Not," *The New York Times*, July 4, 2012, http://www.nytimes.com/2012/07/05/books/a-farewell-to-arms-with-hemingways-alternate-endings.html?_r=0.

"Michael Chabon, 'Two Years into Writing This I Felt Like It Was an Utter Flop,'" interview by Killian Fox, *The Observer*, September 8, 2012, http://www.theguardian.com/books/2012/sep/09/michael-chabon-telegraph-avenue-interview.

McEwan's description of his book *Saturday* appears on his Web page. http://www.ianmcewan.com/bib/books/saturday.html.

"Zadie Smith Talks with Ian McEwan," in *The Believer Book of Writers Talking to Writers*, ed. Vendela Vida (San Francisco, CA: Believer Books, 2005–2007), p. 167.

Part One: Getting Ready to Write

Introduction

"Margaret Atwood, The Art of Fiction No. 121," interview by Mary Morris, *The Paris Review*, Winter 1990, http://www.theparisreview.org/interviews/2262/the-art-of-fiction-no-121-margaret-atwood.

Lorna Bradbury, "Margaret Drabble on Jigsaw Puzzles," *The Telegraph*, July 17, 2009, http://www.telegraph.co.uk/culture/books/booknews/5852395/Margaret-Drabble-on-jigsaw-puzzles.html.

Twyla Tharp with Mark Reiter, *The Creative Habit: Learn It and Use It for Life* (2003; repr., New York: Simon & Schuster Paperbacks, 2006), p. 80.

Michael Chabon, *Maps and Legends: Reading and Writing Along the Borderlands* (New York: Harper Perennial, 2008, 2009).

Orhan Pamuk, "'A Blank Page Gives Me Freedom': Orhan Pamuk Interviewed," by Kevin E. G. Perry, *The Quietus*, November 25, 2012, thequietus.com/articles/10733-orhan-pamuk-silent-house-interview.

Nicole Krauss, "Interview: On *The History of Love*," http://nicolekrauss.com/press.html.

Virginia Woolf, *Pointz Hall: The Earlier and Later Typescripts of*

"*Between the Acts*," ed. Mitchell A. Leaska (1981; repr., New York: University Publications, 1983), p. 33.

Virginia Woolf, *Between the Acts* (New York: Harcourt Brace & Company, 1941), p. 3.

1. Learning How to Work at Writing

Kathryn Harrison, *The Mother Knot* (New York: Random House, 2004).

2. Finding Our Own Rhythm

Alison Leigh Cowan, "Unsealed Letters Offer Glimpse of Salinger," *The New York Times*, February 11, 2010, http://www.nytimes .com/2010/02/12/books/12salinger.html?pagewanted=all.

"Margaret Atwood, The Art of Fiction No. 121."

"Peter Carey, The Art of Fiction No. 188," interview by Radhika Jones, *The Paris Review*, Summer 2006, http://www.theparis review.org/interviews/5641/the-art-of-fiction-no-188-peter -carey.

"Jonathan Franzen, The Art of Fiction No. 207," interview by Stephen J. Burn, *The Paris Review*, Winter 2010, http://www.thep arisreview.org/interviews/6054/the-art-of-fiction-no-207-jona than-franzen.

Edward M. Hallowell, M.D., *Crazy Busy: Overstretched, Overbooked, and About to Snap!* (New York: Ballantine Books, 2006).

Virginia Valian, "Learning to Work," in *Working It Out: 23 Women Writers, Artists, Scientists, and Scholars Talk About Their Lives and Work*, eds. Sara Ruddick and Pamela Daniels (New York: Pantheon Books, 1977), pp. 162–78.

"Michael Chabon Q&A: Fatherhood and Writing at Midnight," interview by Carolyn Kellogg, *Los Angeles Times*, October 13,

2009, http://latimesblogs.latimes.com/jacketcopy/2009/10/
michael-qa-fatherhood-and-writing-at-midnight.html.

"Great Instincts: Interview with Colum McCann," by Gabriel
Packard, *The Writer*, September 29, 2011, http://www.writer
mag.com/2011/09/29/great-instincts-interview-colum
-mccann/.

3. Where to Begin

"Anne Tyler: A Life's Work," interview by Lisa Allardice, *The
Guardian*, April 13, 2012, http://www.theguardian.com/books/
2012/apr/13/anne-tyler-interview.

Anne Tyler, "Still Just Writing," in *The Writer on Her Work*, ed.
Janet Sternburg (New York: W. W. Norton, 1981), p. 6.

Zadie Smith, "That Crafty Feeling," in *Changing My Mind: Occa-
sional Essays* (New York: Penguin Press, 2009), pp. 100–101.

Charlotte Higgins, "Zadie Smith Returns to Her Native London
for Her Fourth Novel," *The Guardian*, August 26, 2012, http://
www.theguardian.com/books/2012/aug/26/zadie-smith-london
-fourth-novel.

"Zadie Smith," interview by Christopher Bollen, *Interview*, October 2012, http://www.interviewmagazine.com/culture/zadie
-smith/.

Mark Hussey, *Virginia Woolf, A to Z: A Comprehensive Reference for
Students, Teachers, and Common Readers to Her Life, Works, and
Critical Reception* (New York: Facts on File, 1995), pp. 169–79,
301–19.

4. Routine

"Interview: Carol Shields, Pulitzer Prize for Fiction," Academy of
Achievement, May 23, 1998, http://www.achievement.org/
autodoc/printmember/shi1int-1.

"Jeffrey Eugenides," interview by Jonathan Safran Foer, *Bomb*, Fall 2002, http://bombsite.com/issues/81/articles/2519.

Eviatar Zerubavel, *The Clockwork Muse: A Practical Guide to Writing Theses, Dissertations, and Books* (Cambridge, MA: Harvard University Press, 1999), p. 24.

David Allen, *Getting Things Done: The Art of Stress-Free Productivity* (New York: Viking Penguin, 2001), p. 26.

5. Tools of the Trade

"Paul Auster, The Art of Fiction No. 178," interview by Michael Wood, *The Paris Review*, Fall 2003, http://www.theparisreview.org/interviews/121/the-art-of-fiction-no-178-paul-auster.

Paul Auster, *The Story of My Typewriter*, illus. Sam Messer (New York: Distributed Art Publishers, 2002). All quotes about Auster's typewriter are taken from *The Paris Review* interview.

"Norman Rush, The Art of Fiction No. 205," interview by Joshua Pashman, *The Paris Review*, Fall 2010, http://www.theparisreview.org/interviews/6039/the-art-of-fiction-no-205-norman-rush.

"Anne Tyler: A Life's Work," *The Guardian*.

"Margaret Atwood, The Art of Fiction No. 121."

"Ian McEwan, The Art of Fiction No. 173," interview by Adam Begley, *The Paris Review*, Summer 2002, http://www.theparisreview.org/interviews/393/the-art-of-fiction-no-173-ian-mcewan.

6. A Writer's *Mise en Place*

Twyla Tharp, *The Creative Habit*, p. 82.

Samuel Hynes, *Flights of Passage: Recollections of a World War II Aviator* (1988; repr., New York: Penguin Books, 2003), p. 258.

"Peter Carey, The Art of Fiction No. 188."

Peter Carey's Web site, http://petercareybooks.com/all-titles/par
    rot-olivier-america/authors-bookshelf.

7. Deliberate Practice

Geoff Colvin, *Talent Is Overrated: What Really Separates World-
    Class Performers from Everybody Else* (New York: Portfolio,
    2008), pp. 65–83.

Daniel Coyle, *The Talent Code: Greatness Isn't Born. It's Grown.
    Here's How* (New York: Bantam Books, 2009), pp. 74–94.

Lucy Corin, "Material," in *The Writer's Notebook: Craft Essays from
    Tin House* (Portland, OR: Tin House Books, 2009), pp. 75–92.

Mark Doty, *Firebird: A Memoir* (New York: HarperCollins, 1999),
    p. 55.

Kathryn Harrison, *The Mother Knot*, pp. 4, 14, 55.

8. Writing and Real Life

Anne Tyler, "Still Just Writing," in *The Writer on Her Work*, pp. 3–9.

"Mary Karr: The Art of Memoir, No. 1," interview by Amanda
    Fortini, *The Paris Review*, Winter 2009, http://www.thepar
    isreview.org/interviews/5992/the-art-of-memoir-no-1-mary
    -karr.

"Alice Munro, The Art of Fiction No. 137," interview by Jeanne
    McCulloch and Mona Simpson, *The Paris Review*, Summer
    1994, http://www.theparisreview.org/interviews/1791/the-art
    -of-fiction-no-137-alice-munro.

"Zadie Smith Returns to Her Native London for Her Fourth
    Novel," *The Guardian*.

9. Raw Material

Elizabeth Jolley, "Dipt Me in Ink," in *The Writer on Her Work*, pp.
    125–39.

"Norman Rush, The Art of Fiction No. 205."

"Isabel Allende," in *Writers Dreaming: Twenty-six Writers Talk About Their Dreams and the Creative Process*, ed. Naomi Epel (1993; repr., New York: Vintage Books, 1994), p. 20.

"Margaret Atwood's Creative Process," video interview by Max Miller, Big Think, October 21, 2010, transcript at http://bigthink .com/videos/margaret-atwoods-creative-process.

"Alice Munro, The Art of Fiction No. 137."

"Writer Series: Interview with Margaux Fragoso," by Caroline Cox, http://skirt.com/print/114719.

10. Walking and Inspiration

"Ian McEwan, The Art of Fiction No. 173."

"Alice Munro, The Art of Fiction No. 137."

"Alice Munro's Nobel Win Likely Won't Change Her Plans to Stop Writing: Editor," *Calgary Herald*, October 11, 2013, http://www.calgaryherald.com/news/Alice+Munro+Novel+l ikely+change+plans+stop+writing+editor/9027603/story .html.

Virginia Woolf, *The Diary of Virginia Woolf*, ed. Anne Olivier Bell, vol. 3, *1925–1930* (New York: Harcourt Brace Jovanovich, 1980), pp. 131, 132, 129.

Virginia Woolf, "A Sketch of the Past," in *Moments of Being*, ed. Jeanne Schulkind (New York: Harcourt Brace, 1976, 1985), p. 81.

Virginia Woolf, *The Diary of Virginia Woolf*, vol. 3, p. 130.

"Robert Stone, The Art of Fiction No. 90," interview by William C. Woods, *The Paris Review*, Winter 1985, http://www.thepa risreview.org/interviews/2845/the-art-of-fiction-no-90-robert -stone.

"Robert Stone," in *Writers Dreaming*, pp. 269, 268.

"Robert Stone, The Art of Fiction No. 90."

Part Two: A Writer's Apprenticeship

Introduction

Margaret Atwood, "Nine Beginnings" in *The Writer on Her Work*, vol. II, *New Essays in New Territory*, ed. Janet Sternburg (New York: W. W. Norton, 1991), p. 153.

Michael J. A. Howe, "The Expertise of Great Writers," in *Genius Explained* (1999; repr., Cambridge, UK: Cambridge University Press, 2001), p. 165.

W. Somerset Maugham, preface to *The Painted Veil* (1925; repr., New York: Penguin Books, 1952), p. 8.

Louise DeSalvo, introduction to *Tropic of Cancer* by Henry Miller (New York: Signet Books, 1995), pp. vii–xvii.

"Mary Karr: The Art of Memoir, No. 1."

"Celebrating the Possibilities of Fiction: A Conversation with Jennifer Egan," interview by Robert Alford, *PopMatters*, February 20, 2012, http://www.popmatters.com/column/154523 -celebrating-the-possibilities-of-fiction-a-conversation-with -jennife/.

"Sue Grafton," in *Writers Dreaming*, p. 64.

11. Apprenticeship

Howard Gardner, *Creating Minds: An Anatomy of Creativity Seen Through the Lives of Freud, Einstein, Picasso, Stravinsky, Eliot, Graham, and Gandhi* (New York: Basic Books, 1993), p. 370.

Virginia Woolf, *A Passionate Apprentice: The Early Journals, 1897–1909*, ed. Mitchell A. Leaska (New York: Harcourt Brace Jovanovich, 1990), pp. 321 ff.

Virginia Woolf's Reading Notebooks, ed. Brenda R. Silver (Princeton, NJ: Princeton University Press, 1983), p. 83.

Virginia Woolf, *Melymbrosia: An Early Version of "The Voyage Out,"* ed. Louise DeSalvo (1982; repr., San Francisco, CA: Cleis Press, 2002), pp. xii–xlii.

Zadie Smith, "That Crafty Feeling," in *Changing My Mind*, p. 104.

Louise DeSalvo, introduction to *Tropic of Cancer*, pp. vi–xvi.

Henry Miller, *The Books in My Life* (1952; repr., New York: New Directions, 1969), pp. 257, 40–41.

"Interview: Carol Shields, Pulitzer Prize for Fiction," Academy of Achievement.

12. Writing Outside and Elsewhere

Ernest Hemingway, *A Moveable Feast: The Restored Edition* (New York: Scribner, 2010), pp. 73, 72.

Louise DeSalvo, "D. H. Lawrence, Forever on the Move: Creative Writers and Place," in *A Companion to Creative Writing*, ed. Graeme Harper (Oxford, UK: Wiley-Blackwell, 2013), pp. 307–19.

13. Process Journal

Dawn Powell, "Diaries," http://www.dawnpowelldiaries.com.

"Sue Grafton," in *Writers Dreaming*, pp. 61–63.

14. Patience, Humility, and Respect

"Michael Chabon: 'Two Years into Writing This I Felt Like It Was an Utter Flop,'" *The Observer*.

Katharine Viner, describing Donna Tartt's ten-year hiatus in "A Talent to Tantalise," *The Guardian*, October 18, 2002, http://www.theguardian.com/books/2002/oct/19/fiction.features.

Pamela Paul, interview with Donna Tartt, "Inside *The New York Times Book Review*" podcast, October 20, 2013, http://podcasts.nytimes.com/podcasts/2013/10/18/books/review/20books_pod/18BOOKREVIEW.mp3.

"Interview with Colum McCann," by Brett Anthony Johnston, National Book Foundation, http://www.nationalbook.org/nba2009_f_mccann_interv.html#.UgOujeChDzK.

Jody Hoy, "To Be Able to See the Tao," in *Conversations with Maxine Hong Kingston*, eds. Paul Skenazy and Tera Martin (Jackson: University Press of Mississippi, 1998), p. 57.

"David L. Ulin Talks to Maxine Hong Kingston," *Los Angeles Times*, February 6, 2011, http://latimesblogs.latimes.com/jacketcopy/2011/02/david-l-ulin-talks-to-maxine-hong-.html.

15. Learning How to Learn

Ira Glass, "On Good Taste . . . ," part 3 of "Ira Glass on Storytelling," YouTube video, 5:20, youtube.com/watch?v=BI23U7U2aUY.

"Peter Carey, The Art of Fiction No. 188."

"Interview with Colum McCann," National Book Foundation.

"A Conversation with Jo Ann Beard," interview by Amy Yelin, *The Missouri Review* 34, Spring 2011, p. 136.

"Jo Ann Beard," interview by Astri von Arbin Ahlander, *The Days of Yore*, http://www.thedaysofyore.com/jo-ann-beard/.

"An Interview with Jo Ann Beard," by Jessica Nelson, *The Fiddleback*, http://thefiddleback.com/issue-items/an-interview-with-jo-ann-beard (no longer available).

16. Labor and Management

John Steinbeck, *Journal of a Novel: The "East of Eden" Letters*, pp. 53, 54.

John Steinbeck, *Working Days: The Journals of "The Grapes of Wrath" 1938–1941*, ed. Robert DeMott (New York: Viking Press, 1989).

Anthony Trollope, *An Autobiography* (1883; repr., London: Oxford University Press, 1953), pp. 102, 103.

Anthony Robbins: http://training.tonyrobbins.com/morning-ques tions-use-the-power-of-questions-to-change-your-life/

17. Game Plan

Louise DeSalvo, "A Desperado of Love," in *Conceived with Malice: Literature as Revenge in the Lives and Works of Virginia and Leonard Woolf, D. H. Lawrence, Djuna Barnes, and Henry Miller* (New York: Dutton, 1995), pp. 277 ff.

Virginia Woolf, *The Diary of Virginia Woolf*, ed. Anne Olivier Bell, vol. 4, *1931–1935* (New York: Harcourt Brace Jovanovich, 1982), pp. 63, 142, 149, 271.

Brian P. Moran and Michael Lennington, *The 12 Week Year: Get More Done in 12 Weeks Than Others Do in 12 Months* (Hoboken, NJ: Wiley, 2013), p. 15.

18. No Excuses

"Ian McEwan, The Art of Fiction No. 173."

Nawal El Saadawi, *Memoirs from the Women's Prison*, trans. Marilyn Booth (1986; repr., Berkeley: University of California Press, 1994), pp. 199–204.

E. B. Sledge, *With the Old Breed at Peleliu and Okinawa* (Novato, CA: Presidio Press, 1981).

"The Hedge Schools," Irish Cultural Society of the Garden

City Area, http://www.irish-society.org/home/hedgemaster
-archives-2/groups-organizations/the-hedge-schools.

19. Writing Rehab

Stephen King, *On Writing: A Memoir of the Craft* (New York:
Scribner, 2000), pp. 264, 265, 266, 264, 268, 269.

20. A Writer's Notebook

Joan Didion, "On Keeping a Notebook," in *Slouching Towards Beth-
lehem: Essays* (1968; repr., New York: Farrar, Straus, and Giroux, 2008), pp. 133, 135, 136, 139.

21. The Creative Act

Margaret Atwood, "Nine Beginnings," in *The Writer on Her Work*,
vol. II, p. 151.

Christopher R. Beha, "Do Something," in *The Writer's Notebook II:
Craft Essays from Tin House* (Portland, OR: Tin House Books,
2012), pp. 187, 193.

22. Support for Our Work

Howard Gardner, *Creating Minds*, p. 43.

"Peter Carey, The Art of Fiction No. 188."

Louise DeSalvo, "'Tinder-and-Flint': Virginia Woolf & Vita
Sackville-West," in *Significant Others: Creativity & Intimate Part-
nership*, eds. Whitney Chadwick and Isabelle de Courtivron (New
York: Thames and Hudson, 1993).

23. Radical Work Takes Time

Carol Vogel, "High-Tech Matisse: New Electronic Methods Provide Fresh Insights into How a Master Honed His Technique," *The New York Times*, July 11, 2010, AR1. In the online

version, the quotes come from the interactive site link from the article (http://www.nytimes.com/interactive/2010/07/11/arts/20100711-matisse-bathers-moma.html?ref=design).

"Jeffrey Eugenides, The Art of Fiction, No. 215," interview by James Gibbons, *The Paris Review*, Winter 2011, http://www.theparis review.org/interviews/6117/the-art-of-fiction-no-215-jeffrey -eugenides.

"Questions for Jeffrey Eugenides," interview by Jessica Grose, *Slate*, October 2011, http://www.slate.com/articles/arts/interrogation/2011/10/jeffrey_eugenides_interview_the_marriage_plot_and _david_foster_w.html.

"Jeffrey Eugenides," *Bomb*.

"Jeffrey Eugenides, The Art of Fiction, No. 215."

Part Three: Challenges and Successes

Introduction

"Mary Karr, The Art of Memoir No. 1."

Michael Chabon, "Diving into the Wreck," in *Maps and Legends*, pp. 147, 148, 149.

Michael Chabon, *Wonder Boys* (New York: Random House, 1995), pp. 134, 362.

"Michael Chabon: How to Salvage a 'Wrecked' Novel," interview by Douglas Gorney, *The Atlantic*, December 29, 2010, http://www.theatlantic.com/entertainment/archive/2010/12/michael-chabon-how-to-salvage-a-wrecked-novel/68665/.

John Steinbeck, *Journal of a Novel: The "East of Eden" Letters*, pp. 4, 23, 12.

24. Failure in the Middle

"Julie Orringer Talks with Tobias Wolff," in *The Believer Book of Writers Talking to Writers*.

Chip Heath and Dan Heath, *Switch: How to Change Things When Change Is Hard* (New York: Broadway Books, 2010), pp. 164, 168, 169. Quotations from Kanter and Brown are from *Switch*.

"Michael Chabon: 'Two Years into Writing This I Felt Like It Was an Utter Flop,'" *The Observer*.

25. Doubt

"Krauss' 'Great House' Built on 'Willful Uncertainty,'" *All Things Considered*, October 14, 2010, http://www.npr.org/templates/story/story.php?storyId=130564695.

Virginia Woolf, *A Room of One's Own* (1929; repr., New York: Harcourt, Brace & World, 1957), pp. 25, 71, xi.

Virginia Woolf, *Three Guineas* (London: The Hogarth Press, 1938).

Virginia Woolf, "The Art of Fiction" and "The Leaning Tower," in *The Moment and Other Essays* (New York: Harcourt Brace, 1947).

D. H. Lawrence, "Surgery for the Novel—or a Bomb," "Art and Morality," "Morality and the Novel," "Why the Novel Matters," "Love," "We Need One Another," and "Women Are So Cocksure," in *Phoenix: The Posthumous Papers of D. H. Lawrence: 1936*, ed. Edward D. McDonald (New York: Viking Press, 1936, 1968), p. 537.

26. Writing as Collaboration

Dear Scott/Dear Max: The Fitzgerald-Perkins Correspondence, eds. John Kuehl and Jackson R. Bryer (New York: Charles Scribner's Sons, 1971).

F. Scott Fitzgerald, *The Great Gatsby* (New York: Charles Scribner's Sons, 1925).

F. Scott Fitzgerald, *Trimalchio: An Early Version of "The Great Gatsby,"* ed. James L. W. West III (Cambridge, UK: Cambridge University Press, 2000).

Don Lee, "About Mary Gordon: A Profile," *Ploughshares,* http://www.pshares.org/read/article-detail.cfm?intArticleID=4294.

Wyatt Mason, "Norman Rush's Brilliantly Broken Promise," *The New York Times Magazine,* August 29, 2013, http://www.nytimes.com/2013/09/01/magazine/norman-rushs-brilliantly-broken-promise.html?_r=0.

27. Creative Problem Solving

"Ian McEwan, The Art of Fiction, No. 173."

David W. Ecker, "The Artistic Process as Qualitative Problem Solving," in *The Journal of Aesthetics and Art Criticism* 21:3 (Spring 1963), pp. 283–90. http://www.jstor.org/stable/427437. I studied with Ecker during my Ph.D. work; this article was essential to my understanding of the writing process.

Louise DeSalvo, *Crazy in the Kitchen: Food, Feuds, and Forgiveness in an Italian American Family* (New York: Bloomsbury, 2004).

Eric Maisel, Ph.D., *Fearless Creating: A Step-by-Step Guide to Starting and Completing Your Work of Art* (New York: Jeremy P. Tarcher/Putnam, 1995).

28. Rejection Letters

One Hundred Famous Rejections, http://www.onehundredrejections.com.

Elizabeth Gilbert, "Thoughts on Writing," http://elizabethgilbert.com/thoughts-on-writing/.

"Jo Ann Beard," *The Days of Yore.*

Stephen King, *On Writing,* pp. 40–41.

29. Hailstorms

"The Rumpus Interview with Colum McCann," by Dylan Foley, *The Rumpus*, June 17, 2009, http://therumpus.net/2009/06/rumpus-interview-with-colum-mccann/.

"Great Instincts: Interview with Colum McCann."

"The Rumpus Interview with Colum McCann," by Alec Michod, *The Rumpus*, June 4, 2013, http://therumpus.net/2013/06/the-rumpus-interview-with-colum-mccann/.

Erica Wagner, "Cross Over: 'TransAtlantic,' by Colum McCann," *The New York Times Book Review*, June 20, 2013, http://www.nytimes.com/2013/06/23/books/review/transatlantic-by-colum-mccann.html?pagewanted=all&_r=0.

30. Turning the Corner

Zadie Smith, "That Crafty Feeling," in *Changing My Mind*, pp. 104–05.

"Michael Chabon: 'Two Years into Writing This I Felt Like It Was an Utter Flop,'" *The Observer*.

31. Practice Deciding

Barry Schwartz, *The Paradox of Choice: Why More Is Less* (2004; repr., New York: Harper Perennial, 2005).

D. H. Lawrence, *Sea and Sardinia* (1921; repr., New York: Penguin Books, 1999).

D. H. Lawrence, *Women in Love* (1920; repr., New York: Signet Classics, 1995).

D. H. Lawrence, *Lady Chatterley's Lover* (1928; repr., New York: Bantam Dell, 1928).

Antonya Nelson, "Short Story: A Process of Revision," in *The Writer's Notebook II*, pp. 144, 145, 147.

32. Successful Outcomes

David Allen, *Getting Things Done*, pp. 67 ff.

"Joan Didion, The Art of Fiction No. 71," interview by Linda Kuehl, *The Paris Review*, Fall–Winter 1978, http://www.thepa risreview.org/interviews/3439/the-art-of-fiction-no-71-joan -didion.

33. Ship's Log

"Ernest Hemingway, The Art of Fiction, No. 21," interview by George Plimpton, *The Paris Review*, Spring 1958, http://www .theparisreview.org/interviews/4825/the-art-of-fiction-no-21 -ernest-hemingway.

Leonard Woolf, *Downhill All the Way: An Autobiography of the Years 1919 to 1939* (New York: Harcourt Brace Jovanovich, 1967), pp. 169, 184.

34. What Worked and Why

Mark Williams, John Teasdale, Zindel Segal, and Jon Kabat-Zinn, *The Mindful Way Through Depression: Freeing Yourself from Chronic Unhappiness* (New York: Guildford Press, 2007), pp. 124–25.

"Q&A: Positive Psychologist Martin Seligman on the Good Life," interview by Maia Szalavitz, *Time*, http://healthland.time.com/ 2011/05/13/mind-reading-positive-psychologist-martin-selig man-on-the-good-life/.

Rick Bass, "When to Keep It Simple," in *The Writer's Notebook*, pp. 29–31.

Part Four: Writers at Rest

Introduction

Arturo Islas with Marilyn Yalom, "Interview with Maxine Hong Kingston," in *Conversations with Maxine Hong Kingston*, p. 26.

"Toni Morrison Returns 'Home' to Read from New Novel," http://www.princeton.edu/main/news/archive/S34/92/80Q99/.

Carolyn See, *Making a Literary Life: Advice for Writers and Other Dreamers* (2002; repr., New York: Ballantine Books, 2002).

"Amy Hempel, The Art of Fiction No. 176," interview by Paul Winner, *The Paris Review*, Summer 2003, http://www.theparisreview.org/interviews/227/the-art-of-fiction-no-176-amy-hempel.

Manuel Cuenca Cabeza, Roberto San Salvador del Valle, Eduardo Aguilar, and Cristina Ortega, "Contribution of Leisure to Creativity and Innovation of a Region," http://ec.europa.eu/education/lifelong-learning-policy/doc/creativity/report/leisure.pdf.

John Steinbeck, *Working Days: The Journals of "The Grapes of Wrath,"* p. 37.

Zadie Smith, "That Crafty Feeling," in *Changing My Mind*, p. 107.

Ray Bradbury, *Zen in the Art of Writing: Releasing the Creative Genius Within You* (1973; repr., New York: Bantam Books, 1992).

"Junot Díaz: By the Book," *The New York Times*, August 30, 2012, http://www.nytimes.com/2012/09/02/books/review/junot-diaz-by-the-book.html?pagewanted=2&_r=0&pagewanted=all.

35. Dreaming and Daydreaming

"Charles Johnson," in *Writers Dreaming*, pp. 120, 121.

"Bharati Mukherjee," in *Writers Dreaming*, pp. 161, 162.

"Gloria Naylor," in *Writers Dreaming*, pp. 168, 169, 171.

"William Styron," in *Writers Dreaming*, pp. 172–74.

36. Dumbstruck

Matthew J. Loscalzo, quoted in Philip Vassallo, "Writing Through Tragedy," *Words on the Line*, http://wordsontheline.blogspot .com/2013/05/writing-through-tragedy.html.

"Reynolds Price," in *Writers Dreaming*, pp. 201, 207.

Blake Morrison, "*Levels of Life* by Julian Barnes—Review," *The Guardian*, April 10, 2013, http://www.theguardian.com/books/ 2013/apr/10/levels-life-julian-barnes-review.

Hannah Furness, "Julian Barnes: I Contemplated Suicide After the Death of My Wife," *The Telegraph*, March 22, 2013, http:// www.telegraph.co.uk/culture/books/9948990/Julian-Barnes -I-contemplated-suicide-after-the-death-of-my-wife.html.

Joyce Carol Oates, "Julian Barnes and the Work of Grief," *Times Literary Supplement*, May 1, 2013, http://www.the-tls.co.uk/ tls/public/article1253123.ece.

Mary Cappello, *Called Back; My Reply to Cancer, My Return to Life* (New York: Alyson Books, 2009).

37. Taking a Break

"Breakaway Minds: Howard Gruber, Interviewed by Howard Gardner," *Psychology Today*, July 1981, available at http:// davidlavery.net/Gruber/Pages/hgbm.htm.

William Boyd, "'Must We Dream Our Dreams?,'" *The Guardian*, September 10, 2010, http://www.theguardian.com/books/2010/ sep/11/william-boyd-elizabeth-bishop-brazil.

"Breakaway Minds," *Psychology Today*.

Virginia Woolf, *A Passionate Apprentice*.

John Worthen, *D. H. Lawrence: The Life of an Outsider* (New York: Counterpoint, 2005), pp. xxi–xxvi.

Dale Chihuly, *Chihuly DVD Collection*, Ent. Software, 2009.

38. Why I'm a Writer Who Cooks

Diane Johnson, "Aspiradora," in *The Writer on Her Work*, vol. II, p. 141.

Michael Chabon, "Art of Cake," in *Manhood for Amateurs: The Pleasures and Regrets of a Husband, Father, and Son* (New York: Harper, 2009), p. 141.

"Michael Chabon Q&A: Fatherhood and Writing at Midnight," *Los Angeles Times*.

Michael Chabon, "Art of Cake," in *Manhood for Amateurs*, p. 151.

Howard Gardner, *Creating Minds*, p. 33.

39. Slow Reading

Bill Gates, The Gates Notes, www.thegatesnotes.com/summer -reading-bookshelf.

Steven Johnson, *Where Good Ideas Come From: The Natural History of Innovation* (New York: Riverhead, 2010).

Michael Cunningham, *The Hours* (New York: Farrar, Straus & Giroux, 1998), pp. 141 ff.

Robert Ferguson, *Henry Miller: A Life* (1991; repr., New York: W. W. Norton, 1993), p. 16.

Henry Miller, *The Books in My Life*, pp. 131, 40, 132, 36, 28.

"Jeffrey Eugenides, The Art of Fiction, No. 215."

40. Fresh Air

Sue Monk Kidd, "Thoughts on Writing: Ten Most Helpful Things I Could Ever Tell Anyone About Writing," http://www.thesecret

lifeofbees.com/Reflections.aspx?t=w&i=1 http://suemonkkidd
.com/Reflections.aspx?t=w&i=1.

Virginia Woolf, *The Diary of Virginia Woolf,* ed. Anne Olivier Bell, vol. 2, *1920–1924* (New York: Harcourt Brace Jovanovich, 1978), pp. 133, 152.

"Toni Morrison, The Art of Fiction No. 134," interview by Elissa Schappell, with additional material from Claudia Brodsky Lacour, *The Paris Review,* Fall 1993, http://www.theparisre view.org/interviews/1888/the-art-of-fiction-no-134-toni-mor rison.

Christoph Keller, *The Best Dancer,* trans. Alison Gallup (2003; repr., Portland, OR: Ooligan Press, 2009), p. 217.

Jody Rosen, "Man of Many Words: Up Close and Personal with Peter Ackroyd . . . ," *The New York Times Style Magazine,* September 15, 2013, pp. 110, 112, 114; available online as "Peter Ackroyd's London Calling," http://tmagazine.blogs.nytimes.com /2013/09/12/arts-and-letters-peter-ackroyds-london-calling/.

41. Waiting for an Answer

"Ian McEwan, The Art of Fiction No. 173."

Stephen Nachmanovitch, *Free Play: Improvisation in Life and Art* (New York: Jeremy P. Tarcher/Putnam, 1990), pp. 147–51.

Ray Bradbury, *Zen in the Art of Writing,* pp. 147, 146, 147.

Victoria Nelson, *On Writer's Block: A New Approach to Creativity* (Boston: Houghton Mifflin, 1993), p. 99.

42. A New Perspective

Joseph Brodsky, *Watermark* (New York: Farrar, Straus & Giroux, 1992), pp. 5, 23, 59ff, 50ff, 22, 111, 28, 47.

43. What's in Your Drawer?

Diana Athill, *Somewhere Towards the End* (London: Granta Publications, 2008).

"Jeffrey Eugenides, The Art of Fiction No. 215."

"Virginia Woolf's *The Journal of Mistress Joan Martyn*," eds. Susan M. Squier and Louise DeSalvo, *Twentieth Century Literature* 25 (Autumn/Winter 1979), pp. 237–69.

Part Five: Building a Book, Finishing a Book

Introduction

John Steinbeck, *Journal of a Novel: The "East of Eden" Letters*.

John Steinbeck, *Working Days: The Journals of "The Grapes of Wrath,"* p. 61.

Robin W. Winks, *The Historian as Detective: Essays on Evidence* (New York: Harper & Row, 1969).

44. How Long Does It Take?

"Questions for Jeffrey Eugenides," *Slate*.

"Charles Johnson," in *Writers Dreaming*, p. 120.

"John Barth," in *Writers Dreaming*, p. 45.

Steve Almond, "Eat, Pray, Love, Get Rich, Buy Up a Town in New Jersey, Write a Novel No One Expects: The Post-Guru Literary Career of Elizabeth Gilbert," *The New York Times Magazine*, September 22, 2013, pp. 22, 24–25, 44–45.

"Joan Didion, The Art of Nonfiction No. 1," interview by Hilton Als, *The Paris Review*, Spring 2006, http://www.theparisreview.org/interviews/5601/the-art-of-nonfiction-no-1-joan-didion.

"Norman Rush's Brilliantly Broken Promise," *The New York Times Magazine*.

"Interview with Margaux Fragoso," by Krystal Anada Sital, *Tottenville Review,* http://www.tottenvillereview.com/interview-with-margaux-fragoso/.

"Writer Series: Interview with Margaux Fragoso," by Caroline Cox.

Margaux Fragoso to Louise DeSalvo, e-mail communication, September 3, 2012.

Leonard Woolf, *The Journey Not the Arrival Matters: An Autobiography of the Years 1939 to 1969* (London: Hogarth Press, 1969).

45. Over Time

"Jeffrey Eugenides," *Bomb.*

"Jeffrey Eugenides, The Art of Fiction, No. 215."

Louise DeSalvo, "Old Flame," in *Ploughshares,* Fall 2009, vol. 35, No. 2, ed. Kathryn Harrison, pp. 10–22.

46. Architecture and Design

Stephen King, *On Writing,* pp. 135, 136.

Virginia Woolf, *To the Lighthouse: The Original Holograph Draft,* p. 2.

47. Turning Pages into Books

E. M. Forster, *Aspects of the Novel* (New York: Harcourt, 1927), p. 86.

"Ian McEwan, The Art of Fiction No. 173."

48. Structuring Our Work

Anne Lamott, *Bird by Bird: Some Instructions on Writing and Life* (New York: Pantheon Books, 1994). Alice Adams's structure appears on p. 62 of Lamott's book.

Adam Braver, "The Experience In Between: Thoughts on Nonlinear Narrative," in *The Writer's Notebook II,* pp. 107, 110, 111.

Cheryl Strayed, *Wild: From Lost to Found on the Pacific Crest Trail* (New York: Alfred A. Knopf, 2013), p. 4.

Louise DeSalvo, "Old Flame," p. 10.

49. The Second Sleeve

"Donna Tartt," interview by Jill Eisenstadt, *Bomb* 41, Fall 1992, http://bombsite.com/issues/41/articles/1584.

"Zadie Smith Returns to Her Native London for Her Fourth Novel," *The Guardian*.

"Zadie Smith," *Interview*.

"Alice Munro, The Art of Fiction No. 137."

50. Tied Up in Knots

"Karen Russell," interview by Lucas Kavner, *The Days of Yore*, February 13, 2012, http://www.thedaysofyore.com/karen-russell/.

Virginia Woolf, *The Pargiters: The Novel-Essay Portion of "The Years,"* ed. Mitchell A. Leaska (New York: New York Public Library, 1977).

51. Writing Partners

"Jonathan Franzen, The Art of Fiction No. 207."

52. Revision

"Jack Kerouac," *Encyclopaedia Britannica*, http://www.britannica.com/EBchecked/topic/315512/Jack-Kerouac/278952/Assessment.

Robert Birnbaum, "The Millions Interview: Robert Birnbaum and Darin Strauss," *The Millions*, September 8, 2011, http://www.themillions.com/2011/09/robert-birnbaum-and-darin-strauss.html.

"Jonathan Lethem Talks with Paul Auster," in *The Believer Book of Writers Talking to Writers*, p. 40.

"Paul Auster, The Art of Fiction No. 178."

53. The Toughest Choice

"Mary Karr: The Art of Memoir, No. 1."

Louise DeSalvo, introduction to *Melymbrosia*.

William Troy, "Stephen Dedalus—in the Rough," *The New York Times*, February 11, 1945, http://www.nytimes.com/books/00/01/09/specials/joyce-stephen.html.

"William Faulkner, The Art of Fiction No. 12," interview by Jean Stein, *The Paris Review*, Spring 1956, http://www.theparisreview.org/interviews/4954/the-art-of-fiction-no-12-william-faulkner.

54. Self-Censorship

"Joan Didion, The Art of Nonfiction No. 1."

"Interview: Carol Shields, Pulitzer Prize for Fiction," Academy of Achievement.

"Jeffrey Eugenides," *Bomb*.

55. The Finish Line

Zadie Smith, "That Crafty Feeling," in *Changing My Mind*, p. 107.

Nicole Krauss, "Essay on Writing *Great House*," http://nicolekrauss.com/press.html.

"Jeffrey Eugenides, The Art of Fiction, No. 215."

John Steinbeck, *Journal of a Novel: The "East of Eden" Letters*, pp. 174, 175.

John Steinbeck, *Working Days: The Journals of "The Grapes of Wrath*," pp. 127–28.

Epilogue: Beginning Again

"John Banville, The Art of Fiction No. 200," interview by Belinda McKeon, *The Paris Review*, Spring 2009, http://www.theparis review.org/interviews/5907/the-art-of-fiction-no-200-john -banville. All Banville quotations in the epilogue are taken from this article.

Arturo Islas with Marilyn Yalom, "Interview with Maxine Hong Kingston," in *Conversations with Maxine Hong Kingston*, p. 26.

"Anne Tyler: A Life's Work."

"Norman Rush, The Art of Fiction No. 205."

"Alice Munro, The Art of Fiction No. 137."

Zadie Smith, "That Crafty Feeling," in *Changing My Mind*, p. 102.

Acknowledgments

The greatest thanks to my husband, Ernest DeSalvo, who saw me through the most difficult time in our lives with hard work, grace, and courage, and who sent me back to the desk. To Edvige Giunta, my writing partner, who understands how I work better than I do, and who reminds me of where I am in the process when I'm stumbling. To Amy Jo Burns, who assisted me with research, organization, and conceptualization, and without whom there wouldn't have been a book.

Thank you to Debra Cottone for helping me understand how long it would take. To Audrey Goldrich, my lifeline. To Christoph Keller for conversations about how to work at writing. To Jan Heller Levi for support and for being a role model of diligence and effort. To Christina Baker Kline for always steering me in the right direction when I don't know what to do next. To Pamela Satran for buoying my spirits. To Lia Ottaviano for help with research early in the process. To Amy Robbins for helping me gather courage and move on. To Michele and Charles Scicolone for their friendship. To Sharon Dennis Wyeth for continuously checking in about my work. To Vanessa Smith, who knows me better than I know myself, for our priceless conversations.

Thanks to all my writing students at Hunter College, who have been so generous in sharing their insights about their work and who have taught me so much about the writing process. Thank you, President Jennifer Raab, Cristina Alfar, and Peter Carey, for encouraging me to begin, and build, the MFA in Memoir at Hunter College, and for their generous support through the years. Thanks to Thom Taylor, for everything he's done.

Thank you to my incomparable family. My sons, Jason DeSalvo and Justin DeSalvo, are a continual source of joy, pride, and encouragement and models of dedication to their art. My daughters-in-law, Deborah DeSalvo and Lynn DeSalvo, demonstrate daily the impact excellent teaching has on young people's lives. My grandchildren, Steven Louis DeSalvo and Julia Frances May DeSalvo, are models of persistence, good humor, and courage.

Thank you to Joanne Wyckoff, my agent, who helped me understand what this book was about, who guided me throughout the process of bringing it to completion, and who asked the right questions. To Daniela Rapp, my editor, for helping me turn my manuscript into a book, and for her care and generosity in the final stages of the process. Thank you to David Stanford Burr, production editor, for guiding this work through publication. Thank you to Martha Schwartz, copy editor, for the care with which she read the manuscript.

Finally, thank you to Nancy Elliott, M.D.; Dana Holwitt, M.D.; Melissa Lee, M.D.; and Richard Michaelson, M.D., for their exceptional care during a very difficult time.